Savi

The
Tsar's Palaces

Christopher Morgan
&
Irina Orlova

ISBN 09549137-1-X

Also by Christopher Morgan

Don Carlos and Company (1996)
The Invisible Crying Tree, with Tom Shannon (1996)

Published by
Polperro Heritage Press
Clifton-upon-Teme
Worcestershire WR6 6EN
United Kingdom
polperro.press@virgin.net

Cover design by Steve Bowgen

Printed in Great Britain by Orphans Press, Leominster, Herefordshire HR6 8JT

PREFACE

The story of the Tsars' country palaces, of their destruction in World War II and of their faithful rebuilding in the years that followed has been told before. We welcome this book however because its aim is to celebrate the ordinary Russians without whose courage, skill and devotion this resurrection from the ruins could not have taken place. We would like every visitor to the palaces, be they Russian or from overseas, to take away with them some awareness of what these people did.

It contains a story of some drama and, at moments, high adventure, but above all, it introduces the reader to the men and women who played key roles in the saving of the palaces. It would not, of course, be possible for it to cover in detail all the contributions of all the many talented curators and restorers who devoted their lives to these projects but it does bring home to the reader the amount of talent, of persistence and of love which so many willingly and for little material reward gave to save their country's heritage.

They were our comrades and we are proud to contribute to this book about them.

Adolf Zabrovsky

Valeria Belanina

Galina Khodasevich

"While I work, my heart shall not sink"

Vera Imber

Leningrad 1942

CONTENTS

Courage

We know what trembles in the scales,
What has to be accomplished.
The hour for courage. If all else fails,
With courage we are not unfurnished.
What though the dead be crowded, each to each,
What though our houses destroyed?
We will preserve you, Russian speech,
Keep you alive, great Russian word.
We will pass you to our sons and heirs
Free and clean, and they in turn to theirs,
And so forever.

Anna Akhmatova 1942

INTRODUCTION

The aim of this book is to tell the story of the small multitude of ordinary, but talented, dedicated and brave Russians, who between them retrieved the necklace of Tsarist palaces around St Petersburg from all the horrors of the twentieth century, starting with the revolution and climaxing with the destruction of the second world war.

One problem with such an aim is that it can result in what is sometimes called an 'excess of Oblomovs'.* Our policy has been to avoid first names, nicknames and patronymics, which are second nature to Russians but confusing in the west, although we do use first names for those characters in the book [eg Irina Benois or Valeria Belanina] who had also become our friends. Even so, over the course of the 80 years it covers, a great many people cavalcade through the story. We have wished to name them all, because they are the very people we want to celebrate. The vast majority have short walk-on parts, explained by the context, but a few keep reappearing and form the central core about which the kaleidoscope revolves. To help readers get to know these, we have provided a dramatis personae at the start. And for the smaller parts, we indicate each person's contribution in the index; unless, of course, to do so would insult the reader's intelligence. We do not feel we should explain who Lenin or Stalin were.

Another problem we have faced is the Russian habit of renaming places. During the course of the twentieth century, the city at the heart of our story was called successively St. Petersburg, then Petrograd [to make it sound less German in the same spirit that caused English dachshunds such trouble in the first world war], then Leningrad and at the end St Petersburg again. We have referred to it by whatever name was current at the time we are writing about. For less well known places [eg Gatchina > Trotsk > Krasnoyeguardesk > Gatchina again] we explain the changes in the text.

When we started to work on this book, we found that we were universally welcomed in St. Petersburg. It was as though all the city was waiting for someone to retell the story of how the palaces were saved and by whom. There had been books about it, notably a beautifully illustrated

---

* The original Oblomov dates from a book by Goncharov published in 1859. Its hero suffers from lassitude, giving rise to a noun oblomovschina describing the disease of boredom to which the Russian country aristocracy was prone. In English, however, the word became associated with the bewilderment English readers can suffer, trying to cope with Russian names.

Risen from the Ashes by a group of curators, but everyone wanted to help and no-one wanted any compensation other than the chance to contribute to a book they wanted written. Sadly, not all are still alive to see the results but we hope that those who are will feel that their efforts were worthwhile. It is with great gratitude that we list our many helpers;-

Ivan Alexeev, painter/restorer
Julia Bakareva,, Archive of the Inspectorate for Art and History Monuments
Valeria Belanina, former Deputy Director of Pavlovsk
Irina Benois, architect
Michael Bobrov, former mountain climber
Adia Bonitenko, Central State Archive of the art and literature documents
Valery David, Museum of the Defence of Leningrad
Tatiana Emilianova, Committee of International Affairs
Elena Felixovna, State Archive of film and photo documents
Natalia Fomichiova, gilder
Alexander Kedrinsky, architect
Galina Khodasevich, archive keeper of Tsarskoye Selo
Tatiana Kishlashko, Switchback Pavilion curator
Vladimir Klementiev, senior curator of Chinese Palace
Constantine Kochuev, wood carver
Nichola1 Lancere, architect
Boris Lebedev, painter/restorer
Leonid Lubimov, painter/restorer
Nadezhda Ode, moulder/restorer
Lilia Shvedskaya, sculptor
Valentina Soldatova, ceramics restorer and sculptor
Lidia Strizhova, modeler and sculptor
Anna Studeynikova, photographer
Tatiana Telukova, gilder
Anastasia Vasilieva, painter/restorer
Andrey Waitens, architect
Adelaida Yolkina, former curator of Gatchina, now at Pavlovsk
Adolf Zabrovsky, wood-carver
Vitaly Zhuravliov, painter/restorer

DRAMATIS PERSONAE

Belaeva, Seraphima, Gatchina's curator during the war.
Belanina, Valeria, Art historian, close collaborator of Anna Zelenova in Pavlovsk who has overseen events there since Anna's death.
Belekhov, Nikolai, Head of the Inspectorate of the Preservation of Art and History Monuments throughout and after the siege.
Benois, Irina, architect involved in the restoration of the palaces, notably the Cottage Palace.
Bernstam, Feodor, art historian, appointed first curator of Peterhof in 1917.
Grabar, Igor, artist and art administrator, curator of the Tretiakov Gallery.
Kazanskaya, Evgennia, architect mainly active in Peterhof.
Kedrinsky, Alexander, architect, extremely influential in all palaces but mainly associated with the restoration of Catherinehof.
Kuchumov, Anatoly, expert on treasures contained in palaces. Keeper of Storages and senior curator of Pavlovsk.
Lubimov, Leonid, artist, leader of a team active everywhere but most of all in Pavlovsk after the death of Treskin.
Lukomski, George, aesthete, appointed first curator of Tsarskoye Selo in 1917 by Kerensky.
Lunacharski, Anatoly, friend of Lenin and first Commissar for the Enlightenment in 1917.
Makarov, V. N., influential academic, succeeded Zubov as curator of Gatchina.
Maria Feodorovna, tsarina, wife of Tsar Paul. Her aesthetic influence is detectable in all palaces but notably, Pavlovsk, her creation.
Ode, Nadezhda, moulder, responsible for restoration of the Gala staircase in Peterhof.
Oleinik, Feodor, architect, responsible for rebuilding Pavlovsk.
Polovtsov, Alexander, aristocrat who, in 1917, first sprang to the defence of the Tsar's country palaces.
Popova-Gunich, Sophia, architect, active in several locations but mainly as Oleinik's successor in Pavlovsk.
Rosenberg, Alfred, Head of the Kunstkommission which organised Nazi looting during war.
Shvedskaya, Lilia, sculptress and moulder. Her son Roma was the model for most of the putti in the palaces.
Tikhomirova, Marina, curator of Peterhof before, during and after the siege.
Treskin, Anatoly, gifted artist responsible for most of the paintings restored at Pavlovsk.
Turova, Evgenia, curator of Tsarskoye Selo before, during and after the siege.
Vasilieva, Anastasia, painter notable for developing silk painting and, among other things, for her work at Monplesir.
Weiss, Nikolai, junior curator of Pavlovsk during the siege.
Zelenova, Anna, director of Pavlovsk during and after the siege.
Zubov, Count Valentin, Aristocrat and first curator of Gatchina in 1917.

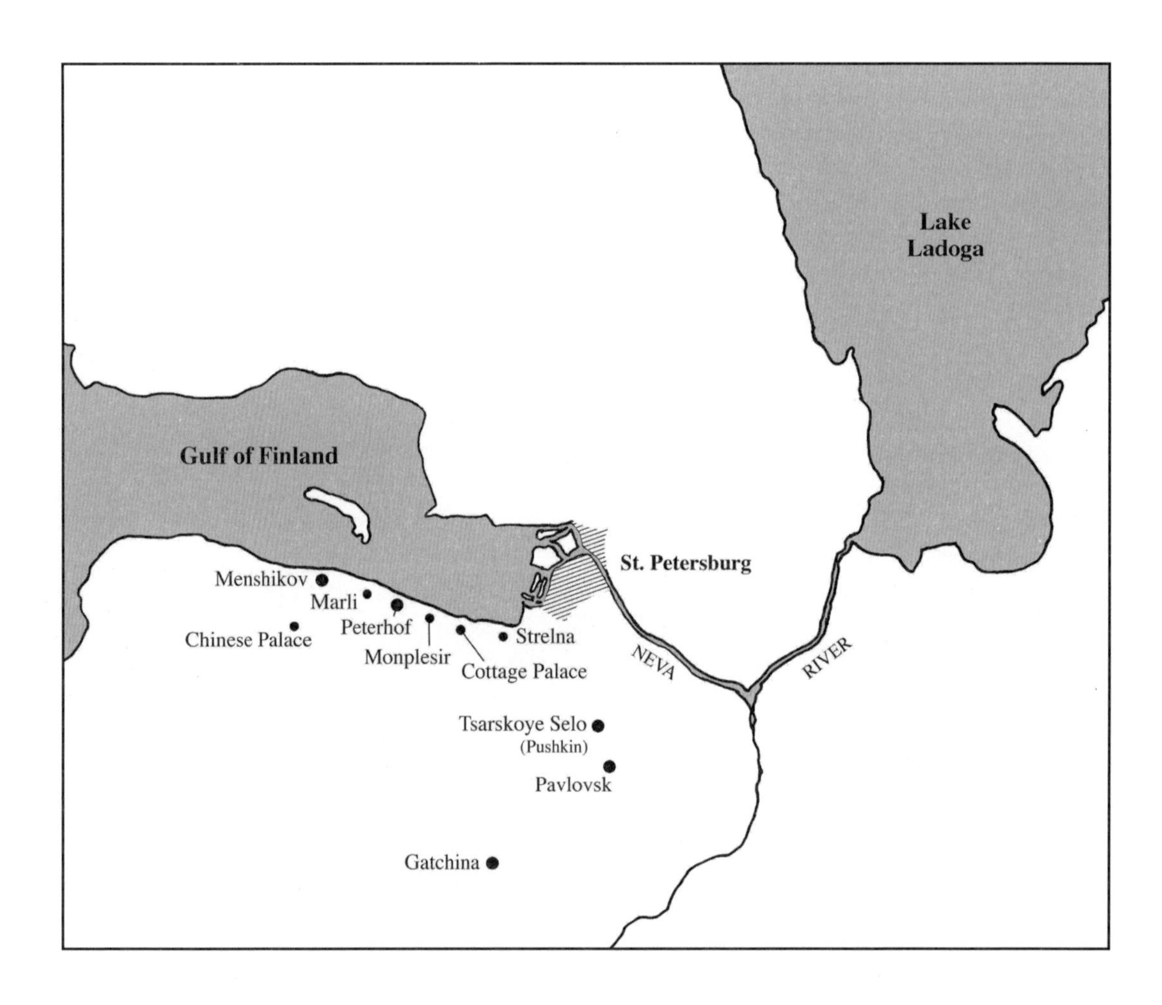

Map showing the location of the main tsars' palaces in relation to St. Petersburg.

Chapter 1

REVOLUTION

Sometimes when we read about doomed historical characters about to take some fatal step, we want to call out to them across the years: "Stop! Don't do it!" Of no-one is this more true than the hapless Tsar Nicholas II on 2nd March 1917. Trapped in his carriage by mutinous railwaymen, his armies crumbling, shaken by ever more panicky messages from his capital, surrounded by gloomy counsellors and, worst of all, cut off from his strong if foolish wife, he was not the man for such a moment. In the Stroganov Palace just off the Nevski Prospekt, there is a tableau of waxworks of the Romanov tsars. Starting with the towering Peter the Great, they stand in a circle of formidable women and inadequate men until returning to where the nervous little figure of Nicholas nestles under the sorrowing gaze of his massive ancestor. Looking at him, one feels that perhaps whatever he did would have been wrong. As absolute Tsar and in the field as commander-in-chief of his disintegrating armies, he had still insisted that he should not be disturbed in the afternoon when he walked his dogs or in the evening when he liked to watch films. After many years on the throne, he does not appear to have had much of a grasp of the job.

He probably had no choice but to abdicate, but it might have saved a lot of trouble if he had nominated a successor. If he thought the crown was too heavy for his sickly son, there was his brother Michael, who had greatly distinguished himself in the war, commanding a division of Chechens and Ingushetians in battle. But Nicholas had quarrelled with Michael who, balked by the Orthodox Church from marrying an English cousin, had renounced all his rights and married a fascinating divorcee. If Nicholas could not overcome his disgust, why did he not propose a daughter? Russia already had plenty of experience of empresses. Then there were numerous Romanov cousins, many of whom would have been willing and suitable, but in this extreme crisis of state, his thoughts could not reach beyond the small circle of his immediate family. He just wanted to do what seemed best for them and left it to others to sort out the mess in which he left his country.

Conceivably he thought he would be allowed to retire to become a country gentleman, enjoying the inheritance that had been accumulated by his forebears, but he soon found he had abdicated that too. The Provisional Government, under Prince Lvov, at once occupied the Winter Palace in Petrograd and appointed a Commissar of the Arts, one Golovine, to look after its fabulous contents. Preoccupied by the indiscipline in the city, Golovine had no time to worry about the string of country palaces that lay like a necklace around it, but it was these that were most threatened by the German advance. Who would evacuate their treasures? Who, indeed, would stop the servants pilfering? What if law and order began to break down? Who had much idea of what they contained anyway? No-one did, but there were some people aching to find out.

Amongst these were three rich patricians, all eminent connoisseurs with time on their hands. Together they went to see Golovine to offer their help. They were acquaintances rather than friends. Indeed, to judge by their memoirs, they did not much like each other, but they all shared a passion for art, for art history and especially for artefacts of the eighteenth century.

One, Alexander Polovtsov was a senior diplomat and the director of the Museum and Institute of Applied Arts which had been founded by his wealthy father-in-law, the banker Baron Stieglitz. Polovtsov was hugely rich, living with his wife and a great many servants partly in a palladian palace on the exclusive Stone Island beside the Bolshaya Nevka and partly in his town mansion on Bolshaya Morskaya Street. He owned factories in the Urals and, about 100 miles east of Petrograd, a vast estate with a mansion crammed with eighteenth century treasures to rival the Tsar's.

The second, also wealthy, was Count Valentin Zubov, a descendant of Catherine the Great's last lover. Though quite young, he had already been married and had a daughter who lived with his mother. He was much more interested in the arts and had already founded an Institute of Art History, of which he was the Director. These two took with them Peter von Weiner, who was the editor of the city's leading art magazine *Times Past.* Golovine was delighted to see them. They agreed that the palaces should become museums.

After some discussion, it was decided that they would work as a team. There were six main country residences, each with a park containing satellite palaces, pavilions and monuments. Of these, two were privately owned. The Great Palace in Oranienbaum, sometimes called the Menshikov because it had been built by Peter the Great for his favourite, now belonged to the Mecklenburg-Strelitz family. The other, Pavlovsk, was in Romanov hands but its owner, the Grand Duke Ivan, was only a distant cousin of the Tsar. Neither of these houses had exactly been orphaned by the Tsar's abdication. Meanwhile Nicholas himself was still in residence in Tsarskoye Seloe in the Alexander Palace and it hardly would do to barge in and start organising his things there or, indeed, in the nearby Catherine Palace. So the choice lay between Peterhof and Gatchina. Gatchina lies about 70 kilometres to the southwest of the city while Peterhof is not far beyond its suburbs along the coast. Gatchina, therefore, was far nearer the German front line. True, the Tsar's brother Michael lived in a private house in Gatchina but, since his morganatic marriage, he had no claim on any Romanov inheritance. He had recently confirmed this decision when the Russian parliament, the Duma, had asked him rather half-heartedly if he would take Nicholas's place. He was certainly not responsible for Gatchina. Nor was there a curator as such. So it was agreed that they should go to Gatchina.

The central block of Gatchina, half circular, had been built by the Italian Rinaldi, in the renaissance style, for another of Catherine's lovers, Gregory Orloff, and it had been provided with plenty of secret staircases and underground passages, some leading out to the park, through which he could escape unseen, not so much from danger as to keep assignations with other ladies, whose existence he felt best kept secret. When Orlov died, Catherine bought the palace back from his family and gave it to her endearingly dotty son Paul I, probably in the hope of not having to see him every day at court. He employed another Italian, Brenna, who roofed over Rinaldi's galleries and added two wings to the palace, forming a half circle round the parade ground where Paul daily drilled his private army. His strutting statue still dominates it. Paul had no time for his mother and her many lovers, and dreamt of emulating Frederick the Great of Prussia. One of the wings, known as the Arsenal, contained apartments that had subsequently been used by several Tsars and still contained many of their personal effects. The other was called the Kitchen Wing, having originally been a canteen for Paul's private army, but it had been converted into accommodation for guests. The whole is surrounded by a charmingly landscaped park, with lakes and graceful bridges, pavilions, fantasies and follies.

The three connoisseurs established themselves in the Kitchen Wing. After an initial tour, they wondered what to do. They could see that the original contents from Paul's time had been much adulterated by nineteenth century additions. Their first impulse had been to restore it to its eighteenth century glory. They had discovered that this was feasible because, while much had been displaced, nothing had been thrown away. The cellars were an Aladdin's cave of marvels, neglected and sometimes in poor shape, but nothing that could not be saved. But they also realised that many of the rooms were historically important, revealing intimate details of their former occupants' lives and tastes. They hesitated to disturb too much. Zubov could not resist hanging in his room a lovely fragment by Veronese he had found in the cellars, but otherwise, they decided to change nothing until they had made an inventory. This was no mean undertaking. There were 500 rooms containing 4,000 paintings for a start plus a huge collection of Chinese porcelain. There were seventeenth century Gobelins tapestries some of which had been cut up to decorate the backs of chairs which they determined to reassemble, if they could. And heaven knows what else. It was clear that they would need help. Polovtsov recruited some of his students from the Stieglitz, dismissed by Zubov as 'grey people', artistically ignorant and only useful as clerks. He, Zubov, on the other hand, imported some real art historians, including one of his favourite students, the beautiful Countess Shakhovskaya. Once started, they made surprising progress, shutting their ears to the growing sounds of tumult outside.

In early July, more and worse food riots occurred in Petrograd, which were quelled with difficulty and which demonstrated for the first time just how frighteningly well the Bolsheviks had subverted the Petrograd garrison. Prince Lvov stood down in favour of the bombastic lawyer Kerensky, who promised to stamp out the Bolshevik threat. In the meanwhile, the three colleagues at Gatchina did not waver. Their loyalty was to art, no matter what gang was in power. The development of local councils or soviets, claiming in some way to represent the people, was a nuisance. They had to be tactfully disabused of the notion that the palace and its contents now belonged to them. It took time that could ill be spared, but Polovtsov had not been a diplomat for nothing. The soviets were talking shops with no real authority and, at this early stage of the revolution, they were usually led by solid citizens of a petit bourgeois disposition.

Halfway to Petrograd, however, at Tsarskoye Seloe, things were getting more restive. The continued presence of the Tsar and his family in the Alexander Palace stimulated local resentment. Why should they be living in comfort and idleness while the people they had so misruled had to suffer? In late July Kerensky decided that Nicholas and his family must be moved to somewhere safer. Given the tense atmosphere, he was afraid of trouble if the move was botched. It would be done at night, as secretly as possible, and Kerensky decided to supervise it personally. He took with him another art historian called George Lukomski, whom he had chosen to take responsibility for the vacated palaces. Lukomski describes the scene vividly.

'Kerensky arrived on the preceding day to check that everything was in order. The news of the Tsar's departure had leaked out but the Alexander Palace was silent. Gone was the bustle of courtiers and aristocrats - just a few soldiers sitting smoking on the grass and some frightened looking servants. Inside, the Tsar and his family were trying to decide what to take with them. At 11pm there was still no word that the train had left Petrograd. Unable to control his nerves, Kerensky phoned the Ministry. The locomotive had broken down somewhere. This led to frenzied telephoning to the intervening stations or anyone who could tell what was going on. By 2am there was still no certain news and all were becoming nervous.

'In the meanwhile, the Tsar, in a colonel's field tunic, sat with his family on their bags in the deserted ballroom. The night dragged on but they did not sleep. At 4.30, the birds began to sing. Then someone said that a train had left Petrograd - but still it did not arrive. They eventually discovered it was stuck somewhere in a field. Kerensky, desperate to get them away before anything went wrong, sent for cars and lorries. The lorries came and were loaded. No-one was taking much baggage but, even in this extremity, there were 50 people in the family's party. Then, in the grey early light, the family emerged, Nicholas and Alexandra in the lead but subdued, no heroics. Nicholas saluted the soldiers, one of whom said, "Good morning, Mr Colonel". Behind them came the boy who tried to joke with the soldiers. Then came the daughters with cropped hair [there was a measles epidemic] and hideous grey dresses. As their car moved off, I saw Alexandra, in tears, make a cross towards the servants watching on the balcony - or was it to the palace?

'Kerensky went in another car to supervise them board the train where it stood in its field. I returned to the palace where the factor, Mr Benkendorff, was waiting with the keys. Summoning up as much dignity as possible, he handed them to me and said: "I transfer to you this palace, by order of the Government." And so I became Head of the Art and History Commission of Tsarskoye Selo.'

Lukomski at once ordered everybody out of the palaces and sealed them. He knew that this was a moment of high danger of pilfering, when loyalties were collapsing and no-one would know what was supposed to be there. On his initial tour of inspection with Benckendorff, he found Alexandra's German lady's maid still sorting through her mistress's things. She spoke hardly any Russian and it was with great difficulty that she was made to understand that it was all over and that she had to leave. She was hugely offended.

Lukomski was a bachelor in his thirties and already an internationally recognised art expert. He had mounted, to great applause, exhibitions of Russian art in Paris and was a member of the Russian Collegium for Museums and of its Ukrainian equivalent and director of the Khanenko Museum in Kiev. He was able therefore to recruit for his Art and History Commission a formidable team of experts including an artist/architect turned arts librarian called Feodor Bernstam and a good administrator called Yakovlev. These would be responsible not only for the Alexander Palace but also the nearby Catherinehof and the park around. The Commission's most urgent task was to make an inventory of everything. They found that some preparations had been made to pack up valuables for shipment both at the Alexanderhof and the Catherinehof but little if anything had actually been shipped out. Since the family had had little warning of their move, their rooms were in the sort of mess that hurried packing leaves. Toys on the floor, drawers rummaged in, objects lying where rejected. To cut corners, he quickly had everything photographed which was better than nothing. Lukomski then decided to make a photographic record of all the rooms, not only in the Alexander Palace but the Catherine Palace too. He employed the well known photographer called Lebiodkin. Not all the pictures have survived but those that do are excellent testimony of the opulence of the Tsars' lives. Lukomski, having few ties in Petrograd, moved into the Alexander Palace himself.

In the meanwhile, Kerensky's attempts to suppress the Bolsheviks had been meeting with some success. Several leaders were imprisoned and Lenin himself had to go into hiding. However, all was undone and more when, in early August, General Kornilov, whom Kerensky had himself placed in military command, attempted to occupy Petrograd and seize power. The army's loyalty was by now too uncertain for the plan to stand much chance of success but it turned into farce when the railwaymen refused to transport the troops. From this point the situation deteriorated rapidly. Law and order began to crumble and the reviving Bolsheviks made rapid progress. Furthermore, the Germans resumed their advance and, in September, occupied Riga. Golovine ordered the most precious things in the Winter Palace to be crated ready for evacuation to Moscow and urged the curators at Gatchina to do likewise.

In the meanwhile, however, trouble was looming at Pavlovsk. The local town soviet had began to challenge its status as private property. Who had paid for it to be built if not the Russian peasant? And, if a private house, why was it guarded by soldiers? Anyway, Prince Ivan and his family were Romanovs, weren't they? The Grand Duke Ivan was an extremely religious and kind man and did not believe that the local people wished him ill, but he had heard about the inventories being made at Gatchina and Tsarskoye Seloe and felt that he ought to have one at Pavlovsk. As a young man, he had served in the guards with Polovtsov and so he asked him to recommend someone. Now, Pavlovsk had been the creation of the Empress Maria Feodorovna, the wonderfully talented wife of Paul I, and was considered artistically to be the jewel of all the palaces, having escaped the invasion of nineteenth century taste. Polovtsov almost swooned with excitement and volunteered to do it himself. Most of the work at Gatchina was complete and, indeed, Peter von Weiner had already returned to Petrograd. Polovtsov happily moved across next day, leaving Zubov to cope with an ever more officious Gatchina town soviet, now insisting on weekly 'supervisory' meetings with the curators.

Pavlovsk by comparison, seemed an island of peace. The soviet there, led by a doctor and the local station master, were not really militant and were more than satisfied with the grant of some land in the park to enable townspeople to grow their own vegetables. The garrison regiment, which normally provided the palace guard, had been drawn away by the Kornilov affair but Polovtsov found a local artillery unit prepared to take over. This did not last long because the soldiers found they were being jeered at for 'guarding the Romanovs' and refused guard duty. At this stage, Polovtsov, whose only loyalty was to the treasures he had set out to save, decided that the Grand-Duke had become a liability. Asked to withdraw to Petrograd, Prince Ivan at first pooh-poohed the thought. What did they need guards for anyway? But Polovtsov was adamant. It was either one or the other, he said. He was not prepared to stay and be lynched for a whim of Ivan's. Regretfully Ivan conceded and departed with his family, leaving only his sister Olga, Queen of the Hellenes, who was nursing wounded soldiers in a hospital she had established in the town. The artillerymen resumed their guard duty.

Unlike Zubov and Lukomski, Polovtsov was not able to spend all his time at Pavlovsk. He was still responsible for the Stieglitz museum, already packed up for evacuation, and he felt he must see Golovine regularly. Furthermore, he worried for his wife still living in their town palace. Horrifying reports were beginning to come in of country houses being vandalised and of army units killing their officers and deserting. Although this type of disorder was not yet prevalent in Petrograd, Polovtsov worried more and more about leaving his wife alone. Furthermore, the train journey was getting more unreliable and he feared that one day it might come to a complete standstill. Petrol for private cars was already a distant memory. So he persuaded an architect called Pospolitaki to move to Pavlovsk as his assistant. This was as well, because in mid-October, Golovine decided it was time to send two train loads of treasures from the Winter Palace to safer storage in Moscow and asked Polovtsov to accompany them and see them well housed. Polovtsov, who wanted to scout out a suitable store for the Stieglitz treasures, was delighted to accept. The move was due to take place on October 25th. He left Pospolitaki in charge at Pavlovsk.

According to Zubov, the only people in Russia who did not seem to know that the Bolsheviks were planning a coup on October 25th were the Provisional Government. Of course, they must have known but underestimated the danger. Perhaps it was inconceivable to them that such a ragtag band of ruffians could bring down such a solidly based and complacent society, which was still not letting the troubles interfere with their pleasures. The cabinet had a meeting scheduled for October 25th, so meet they would. Anything else might reveal a loss of nerve, but Kerensky himself slipped out of town to summon loyal troops from nearby garrisons.

Polovtsov, for whom coups and countercoups were of little interest provided he could get on with his job, went to the Winter Palace for final instructions from the Fine Arts Commission before boarding the Moscow train. The palace seemed eerily empty. A few cadets and women soldiers were scattered through the vast building. In the Office of Fine Arts, immediately below the room in which the government was meeting, he found only a secretary, who warned him that events were getting out of hand. They were, he said, probably standing in the most dangerous place in Petrograd. Polovtsov did not hang around and fetched his wife to go to the station. They arrived safely in Moscow next day to stay with friends whose house looked directly across the Moskva River at the Kremlin walls.

They had barely unpacked when all hell broke loose. They found they were in the front line of the siege of the Kremlin, wedged between the Communist Battle HQ on their left and a factory used for marshalling the red brigades on their right. The cadets defending the Kremlin assumed their lodging was part of this Bolshevik fortress and a twitched curtain sufficed to attract a volley of quite accurate fire. A servant who attempted to exit was shot dead on the front door step. Polovtsov, standing well back from the window, watched in anguish the bombardment of historical buildings like the tower from which Ivan the Terrible had so much enjoyed watching the death throes of the boyards. Then, when the shooting stopped and they could safely emerge, they found it extremely difficult to convince their victorious neighbours that they were not white spies. However, ten days later, they were eventually allowed to board a train back to Petrograd.

In the meanwhile, Zubov had been having an even more harrowing experience in Gatchina. Shortly after Polovtsov's departure for Moscow, the cruiser *Aurora* had fired her historic shell [wildly missing the target unless, as many believe, it was a blank]. Like a starter's pistol, it was the signal for the red guards to storm the Winter Palace, intent on capturing the government intact. With each successive film version of this action, the fight has become more desperate. In reality, it was hardly a skirmish. The cadets put up a brief show but the women surrendered at once. The attackers' main problem was to discover which of the 117 staircases led to the room where the government still sat debating. In the end a dignified flunky, liveried and bewigged, led them to the room. The ministers meekly let themselves be led away but, to the Bolsheviks' dismay, the hated Kerensky was not there. They learned that he had left to try to rally a Cossack division, stationed in Pskov, nearly 200 miles to the south. They did not think he would get far because, earlier on, they had demobilised all vehicles in central Petrograd but they were wrong.

Zubov was breakfasting at Gatchina on the 25th when he was astonished to see a British Embassy car flying the Union Jack drive up to the palace. Out of it stepped Kerensky and his ADC, a man called Knirsha whom Zubov was relieved to recognise as an old friend. Desperate for transport, Kerensky had sought diplomatic help and the British had lent him a car.* The news from the Winter Palace had not yet reached Gatchina and the garrison there willingly lent him another car to continue his journey to Pskov. Kerensky was back on the 27th, followed rather sulkily by the cavalry division, which suspected that he had betrayed Kornilov. Zubov was appalled at the possibility that they might expect all to be billeted in the palace. With Knirsha's help, however, he persuaded them to limit themselves to the Kitchen Wing. Only Kerensky and the officers would be allowed in. The soldiers slept on the parade ground, using their horses as pillows.

Up to this point, Zubov had been ignoring an instruction from Golovine to prepare for the evacuation of the most precious treasures. He secretly believed they would be safer in German

---

* There is some controversy about whether it was the British or American ambassador's car. We assume that Zubov, who saw it, was right.

hands than entrusted to the Russian railways, but could hardly use this argument. As a cover plan, he had been collecting some of his favourite items in a relatively secure room in the centre block of the palace. They were supposedly awaiting packing materials but he had not ordered any. The Bolshevik coup and the arrival of the Cossacks made him wonder how wise he had been but it was now too late. All he could do was hasten the collection of treasures into his inner sanctum and start to board up ground floor windows and lock the public doors. To cover his tracks, he took to using Orlov's secret doors and passages. He made great efforts to make friends with the Cossack officers, making good use of some alcohol allocated to him for picture restoration. This made him quite popular because sales of vodka had been banned by the Government, knowing how liquor could transform the Russian proletariat. Nevertheless, he was relieved when, on the 28th, the Cossacks resumed their advance on the capital.

Never one of Kerensky's admirers, Zubov describes him rather unkindly as behaving like some toy Napoleon, striking heroic poses to mask his terror. Nevertheless, when an officer of the Gatchina garrison, an ardent monarchist called Pechionkin, arrived in Zubov's study, festooned with hand grenades and full of drink, and implored him to come and assassinate Kerensky, Zubov demurred. Indeed, he put himself out to dissuade him with such success that Pechionkin tearfully flung down his grenades and stormed off. Thankfully they did not go off. He deemed it wiser to arrange for Pechionkin to be locked up while in so violent a mood, which turned out very well for him. When the reds arrived and found him under arrest, they assumed he was a sympathiser and treated him like a hero.

The Cossacks had the greatest difficulty in persuading Kerensky to advance any further with them. He must have guessed they would soon meet some opposition but he eventually agreed to go with them. It turned out he was right. That night they were all back and not too proud of themselves, while Kerensky was in a pitiful state. They had encountered unexpectedly fierce resistance near Tsarskoe Seloe. Nevertheless, they resolved to try to do better next day. The officers could not believe they could not deal with a rabble of militiamen but it was a fight for which the Cossacks had little stomach. They had supposed that all that was expected of them was a triumphal re-entry into Petrograd, virtually unopposed. It had been a shock to meet such an organised and determined enemy. They began to wonder what they were doing here. They were Don Cossacks from the open steppes. What had these quarrels between city folk to do with them? Nevertheless, on the next day, the 29th, they assembled to try again but their mood was not improved when Kerensky was found incapable in his room, stoned out of his mind on sedatives. They advanced nonetheless but they were back again even earlier that evening having achieved even less.

The atmosphere in the palace was now extremely tense. Towards midnight, one of the sentries from the garrison regiment thought he detected red guards taking up positions encircling the palace. He roused the nearest curator which happened to be the Countess Shakhovskaya. She at once warned Zubov whose first thoughts were for the safety of his curators. He got them together and told them they could leave if they wanted to and they mostly did, but not the Countess. 'She was a brave woman,' wrote Zubov later, 'who liked a little excitement.'

Next, he and she turned their attention to the treasures for which they were responsible and which now seemed in grave danger. Somehow they managed to borrow a military car which they loaded with the most priceless of the treasures in their secure room. Golovine had a dacha nearby but well away from the likely battle area. They took them there. Miraculously, they did not meet any of the red guards. Golovine's wife was by no means pleased to see them, feeling the situation was tricky enough already, but Zubov was not in the mood to argue. Having unloaded and hidden the treasures as well as possible, they rode back to Gatchina. Barricading all the entrances to the main block and gathering up a last few canvasses and ornaments, they withdrew into their secure room and locked themselves in. There, perching uncomfortably amongst the jumble of furniture and statues, they waited for the bombardment to begin. Nothing happened.

It had been a false alarm. Nevertheless, in the morning, the news was grim enough. Where the Cossacks remained in contact with the reds, they were getting the worst of it. Feeling nothing but contempt for Kerensky and longing to be home in their Don basin, their discipline started to crumble. This was a great anxiety to Zubov. The tidy arrangement whereby only the officers entered the palace was breaking down. Soldiers were sleeping everywhere in the Kitchen Wing and Zubov began to encounter foraging parties that had somehow got into the main block. Luckily he had made some good friends amongst the officers who helped him get them out. But he was mortally afraid for the many treasures still left in the Kitchen Wing, especially in its cellars. With his curators, he tried to retrieve as many of these as possible but it was not easy. Still he continued to concentrate what he considered most valuable in his strong room.

Daylight of the 30th October had revealed no red guards around Gatchina, but there was no more talk of advancing on Petrograd. While the Cossacks and the curators watched each other suspiciously, a somewhat hung-over Kerensky was having trouble with his nerves. The palace was full of rumours that the Cossacks were secretly negotiating with the reds to hand him and the palace over in exchange for a safe passage back to the Ukraine. Desperate, Kerensky sent his ADC, Knirsha, to Zubov to ask him to hide him and smuggle him out of the palace. Realising that Kerensky was a spent force, Zubov agreed but nothing happened until early on the 31st October when Knirsha rushed in. "We must go!" he gasped. "They are about to betray him." Quickly agreeing on a plan of action, they went to fetch Kerensky from his room but he was not there. Apparently, while they had been deliberating, a sailor had given him his uniform, he'd found a car and, wearing goggles, had been driven off, out past the guards on the gate and away to flight and safety, leaving Knirsha to his fate. There is a version of the story that he escaped through a secret passage, dressed as a nurse, but Zubov was there and is probably right. Perhaps the nurse story was invented as a cover by the guards who should have intercepted him. There was no more fighting. In due course, the Cossacks did withdraw and not long after, red brigades started to arrive. Zubov, Shakhovskaya and Knirsha were all put under arrest. The latter was sure that he at any rate would be shot but they were all saved by the arrival of Trotsky who knew Knirsha well. At this stage, the week old revolution still had a human face.

The red guards turned out to be far more demanding guests than the Cossacks. Here was a vast palace full of unimaginable luxury. Why should they be denied the run of it? With great difficulty

Zubov managed to convince some of their officers that the treasures he was guarding were now the property of all the people and not to be looted by those few who happened to be on the spot. Even so, the tramp of boots through the corridors and the sound of locks being rattled became a regular emergency. Many of the servants had learnt to respect Zubov and now played an invaluable role, diverting intruders or delaying them until sympathetic red officers could be found and brought to the rescue. The kitchen wing had to be sacrificed, however. It became a nightmare of drunken and ribald soldiers and sailors, vandalising portraits with their bayonets and smashing valuable porcelain for the sake of its bronze handles. Zubov and his team withdrew into their safe rooms and waited for something to turn up.

When eventually Polovtsov and his wife were able to leave Moscow, he managed to buy an evening paper to read on the train back to Petrograd. Therein he found an article about a man called Lunacharski, a close companion, it seemed, of Lenin's. Lunacharski had pronounced anathema on the vandals responsible for damaging the Kremlin. He declared that, although himself a long serving Bolshevik, he would refuse any participation in their government unless they at once made arrangements to preserve the nation's artistic heritage. And so he had been made Commissar for Enlightenment based in the Winter Palace. For Polovtsov, he seemed to be a candle in a darkening world. As soon as they reached Petrograd, he sent his wife home and hurried to find him. He was introduced into a meeting, if meeting is the right word. It creates an image of something far more orderly than what Polovtsov found. In a large room were gathered a multitude of artistic and semi-artistic people and many who were unknown to him. There were several groups arguing noisily or rather haranguing each other in a quite undisciplined way. There was much talk about the glory of the revolution which would bring enlightenment to the people held too long in darkness. Polovtsov was to discover that long speeches on these lines were much favoured by the early Bolsheviks. He asked if someone called Lunacharski was present and was shown a harassed looking man with spectacles in a corner surrounded by petitioners. He joined the queue. Eventually reaching the great man, he said: "We must save Pavlovsk!" Lunacharski started. "I quite agree," he said, "but how?" "Make me its commissar!" "With pleasure! But who are you? Just write your name. It will be done." And it was. A few days later, Polovtsov received a document, covered in convincing looking seals, nominating him curator of Pavlovsk Palace and park.

He stayed on at the meeting hoping to find out what had been happening. After a while, the talk turned to Gatchina and the rumour that it had been engulfed in anarchy. Lunacharski proposed sending out a patrol of discovery. Was there anyone present who knew anything about Gatchina? Polovtsov raised his hand and next day found himself in a car heading thither with two committed Bolsheviks called Yatmanov and Mandelbaum, both later to become influential players in Russia's cultural scene. He prayed they would find nothing compromising.

Entering the kitchen wing, he was aghast at what he saw. In every room lounged four or five unshaven and loutish soldiers and sailors surrounded by the detritus of several days eating and drinking. Happily, the furniture in the kitchen wing was expensive rather than valuable but it was a sorry sight. There had been much wanton damage. But a quick glance told him that nothing was there of top quality. The bayoneted portrait of Catherine the Great was only a copy. In his former room he found no trace of his own possessions but the floor was adrift in papers which, to his horror, he recognised as the precious inventory. There were pages missing, used, he discovered, for cigarette paper. Yet he felt he could recognise Zubov's hand in that what was valuable, including the Veronese, appeared to have been removed. Leaving his Bolshevik companions to deal with the squatters, he set off in search of him. He had a shrewd idea of where to look and how to get there and soon found him with the countess and one or two faithful followers, camping uncomfortably in their treasure room. They were very, very glad to see Polovtsov.

While Polovtsov briefed Zubov and his companions about Lunacharski and the new situation in Petrograd, the two Bolsheviks went from room to room through the kitchen wing, pouring such torrents of words over the sleepy inmates that, to Polovtsov's amazement, it was eventually agreed to evacuate the palace within ten days. And, in 15, they were gone. Zubov and his companions in the meanwhile had emerged from their refuge, and resumed the use of the public doorways. On Polovtsov's advice, he wrote a report to Lunacharski, putting his 'museum' at the disposal of the new government and asking to be formally appointed commissar-curator. He sent his report with the attractive countess who duly brought back his commission. Provided he could get on with his task of saving Gatchina, Zubov did not care what government was temporarily in power. No-one expected the Bolsheviks to last more than a few weeks.

As soon as things were reasonably settled at Gatchina, Polovtsov left for Pavlovsk, dreading what he might find there. It was known that bands of red sailors had descended on that palace too, but all was well. Pospolitaki, supported by the Queen of the Hellenes, had managed to persuade them not to enter en masse but to select a delegation to be shown round by the curators. Their declared aim was to seize the armories of weapons which they supposed the Tsar's palaces must contain in order to suppress the poor. Not finding them, they had gone away satisfied with a few modern sabres. Once again, Pavlovsk seemed to Polovtsov a haven of tranquillity. Nevertheless, his first act was to visit the 'House of the People' which was a new feature of the little town. He found it full of soldiers and proletarians, but he was relieved to see the doctor he knew. In due course, he was invited to speak and made an impassioned speech, waving his curatorship in the air and declaring that his only aim was to save for the people what belonged to them. In conclusion, he asked for a vote of confidence which was passed unanimously. He nevertheless thought it prudent to persuade Princess Olga to depart for the relative safety of Petrograd. It was no longer wise to consort too closely with a Romanov.

These local difficulties helped to concentrate the minds of the curators. The Germans no longer seemed the only danger to the palaces, or even the greatest. Peterhof might be the furthest from the front but it lay opposite the Kronstadt naval base teeming with mutinous sailors. It now needed its own protector urgently. Lukomski, not entirely unselfishly, proposed Bernstam, whom he had come much to dislike. Whatever his motives, it made the other two and especially Bernstam happy. They were not exactly warming to each other as individuals but as the storm clouds gathered they felt increasingly the need to hang together as a team. It was no problem to get Lunacharski's approval for Bernstam's appointment.

It was never difficult to get Lunacharski's approval. His method of working, if it can be called that, was totally chaotic. His office in the Winter Palace was a scrimmage of supplicants amidst a swirl of papers. The only problem was to get his attention. Polovtsov, who perforce spent part of each week in Petrograd, found the best answer was to catch him at breakfast. Zubov, who rarely went to the city, used simply to take some of the official paper lying around, type out whatever he needed, locate Lunacharski's stamp amongst the papers awash on the tables, apply it to his memo and shove it under Lunacharski's nose. He usually signed it unread.

Lunacharski was a rather odd Bolshevik. Describing himself as 'a Bolshevik amongst intellectuals and an intellectual amongst Bolsheviks', he had been close to Lenin in exile. Regarding him as too soft and idealistic for the dirty work of organising a revolution, Lenin nevertheless liked him very much and admired his erudition. He appointed him Commissar of Enlightenment, a job which Lunacharski embraced with delight. He truly believed in the suppressed genius of the poor which universal education would bring into instant flower. One of his faults was to make long speeches on this subject and Polovstov soon learned what not to say, lest he set him off. Perhaps such a romantic title made him worse but it is arguable that one of the communists' best legacies to Russia lay in the field of education which was the Commissar's main responsibility. Lunacharski was of obscure origins, although his name was said to be an inversion of Charnoluski, an aristocratic family which had perhaps once been embarrassed by some illegitimate fruit of their loins. The story could well be true because he combined an instinctive feel for beautiful things with a strong sense of social injustice. He had taught himself. He amazed Polovtsov, who wrote of him, 'How could a man of such discrimination join, of his own freewill, this troupe of orang-utans who are destroying everything that makes life worth living.' Lenin gave him a pretty free hand and he was able to give generous grants not only for conservation work, but for artists and cultural projects of all kinds. As a result, the early years of the revolution saw a flowering of the avant-garde.

It was as well for our curators that they did have Lunacharski's support and a clear line of reporting to the Winter Palace, because the nature of the local soviets soon began to change. The original worthies began to be replaced by less inhibited types, seemingly chosen more for the loudness of their mouths than the span of their attention. They tended to be suspicious of these patrician curators, who seemed more tsarist than the Tsars. They might not be able to cope with all their clever talk but at least they could appoint supervisors to make sure that their every action was accounted for. Polovtsov handled all this with aplomb and came to enjoy it as a game, regretting only that so much of his own wit was wasted on these numskulls. Bernstam also sailed through without too much trouble. He was good with people and quickly won the loyalty of the staff at Peterhof who were supportive when the soviet appointed an oafish apprentice baker as its head. This man, flushed with self-importance, set about arranging an office suite for himself in accordance with his new status. He demanded some of the neo-Gothic furniture from the Cottage Palace but Bernstam warned him that he would be laughed at for choosing such unfashionable stuff and obtained for him some hideous gilded modern things instead. However, when the baker secretly helped himself to some bronzes, he had gently to be warned that he was stealing the people's property. He gave them back but Bernstam could not stop him from sacking the servant who had sneaked on him. Lukomski had more trouble. He was a more abrasive man and soon was at loggerheads not only with the town soviet but also with the somewhat sullen committees that had been set up by the palace servants, by the park staff and by the outside workers. He became absolutely incensed because of the time he had to waste with all these committees. This impatience was eventually his undoing but, in the meanwhile, it was Zubov who got into real trouble.

In February 1918, Trotsky broke off his peace negotiations with the Germans with the petulant cry 'No peace, no war!' Such petulant cries are all very well, but they do not instil confidence in others and it was generally assumed that the Germans would now be in Petrograd within days. The Gatchina Soviet immediately instructed Zubov to take steps to evacuate the treasures from the palace but Zubov's objections to such a reckless step had only been reinforced by the arrival in power of the Bolsheviks. He resolved to disobey as he had previously disobeyed Golovine. Indeed, he hastened the stocking of his strong room and started to brick it up. But he was now being much more closely supervised and, required by the local soviet to defend his disobedience, he lost his cool and shouted what he had meant never to say - that he would rather see the treasures properly cared for by Germans than ruined by Russians. Not long afterwards, some soldiers came to his quarters with a warrant for his arrest. For good measure they also arrested the Grand Duke Michael - merely for being a Romanov. Ironically, after weeks of argument, Zubov had just managed to persuade the Grand Duke to withdraw to Petrograd. This was no longer a simple matter. There was now no way that someone like the Grand Duke would be allowed to buy a train ticket, and Zubov had been busy solving this in his own way. To his horror, he now remembered that his wallet contained the train pass he had just forged for the Grand Duke. Sure that he would soon be searched, he managed to persuade his guard to let him visit the lavatory on his own where he flushed it away. Much relieved in every way, he rejoined the Grand Duke, the morganatic wife and their guards. They were taken to Petrograd, to the Bolshevik HQ in the Smolny Institute for interrogation. The faithful Shakhovskaya managed to get a message through to Lunacharski.

The last time Zubov had seen the Smolny, it had been an elegant academy for the daughters of the nobility. His arrival there was a culture shock. Instead of pretty young girls in white dresses, ugly people were everywhere, scurrying about through disgusting smoke filled corridors, adrift in waste paper, cigarette butts, spit and sunflower kernels. It was this sight which finally brought home to him just what was happening to Russia. He and the Grand Duke were taken to a large room on the first floor where a high ranking Bolshevik, Uritsky, awaited them.

Uritsky was the first Bolshevik chief of the Petrograd police and a founding father of the CHEKA, the first of many acronyms for the political secret police, fear of whom was to hold together the communist experiment through most of the twentieth century. Uritsky was already feared and had survived attempts on his life, but his reputation was not so monstrous as that of some of his successors. He had been born in 1873 into a family of orthodox jewish merchants but had been seduced at university by social-democratic ideas, spending most of his youth in exile, meeting many of the Bolshevik leaders. Although he did not join the party until the very eve of revolution, he was held in such respect that he was at once co-opted onto the Central Committee. Soon afterwards, he was entrusted with the protection of the fledgeling government at a time when a great many were determined, by hook or by crook, to bring it down. He felt he had to do whatever was necessary to defend it, but, unlike some of his successors, he was not a cruel man.

He interrogated the Grand Duke first, which suited Zubov who was praying desperately that Lunacharski was riding to the rescue. He was, but only to reveal how limited, in reality, was his influence. The evidence of the Gatchina Soviet was not very impressive, being mainly that they thought Zubov had been exceeding his authority and had challenged theirs. Lunacharski spoke in his defence about his cooperativeness and qualifications. He went so far as to say that he sympathised with Zubov's outburst, and he earnestly prayed that he be allowed to carry on his good work. Zubov, who did not lack courage, explained his belief that works of art should be protected as a sacred charge. Who owned them was less important than their safety. Uritsky decided to defer judgement. Zubov and the Grand Duke found themselves locked into one of the girls' dormitories, with iron beds and mattresses but no blankets. Zubov had a bad night but the Grand Duke slept like a child. He had fared worse campaigning in the Carpathians. He probably found Uritsky a lot less frightening than his Chechen soldiers.

Uritsky took his time coming to a decision. When he eventually summoned Zubov to the same large room, he acknowledged at once that his only real crime had been to irritate the Gatchina Soviet. Zubov was reacting with relief when Uritsky cut him short. It was no small matter. The whole basis of communism was to devolve power and even he could not easily overrule a town soviet. "It is true that you work with us," he added, "but you are not one of us. You are an aesthete, not interested in our cause but only in works of art. Look at that sentry on the door. He is different from you. You would work with any government but he will only work with us. When we stormed the Winter Palace, if the Venus de Milo had been in the way, we'd have shot her to bits. You would not do that. It is that attitude which irritated the local soviet." The upshot was that Zubov was banned from Gatchina and, indeed, for the time being had to go to Moscow while tempers cooled. Lunacharski, whose support had proved ineffective, was told to find him something useful to do there. At least, Zubov reflected, his team at Gatchina would know how to carry on. The most difficult and dangerous days were past. He was succeeded by an experienced academic called Vladimir Makarov.

Whether it was Zubov's disappearance or just a general feeling that the waters were rising, soon afterwards the curators decided it was time to formalise their position. Under Polovtsov's chairmanship, they formed a Council of Curators of the Country Palaces. The task of liaising with Lunacharski and the government would be Polovtsov's, who in any case had other responsibilities in Petrograd like the Stieglitz Institute, to say nothing of his wife. Since he would not be able to give Pavlovsk his full attention, he recruited another artist-architect called Teleporovski to become curator in his place and to sit on the Council. The other founding members were Lukomski, Bernstam and Makarov. They met formally every month, keeping meticulous minutes which vividly reflect their current concerns and record successive changes in the Council's membership. In their way, these minutes reflect in microcosm the huge events which were starting to convulse Russia.

The winter of 1917/18 was bitterly cold. The curators agreed to let townspeople take trees from the parks but felt it would be too provocative to heat the uninhabited palaces, so they were often working at temperatures of minus 20 or worse, but they were happy. A masterpiece retrieved could compensate for much hardship. And they made astonishing progress, not just with their inventories but also in returning the palaces to what they thought had been their former glory. The nineteenth century Tsars had liked to be fashionable but had never pretended to be connoisseurs. Out went second rate Romanov portraits to make way for the Watteaus and van Ruysdaels emerging from the cellars. Polovtsov's memoirs throb with excitement as he recalls seeing one day a corner of Maria Feodorovna's eighteenth century painted bed poking out from under a pile of junk in a cellar - and then, by detective work, reuniting the whole scattered suite and putting it back where it belonged. Maria Feodorovna's rooms in Pavlovsk are perhaps the most charming and most moving of all the many remarkable things to be seen in the country palaces. But the curators had to be careful. Not everyone shared their enthusiasm for the eighteenth century. Many saw the palaces as historical documents, monuments to the vainglory of the Romanovs to be preserved as little altered as possible. After Polovtsov and his friends had gone, much controversy arose over what they had done.

Lukomski in particular was criticised for destroying the historical integrity of the family's rooms in the Alexanderhof but in this he was by no means solely to blame. In April 1918, Lunacharski, decided that he and his wife would move into the Alexanderhof. He had made many speeches declaring that the palaces belonged to the people, not their new masters, and so this was something of a surprise. The moving spirit was probably his wife, Lunacharskaya, who had taken up the cause of poor children and orphans. At any rate, it soon emerged that as well as occupying a suite in the Alexanderhof themselves, they wanted to use parts of it and of the Catherinehof for an orphanage. The name of Tsarskoye Seloe was to be changed to Detskoye Seloe, meaning Children's Village. Lunacharskaya wanted to distribute the princesses' books to local schools and the Tsarevich's toys to the children of the deserving poor. Lukomski was horrified. He at once sprang to the defence of these personal things, the value of which shortly before he had himself been dismissing, but which he now felt were far too good for the poor, no matter how deserving. And he was genuinely touched by the pathos of these sad, hurriedly abandoned rooms, but Lunacharskaya snapped that it didn't make something historical just because a Tsar had used it. A compromise between him and Lunacharskaya was eventually brokered by her main aide, a man called Telepniov, whom Lukomski liked and trusted. Earlier, when Lukomski had first come to Tsarskoye Seloe, Telepniov had been commander of the garrison unit. Lukomski had had to complain to him about the guards sleeping on duty and together they had solved the problem by allocating each man a small vegetable patch, something far more worth guarding than an old palace. Polovtsov, on the other hand, hated Telepniov, describing him as 'drunken, sly and dishonest'. Perhaps this was because Telepniov had once insulted one of Polovtsov's aristocratic friends whose porcelain collection he was trying to protect, but more likely it was simply because, if Lukomski liked someone, Polovtsov probably did not. In the same way, Polovtsov in his memoirs makes a point of how much he liked and admired Bernstam whom Lukomski could not stand. In the meanwhile, this episode hardly endeared Lukomski to the Lunacharskis. His time as curator of Tsarskoye Seloe was beginning to run out.

Despite these quarrels the work had been proceeding apace and by June 1918, it was felt possible to open parts of the palaces to the public. Given the growing civil disorders, the curators were anxious to take this symbolic step as soon as possible. On the other hand, they had great forebodings about letting in the people. Cautiously, they decided only to allow organised groups with a guide, but they still did not know what to expect. At the last moment, Lukomski came up with his inspired invention, the tapachki, a loose slipper of felt to be tied over the visitors' boots to protect the parquet floors which are a feature of all the palaces. Tapachkis are still obligatory today. The curators need not have worried. The decorous behaviour of the visitors astounded Polovtsov and brought tears to Lunacharski's eyes. They were respectful, full of intelligent interest and seemed determined to be worthy of what they were being allowed to see. They were obviously proud of this part of holy Russia's history. Once a burly red guard refused to put on tapachki. Well then, said the rest, we stay here till you do. He gave in. And the curators were deeply touched by the many appreciative letters they received. They had not done what they had done for the people and now the people's thanks caught them unawares.

In one sense, with the opening of the museums, the curators' task was done. Their palaces had reached some sort of safe haven. There would still be much more to be rescued and restored but the first squall had been weathered. The palaces were now public property and under the protection of the state, in distressing contrast to the private property of the rich. Polovtsov had learned as early as the end of 1917 that his country mansion with all its cherished contents had been ransacked and destroyed. Private property in Petrograd was increasingly threatened by unruly elements, some with the authority of a local soviet. But the Tsar's country palaces could not now be touched. Although only open for a few hours on two or three days a week, during the first five months 33,000 visitors came to Tsarskoye Selo alone and many more to Peterhof and Pavlovsk. They clearly belonged now to the people and a crime against them was a crime against the people. The pride of the curators in their achievement shines out from their memoirs. To quote Lukomski: 'There had been a wholesale change of ownership but little was lost - only some 20-30 paintings, sculptures, snuff-boxes and so on. On the other hand, neglected marvels were found and unquestionably what was saved from oblivion and decay greatly outweighed what was lost . . . This is a source of great satisfaction, especially when compared with the widespread destruction of treasures during the French Revolution.* It leads to the conclusion that at the time of the revolution, Russia was experiencing an artistic rebirth. The desire was strong and widespread that the antiquities must be preserved.'

It was, but the century still had much trouble in store.

* In the aftermath of the storming of the Winter Palace a good deal of looting took place but, some time afterwards the Bolsheviks, Yatmanov and Mandelbaum issued an appeal and practically everything was returned.

Chapter 2

CIVIL WAR

If the Tsar's palaces had reached some sort of safe-ish haven as museums, it was in sharp contrast to what was happening elsewhere. Petrograd was full of magnificent private palaces, full of priceless possessions and the little towns round the country palaces consisted largely of impressive dachas belonging to courtiers. As soon as the existence of the Council of Curators for the Country Palaces became known, they became the object of desperate pleas for help from private owners. Sometimes, when he knew of something particularly valuable, Polovtsov would persuade the owner to let him transfer it to the Hermitage but they could not cope with everyone. One Mr Stal, coming to them on behalf of a number of mansions in Krasnoye Selo [near Tsarskoye Selo] had to be fobbed off with the promise to request Lunacharski to set up a special investigatory group, which no-one believed would happen. More serious, however, was the plight of the Menshikov Palace at Oranienbaum, dangerously close to the mutinous naval base at Kronstadt. It too was privately owned, and within its area lay the delightful Chinese Palace, the Switchback Pavilion and the Palace of Peter III, all belonging to the tsars but with no-one appointed to protect them. Even as early as the spring of 1917, the Provisional Government had withdrawn their security guards from the Menshikov Palace, leaving them to be replaced by some mutinous soldiers from a local unit who regarded it as an invitation to help themselves. The palaces were locked but otherwise defended only by a hapless family retainer called Verkhneustinsky. The so-called guards were soon inside, helping themselves to whatever they could carry and sell, while mindlessly vandalising what they could not. They also broke into the Chinese Palace, stripping the furnishings and looting the Silver Chamber with such enthusiasm that they brought a horse and cart right into the palace the more easily to load up their booty.

One of the less felicitous steps the Bolsheviks took in their early days was to divide the nation's historical buildings between two commissars. Luckily, and perhaps because of Polovtsov's timely action, the Tsar's legacy of palaces and their contents were put under Lunacharski and his Commissariat for Enlightenment. The rest, the aristocratic mansions, the churches and the public buildings went to another Commissariat of Republican Property whose instructions were to lease them to tenants appropriate to the new social order. All Lunacharski could do was protest if this was going to lead to a loss of items of cultural or historical importance. This dual responsibility led to a great deal of confusion. Lunacharski, supported by his team of curators, formed a Collegium of the Museums of Petrograd which included authorities from the city palaces plus two influential party members. One, Isakov, became its chairman while the other, Yatmanov, became responsible for artistic and historical monuments. Lunacharski and this Collegium early on attempted to bring the Menshikov Palace under its control, an intention which lay behind the extension of Bernstam's responsibilities but they were only partially successful. They were able to retrieve the Chinese Palace and the Switchback Pavilion but the main Menshikov Palace had already been leased to an Agricultural College, which had filled it with 500 students and put the beautiful park to the plough. Lunacharski's role was restricted to doing what he could to prevent items of historical or artistic value from being laid waste.

It was no wonder that Bernstam resisted so strenuously this extension of his responsibilities. Poor man, he did not have a chance. The students paid no attention to his bleatings and soon the palace was filthy and disorderly, while the statues in the park were vandalised. He did manage to arrange for a team to make an inventory of the contents of the palace which reported to the Commissariat the terrible damage that was being done but it fell on deaf ears. With society rapidly disintegrating into civil war, such matters were only of importance to really dedicated people. Bernstam was dedicated but his main priority was to hand over responsibility for Oranienbaum to someone else. At meeting after meeting of the Council of Curators he pleaded with his colleagues to find someone else, but it was a long time before he was able to pass the chalice on to an administrator called Balabanov. By this time the country was trembling on the brink of a civil war, in which Oranienbaum would find itself in the front line.

The Treaty of Brest-Litovsk in March 1918 had ended the German threat, but unleashed the full fury of the civil war. It is not the purpose of this book to unravel the wonderfully confused fighting which followed, mostly well away from Petrograd and its palaces. Only once, in October 1919, were the palaces in danger when the British landed a White army under General Yudenich, which passed through Gatchina, briefly overran the suburbs of Petrograd and threatened the city itself. There was talk in Moscow of having to abandon the 'cradle of the revolution'. but an outraged Trotsky rushed to its rescue in his armoured train, rallied the demoralised defenders and within two days had Yudenich in full retreat. The actual fighting did not last long but there is a gap in the records of the Council of Curators from August 1919 for several months and when they did meet, all they could talk about was the lack of adequate guards. Nevertheless, Petrograd was spared the prolonged agony which laid waste to so much of the country over the next two years. Kiev changed hands ten times. But from the outset, the war injected into every corner of society, perhaps most of all in Petrograd, the deadly poison of suspicion and hatred. The Bolsheviks were by their nature conspiratorial and untrusting, and knew how precarious was their grip on power. Their reaction to every setback was to suspect sabotage and very often they were right.

The formerly well-to-do, such as the curators, were naturally suspect. Lunacharski could offer his curators some protection but he could not prevent the seizure of their bank accounts nor save them from the attentions of the red patrols, sent out, usually late at night, by various new revolutionary soviets to check on private houses and their owners. The aims of such raids could be specific or comprehensive, but most patrols were looking for arms, hoarded food or, since liquor sales were still banned, for alcohol. Many a cherished cellar was reduced to a small sea of wine and broken glass. There was no warning of these raids, nor pattern. One night, the Polovtsov found himself entertaining two quite independent patrols at the same time. They surprised each other in the drawing room and had a brief shoot out, before he was able properly to introduce them to each other. The most alarming were the patrols seeking evidence of counter revolutionary behaviour. For Polovtsov, who was trying to keep in touch with a brother serving in the Crimea with Wrangel's White Army, this posed a special risk but, being a diplomat, he was very skilled at covering his tracks. His greatest difficulty was to persuade them to let him open his antiques with the key instead of shooting out the locks.

But it was not only the rich who were oppressed. Peasants bringing their produce for sale were arrested for speculation if someone thought they were charging too much. Soon they stopped coming, forcing the citizens to go out foraging for themselves. At first, their sorties were local and individual but under the chaotic conditions, people soon began to organise large armed foraging parties that might be away for weeks scouring distant parts of the country for whatever they could buy or steal and hoping not to meet a better armed, official party entitled to requisition what they had got. Nothing the Bolsheviks did, however, could stop the black market.

Polovtsov found himself spending much time in the city. It was his job to liaise with the authorities in Petrograd, including Yatmanov and Isakov. And then he not only had to look after his wife and all their servants whom he dared not dismiss - but also his Stieglitz Institute, most of whose treasures were still waiting in their packing cases for some sort of decision. Furthermore, he found himself drawn in to try to prevent increasingly destitute friends from bartering their valuables for a meagre meal. It was one thing to hawk now useless uniforms for the melt down value of the epaulettes, but he could not bear to see real treasures cast before swine. Many agreed, preferring to take their treasures to the safety of the Hermitage, leaving them like unwanted babies outside the door in the hope that they would be taken in and cherished.

The other curators, Lukomski, Makarov and Bernstam, chose to stay in the relatively quiet conditions in the country, although here too, more and more local worthies were being appointed to political and administrative posts relating to the palaces which did not simplify their situations. But they were still dedicated to what they were doing, and had the comfort of a kindly commissar, supporting them both morally and financially. Nevertheless, it was about at this time that Lukomski got into trouble. His position at Tsarskoye Selo had always been subtly different from the others, deriving from his appointment by the Provisional Government as Chairman of the Arts and History Commission. He had, in fact, set this up himself but had arranged for it nominally to report to the Collegium of Museums of Petrograd. Lunacharski had not bothered to amend an arrangement which seemed to be working quite well but the membership of the Collegium was changing. Some began to find Lukomski altogether too high handed, and in the late summer of 1918 they proposed to appoint an administrative commissar over his head. Worse still, they chose his own assistant Yakovlev, for whom he had no regard. Never skilful politically, he tried to counter this by withdrawing his own candidacy as chief curator, believing the Collegium would rally to his side but they did not. They waited for three months for him to climb down and, when he did not, they appointed Yakovlev as curator as well. Using a pass given him by Lunacharski,

Lukomski went abroad to cool down. On his return, he tried to make the best of it. If Yakovlev would stick to the administrative stuff, which he hated anyway, he would happily work under him on the expert artistic work, which he loved. But it was too late. Yakovlev accepted but never let him work in peace and so, after a few weeks, Lukomski walked out with all the drama he could muster, leaving Tsarskoye Selo 'for a long time'. Lunacharski at no stage tried to intervene. From now on, Yakovlev represented Tsarskoye Selo on the Council of Curators.

While these curatorial dramas played themselves out, something much more alarming occurred in Petrograd in August 1918. Late in the month, the social democrats staged a coup, starting with an attempt to assassinate the Bolshevik leaders. It misfired. They killed Uritsky and wounded Lenin, but it was ill planned and uncoordinated, serving only to infuriate the Bolsheviks, whose distrust now turned to paranoia. The death of Uritsky marked a watershed in the development of the revolution. While he disagreed with Uritsky, Zubov admitted to rather liking him. Behind his fanaticism, Uritsky had a warm heart. It did not stop him from doing ruthless things but he did not enjoy them. With his death, such inhibitions fell away and cruelty became an accepted practice. It so happened that one of the assassins, called Kannegisser, fleeing from the scene, fell off his bicycle just in front of the exclusive English Club and ran inside to hide. The reds soon found him and arrested him - and everyone else present in the club. Polovtsov was dining next door in the equally exclusive New Club. Hearing what was happening, he advised all members to leave at once. When the red guards entered, it was virtually empty but they found a list of members. Most were rounded up next day and many were amongst the 500 'reactionaries' shot in cold blood as a warning to others. Polovtsov had wisely decided to go straight to Pavlovsk and escaped arrest, but not for long. However, when they caught up with him, he managed to get word to Lunacharski, who quickly procured his release. He complained bitterly but Lunacharski cut him short. "These things happen," he said cheerfully. "They arrested me a few days ago." Ironically, Kannegisser, despite announcements of his execution, was ransomed by some relatives in Sweden.

Somewhat rattled, Polovtsov decided to spend more time in Pavlovsk. He suspected that his wife might actually be safer without him and, in any case, the short train journey was becoming a nightmare. People could wait for days for a local train and then be squeezed out when one arrived. Not a sentimental man, he tells the moving story of a tiny girl left behind on the platform, the only member of her family too slow to get on board. To reduce pressure, the authorities decreed that an official permit had to be produced to get tickets but so unstable was the situation that a permit validly signed on Monday might be out of date by Friday. Still, he was able to throw himself into his work. He found Teleporovski a most congenial colleague and together they started to tackle the magnificent but neglected park, cutting back the vegetation hiding Maria Feodorovna's charming monuments, restoring her pavilions and evacuating to the relative safety of the palace any of their contents too valuable to leave unguarded. Then they threw themselves into reclaiming the fantasy villa, long neglected, which Catherine the Great had built for her grandson, Alexander. She had surrounded it with a little park of its own, full of temples and follies designed by Cameron to illustrate *Felitsa*, a flattering fairy story dedicated to the Empress herself by her court poet Derzhavin. Like the castle of the Sleeping Beauty, they had to hack their way in through the undergrowth.

One day, while this work was proceeding, Polovtsov noticed that he was being tailed. He went at once to Lunacharski to complain and the latter promised to put it right, but a week later, the tail was still there. Well aware by now that Lunacharski's power was not limitless and confident in Teleporevski's abilities, Polovtsov and his wife decided to leave. Already this was not easy. A cousin of his, trying to escape with some vestiges of his former wealth, had recently been arrested aboard the Stockholm ferry when agents searched it before it sailed. His first step was to make a string of appointments for the next two to three weeks. Next he wrote to Lunacharski that he could not do his job under such surveillance and had decided to take some time off, until his tail had been withdrawn. And then, at the end of October, secretly, without telling the servants, with no papers and hardly any baggage, they walked out of their palace on Stone Island and simply did not come back. He failed to show up at the Council meeting on 24th October which the others put down to the hazards of the time but when he also missed the next one on 16th November, Isakov took the chair and suggested that they should appoint a new chairman. The others still demurred, but when shortly afterwards a party of red guards arrived with a warrant to arrest him they had to accept that he had abandoned his post. Both Lukomski and Zubov, in their memoirs, do not hide their disappointment at his desertion but in fact his timing had been shrewd.

As the civil war developed, conditions of life in Petrograd became more and more impossible. Perhaps it is enough to say that during the period between the October Revolution in 1917 and the end of the civil war in the summer of 1921, the population of Petrograd fell from 2.5 million to 750,000. They were not all killed, of course. Most had left in the hope of finding some place easier to live in, or had joined the many bands roaming the country in search of food. Some left just to get away from the Bolshevik government. Whatever problem might arise, chaotic transport, lack of food, lack of fuel, the Bolsheviks instinct was to blame sabotage and to try to cure it by force. And when this failed, it must be the fault of the red guards who were not ruthless enough. So they recruited and armed Chinese coolies, made redundant from work on the Murmansk railway. Speaking no Russian and without pity for their former masters, they could not be suborned but unfortunately they could not be controlled either. Their brutality achieved new levels. By the time the civil war was ending, the people had had more than enough. Even the very sailors of Kronstadt Island, the heroes of the October Revolution, rose up in protest, seizing a bridgehead on the mainland which included several of the Oranienbaum palaces and pavilions. Conscript soldiers were forced to attack them, driven forward by Chekist policemen following close behind to shoot any waverers. Before the sailors were driven off the mainland, the palaces changed hands several times which did not improve them. In particular, the Switchback Pavilion, which the sailors used as a forward defensive position, was badly damaged. In the end, a series of massive and bloody attacks across the ice overwhelmed the sailors' defences on the island. A few escaped across the ice to Finland but most were treated with no mercy.

The country was in ruins and the people were too frightened and too exhausted to restore it. Even the Bolsheviks saw they could not be forced to do so and introduced the so-called New Economic Policy, which encouraged free enterprise on a small scale as the quickest way to get the devastated country back to work. Forced requisition ceased to be the basis of the economy. All sorts of oppressions were eased. Small shops reappeared and the more energetic peasants seized their opportunity so that grain production had almost returned to pre-war levels by the time the NEP was abolished in 1928. The country was saved by the very types of people the communists most deplored, but the NEP had never been more than a stop gap, 'a breathing space' as Lenin put it, 'that will enable us to advance again soon, on a broad front'. In the meanwhile, a great many people had taken the opportunity to leave the country including, perhaps, Bernstam and Teleporevski whose names disappear from the Council's records from the autumn of 1924.

By early 1919, Zubov had returned to Petrograd but not to Gatchina. He wanted to go there but Lunacharski would not take the risk of more trouble with the local soviet. In a way, he had made himself dispensible by recruiting the young academic V Makarov for his team when he first went to Gatchina. While not so brilliant an art expert as Zubov, Professor V Makarov had been doing a sound job in his place and was now confirmed as head curator. He had the knack of dealing with people and was to remain there through many difficult years, proving a steady hand on the tiller in stormy weather. He did not leave until the mid-thirties when he was promoted to the Museum Collegium in Leningrad. By that time, he had trained an able young woman called Seraphima Belaeva to take his place.

Zubov therefore never returned to Gatchina but Lunacharski liked him and he was given a job in the Department for the Preservation and Registration of Art Monuments as head of the section dealing with painting, sculpture and applied art. He was given a monthly salary of 1,440 roubles which was not bad. A new assistant curator at Peterhof, appointed at the same time, got only 620. Zubov never joined the Council of Curators which continued to meet through this period, although the growing social turmoil made it difficult to obtain funds. Their discussions were increasingly preoccupied with practical problems. One was the pressure from the townspeople to be allowed to cultivate the parks. Allotments for citizens were one thing but when the Agricultural Institute of Pushkin insisted on widespread agriculture, the curators joined battle. They were not given much support by the Commissariat for Public Property but they held the line. Starved of government funds, they resorted to longer and longer opening times, even opening to visitors in the depths of winter. This brought in a pittance but led to a wave of petty thefts for the guards were slack and apathetic.

There is no doubt that a good deal was lost during this period but it is not clear how much. No new inventory was made and probably these losses were less significant than others which came later. But it was something the curators found very difficult to deal with. Furthermore, in the climate of northern Russia, the exteriors of buildings soon start to crumble if not carefully looked after. First to go were the orangeries. The curators were tempted to dismantle them but Bernstam pointed out that they contained valuable glass which could be sold and replaced later if and when things got better.

There was much talk in the Council about these problems but they were dwarfed by the outbreak of a miniature civil war within the membership of the Council itself. This membership had been expanded by the introduction of authorities from the Hermitage and other Petrograd museums who formed a faction, led by their most senior man, O. Waltgauer and supported by none other than Peter von Weiner from the team that had originally gone to Gatchina. This faction believed that any of the contents of the country palaces that had significant artistic merit should be taken away and added to the Hermitage's collection. In their view, if the country palaces were worth keeping at all, it would be as sociological museums, odious examples of the extreme luxury enjoyed by the former classes. They did not need artistic masterpieces for such a purpose. Indeed, such treasures were best kept away from loutish tourists who did not have enough taste to appreciate them anyway. Led by Teleporevski, who had not yet lost his nerve, the country curators fiercely opposed this attempt to emasculate their collections. The argument raged on for meeting after meeting. Exasperated, Teleporovski went so far as to defy an order from the Museum Department to yield up Maria-Feodorovna's set of classic statues, which he held to be an integral part of Pavlovsk's design. Others challenged this view holding that although they had been acquired by Paul I, they had been kept in a separate museum until the 1860s. In the end however, Teleporovski found letters in the archives between Maria Feodorovna and her architects discussing how best the statues should be shown off. It was accepted by all that the statues in question were those acquired by Paul before he built Pavlovsk, putting the Waltgauer faction onto the defensive. To try to calm things down, Alexander Benois was added to the Council, in the belief that someone who could keep harmony within the Diaghilev Ballet, should be able to conciliate these furious curators. He indeed achieved acceptance of a formula whereby works of art, however valuable, should remain in the country palaces, provided they were an integral part of their design or of other historical significance. This saved Paul's classic statues for Pavlovsk and helped tempers to cool down, but it inevitably gave rise to prolonged arguments over which individual pieces fell into what category. There were quarrels about some statues at Gatchina and, in particular, about a statue of Hypnos from Pavlovsk which the Hermitage faction lusted after. This time they won, which was too much for Zubov, watching from outside.

Unable to restrain his feelings, he wrote a reckless article condemning this decision with all the rhetoric in his power, only to find himself isolated from all his colleagues and from the authorities, although supported, much to his surprise, by the trades union for museum workers. A few days later, he was asked to attend a Museum Conference in Moscow. Rather flattered, he supposed that the Hypnos case was to be debated there but, on arrival, he found it was not on the formal agenda. On the other hand, when he returned to his lodgings at the end of the first day, a colleague warned him that his room had been searched, papers taken and the impression left that he was in trouble. Sure enough, next day at the conference, he was approached by a member of the GPU, as the CHEKA was now called, with an order for his arrest. Luckily, the order had been made out in a cousin's name and not valid, but Zubov was taking no chances. Prison rations were only 100grammes of rye bread per day and prisoners had to rely on family and friends to supplement them. He did not know very many people in Moscow so, next day, he took with him a case stuffed with his washbag, a few clothes and as much food as he could lay his hands on. His spy was waiting for him with an amended warrant and they went together to the Lubianka. The next few days were filled with interrogations but no accusation.

After ten days, to his relief, he was moved to Petrograd where friends could bring him food and books and once, even a bottle of wine disguised in a milk carton. Apart from a ghastly fortnight in the notorious Gorokhovaya Street prison, sharing a room with some 200 intellectuals and academics, plus numberless cockroaches, bugs and lice, he almost enjoyed his time in prison. Compared with the hurly-burly outside, it was peaceful and let him catch up with all the books he had not had time to read. He was released after four months with the mystifying explanation that he had been arrested because a white spy, who had been caught and shot, had had a letter to Zubov in his pocket. He never discovered who the spy was nor anything about the letter. It cannot have been very damning because Zubov was soon afterwards allowed to leave the country with his new wife, on a six-month business pass provided by Lunacharski. He found that going abroad was almost more unsettling than gaol. He had not realised just how far Russia had sunk in material terms, notwithstanding the NEP. Even so, before the six months was up, he returned. He did not want to leave Russia and certainly not irresponsibly like Polovtsov, but he could now see that he might be forced to. It was time to make arrangements.

Within Narkompros, his voice was still influential and his responsibilities considerable. Lunacharski had never lost his regard for him and Zubov did not want to let him down by simply deserting him. He felt that he must hand over to someone in an orderly way and so he approached the well-known artist and art administrator, Igor Grabar who had the advantage of living in the new capital, Moscow. Lunacharski knew him and respected him. Although Grabar was never directly involved with the country palaces, his role in between the wars in the defence of Russia's cultural heritage was of the greatest importance. He had been born in Budapest, the son of a Russian lawyer from the Carpathians who was becoming unpopular with the authorities for championing minority slavic rights. In 1879, when Igor was still tiny, the family had fled to Russia where the lawyer eeked out a living as a provincial language teacher. It was soon clear that the boy was extremely gifted and the family made great sacrifices to enable him to attend a private school in Moscow.

He was not exactly happy there because he was so much poorer than the other boys, but not the least of Grabar's many talents was his amiability and knack of making friends. Being poor at least reduced the temptation to waste his time. His interests were omnivorous but he threw himself with most enthusiasm into the study of literature and art. He was an exceptionally gifted artist and throughout his life, whenever he needed a little money, he could paint and sell a few pictures without any difficulty. In due course he had no difficulty getting a place in the university at St. Petersburg. The first sight of the city entranced him. University life stretched his funds, so, in addition to his paintings, he started writing satirical articles for a magazine called *Niva* which soon invited him to illustrate books. These activities led him into contact with bohemian and artistic society. One evening, walking home with Tchaikovsky, the great man gave him some advice which he never forgot. "There are very few untalented people," he said, "but a great many who do not care to work."

After university, Grabar joined the Academy of Arts but he found it too backward looking and set out to tour Europe, mixing with the leading impressionists and finally settling in Munich, where he joined a private art academy. Quite soon the principal begged him to cease being a pupil and become his partner. Finding his paintings were being taken seriously, he forsook his bohemian social life, rose early to paint before dividing his day between teaching and studying architecture and sculpture at the polytechnic. He had taken Tchaikovsky's advice to heart. After five years of this, he returned to St. Petersburg not just an accomplished painter but a considerable expert on all aspects of art. He was at once taken up by the art world. Diaghilev, Alexander Benois, Eugene Lancere, Golovine and all the eminences of the modern movement became his friends. His old friends on the magazine Niva soon approached him with a major project - to update the seminal work *The History of Russian Art.* He accepted and by the outbreak of the first world war, had completed 15 volumes.

This did not hinder him from taking on other projects. He designed buildings, including a hospital. He continued to paint and, in 1912, accepted the post of Director of the Tretiakov Gallery in Moscow, originally set up to house the huge collection of the Tretiakov family. He found it in a chaotic condition and spent his first years there cataloguing its contents and bringing some coherence to their display. When the revolution came, he at once appreciated the twin dangers that Russia might lose many privately owned works of art and many art experts. On his own initiative, he called a meeting of museum workers to persuade them to remain at their posts. Naturally, first Golovine and then Lunacharski welcomed him as an ally. After the government moved to Moscow, he and Lunacharski became firm friends. Lunacharski asked him to set up a Collegium for the Preservation of Artistic and Historic Monuments on the lines of the one already operating under Yatmanov in Petrograd, but Grabar's Collegium soon outgrew its predecessor. He set up a restorer school and workshops, mainly with a view to saving and renovating the huge amount of neglected religious art in Russia's orthodox churches. It soon had offshoots in most of the towns in the empire.

All in all, Zubov could not have found a more accomplished person to hand over his responsibilities to, but the most important thing about Grabar still was that everybody liked him. Nor was he tainted by association with the 'former classes'. He had got where he was entirely by merit. Grabar must certainly have had an shrewd idea of what lay behind Zubov's approach but he would be the last man in the world to betray him. He agreed to look after Zubov's duties for him, at any rate for the time being. Eased in his mind, Zubov now needed a successor for his own Institute for Art History, of which he was still the director. On 15th January 1925 he signed an order appointing a Professor Schmidt in his place and, soon afterwards he left Russia. He left with some regret but it was a wise decision. He would never have been able to contain his wrath when Stalin began to plunder the country's art treasures.

In the meanwhile, Lukomski too had chosen exile. After his walk-out from his collegium, he never resumed a leading role with regard to the country palaces, but it is not clear when or how he left the country. By 1923 he was presumably in Berlin, for that is where he published his account of his experiences. In them, he quotes with some relish an article that had just appeared in *Izvestia* on the current state of the palaces.

> 'Perfectly organised in 1917-18, the palace museums are going through a period of decay in Detskoye Selo. This decay is because G. Lukomski left and, with him, many

knowledgeable curators. A new senior curator has been appointed with little idea of art and culture and this has resulted in a series of unforgivable vandalisms. They have cut down the beautiful lilacs in front of the Alexander Palace and the acacias in the park. Urgent repairs needed by the buildings are neglected. The guides are absolutely incompetent. The palaces are just about kept in order but idiotic rearrangements of the furniture have undone all Lukomski's sensitive work to achieve stylish unity. The superb parquet floors are covered in carpets and many of the most interesting rooms are closed. We urgently need to hire a museum expert who will get to know the palaces well.'

Not everyone today agrees with that *Izvestia* correspondent. Some feel that the first curators had over-indulged their preference for the eighteenth century and been blind to the merits of other periods. After all, the Romanovs had been collecting enthusiastically for over two hundred years and had always been able to afford the best. The high romantic Gothic of the Cottage Palace may one day be as much admired as Cameron's classicism and more so than the flamboyant baroque of the Catherine Palace. The criticism is not quite fair. The curators threw nothing away and were highly sensitive to the historical importance of items whose style they did not appreciate. They may have deplored the heavy art nouveau decoration with which Nicholas II had covered over Quarenghi's spare classic designs for the Alexanderhof, but they did not disturb it. Their main ambition had been to restore to each room its stylistic unity which the eclecticism of the Romanovs had often disturbed. In this, they foreshadowed a controversy which has never fully died away and which will return in later chapters of our story - what should restorers restore to? But such criticisms are mere details beside the first curators' real contribution. Without them, the palaces might have gone the way of Oranienbaum and so many other fine houses and art collections that have been overwhelmed in times of trouble, not only in Russia but elsewhere too. Of course they were helped by faithful friends like Shakhovskaya, Pospolitaki, Teleporovski and many others and could have achieved nothing without Lunacharski. But it was they who had first taken the lead and who were on the spot when needed. The world owes them a huge debt of gratitude.

Chapter 3

ON THE ROPES

Lenin never really recovered from the wound he received in 1918. In May 1922, he suffered his first stroke followed by two more within a year, aggravated, some say, by terminal syphilis. Whatever the truth, during much of 1923 he seems to have been little more than a cabbage, and, in January 1924, he died. This did not bode well for Lunacharski whom Lenin had admired and supported. Zubov is less generous, describing him as a kind but weak man, always keen to help but idealistic to a fault and an intellectual lightweight. As the manoeuvrings to succeed Lenin became more intense and savage, Lunacharski must have wondered what room would be left for his idealism. But where was he to go? He must also have realised that his influence was ebbing away. Still, they let him soldier on at Narkompros until 1927, when he was replaced by a Mr Bubnov. He was sent to join the Soviet delegation to the disarmament talks in Geneva. In 1929, he became involved in a Scientific Committee and finally, in 1933, he was nominated ambassador to Spain. He never got there, dying in France on the way. He was, as Lenin said, richly talented, finding time to write several plays and literary studies. And he led for a decade the educational renaissance of Russia which was his greatest achievement. In the official history of Narkompros, there is much about developing schools and virtually no mention of the country palaces. All the more credit to him that he found so much time for them too.

Apart from the Kronstadt rebellion which had wrecked Oranienbaum, the Civil War and, in particular, Yudenich's advance on Petrograd, seems to have caused little damage to the palaces but it brought a halt to any constructive work. For one thing there was no money, a problem made plain in the minutes of the Council meetings. Yakovlev, Makarov and Teleporovsky who now took the places of Lukomski, Zubov and Polovtsov, were men of a different stamp, less passionate perhaps but far better able to deal with the new circumstances. They were not going to make a scene over 'idiotic arrangements of the furniture'. Their preoccupations were calmer and of a more practical nature, but they did care greatly about keeping the museums open for the public and, despite growing pressures, they succeeded. During the early twenties they even became alarmed by the huge crowds of visitors, more than they could safely handle. On the other hand, they badly wanted the money and tried to solve the problem by extended their opening hours. Nevertheless, the money they took was never enough and the country, reeling after the destruction of the war, could only offer them derisory amounts. And longer hours increased the risk of theft.

Meanwhile, they were getting scant sympathy from the authorities who had many things to preoccupy them. If the curators could not make the palaces pay, they should be shut down or, better still, converted to other, more proletarian uses. Nevertheless, they kept open and managed to fight off the demands of the Hermitage but the wear and tear was beginning to tell. By early 1924 Alexander Benois had had enough. His name disappeared from the records followed by both Bernstam and Teleporevsky six months later. An architect called Arkhipov took over Peterhof and a Mr Dombrovsky, Pavlovsk.

Once the Civil War ended, Lunacharski was able to restart his campaign to rescue Russia's heritage. He reorganised his department, setting up an over-arching organisation called Glavnauka, an untranslatable term but it was to control, amongst other things, all bodies involved in the preservation of monuments anywhere in Russia. Under it, Grabar set up a Restorer Workshop which quickly grew, becoming powerful and well endowed but its priorities were aimed at the traditional medieval monuments of old Russia - the kremlins and cathedrals which had suffered terribly from years of neglect and more recently during the revolution and the war. They collected together as many of the surviving, pre-revolutionary artists and craftsmen as they could find, setting up ancillary branches where the work was needed, but not, apparently, in Petrograd, perhaps because its treasures had escaped the worst of the destruction. Anyway, the task they had set themselves far exceeded their resources. They did, however, lay down a rulebook for the guidance of restorers, enjoining them to clean, strengthen and repair but on no account to improve according to their own fancy. Restorers were required to prepare mock-ups of what they proposed to do, to be approved by an expert panel before touching the original. This established a sensible tradition which pertains to this day.

In the meanwhile, however, only such restoration work was undertaken in the country palaces as could be financed from their receipts from visitors or from tenants using their buildings. The records of the Council of Curators reveal their ambivalence regarding the hiring out of parts of the palaces to orphanages, workers rest homes, clubs for architects and, not least, the agricultural college still occupying Oranienbaum. They needed the money and were under much pressure to accept. Bernstam, ever constructive, produced a list of alternative suggestions - locations for restaurants, art exhibitions in Monplesir, a flower shop in the Aviary and so on. Teleporovsky accepted workers rest homes in the wings of Pavlovsk. Both allowed the making of hay in the parks while drawing the line at more intensive agriculture. But the pressures were all one way. The government, impoverished, had so little to offer the people who had brought them to power with such expectations. The very least they could do, so many felt, would be to let them enjoy a taste of the extraordinary luxury the Tsars had permitted themselves. The curators, dedicated to the preservation of beauty, struggled valiantly but judiciously to protect their palaces. Luckily they were not the sort of people to lose their tempers like Zubov and Lukomski. While all around them private mansions and even some Romanov palaces like Strelna were being converted wholesale into orphanages, rest homes and sanatoria, they fought a sensible rearguard action. However, they did draw the line when the local soviets wanted to change the name of Pavlovsk to Slutsk [after a civil war heroine called Slutskaya] and Gatchina to Trotsk [after Trotsky - later hurriedly changed to Krasnoguardeysk when Trotsky was banished]. Of course the soviets could call their towns what they liked but the curators insisted that the palaces should keep their traditional names.

The heyday of Glavnauka did not last for long. The Civil War had left the country in a state of bankruptcy. In the early twenties, more Russians died of starvation than had been killed by the war. There was a desperate need to raise money to import food and material to repair wrecked factories. In the Kremlin Armoury, they had found the contents of the once fabled and mysterious Diamond Room, which had been evacuated there from the Winter Palace. Under the tsars, few had been allowed to enter the Diamond Room and no-one more than once. It had never been properly catalogued. It contained not just the crown jewels and regalia but also breath-taking hordes of diamonds, rubies, sapphires and every kind of gem and precious metal. They found 25,300 carats of diamonds alone. A National Store [Gokhran] was set up to receive all this loot and in to it came also items confiscated from churches, monasteries and private citizens. Laws had been passed cancelling the right of inheritance and requiring the owners of works of art to register them. They could not take then abroad and could only keep them provided they could look after them properly. At any time, the state could demand that they be given up to it. There was some attempt to classify whatever was obtained by these means into items of artistic value and those which should be melted down but these stores were not the responsibility of the Commissariat of Enlightenment which had very little influence over such decisions. The country desperately needed money and there was a genuine feeling of disgust at the wealth that the church and the tsars had been hoarding. A Treasury official called Laserson, on viewing the contents of the Diamond Room, noted in his diary, 'I walked through halls full of every kind of receptacle - boxes, baskets, trunks and bags - all piled on top of each other to the ceiling. They were all labelled but no-one had yet attempted to open them or sort them out.' Furthermore, there was a new spirit abroad in the arts which pervaded the Commissariat of Enlightenment. One of the new wave artists, Kazimir Malevich, wrote: 'We should go forward boldly into the future, not gazing backwards. Let us discard the past which will only hamper our ability to develop the future.'

Trotsky's wife was put in charge of Gokhran and Maxim Gorky was instructed to use his western friends to arrange for sales. He tried to develop a ring of antique dealers he knew but the whole effort was pretty chaotic to begin with. Nobody knew what was the value of anything. Initially, they tended to break things up, melting down the precious metals for sale by weight. It soon occurred to them that they might make more as works of art although there was not a ready made market for such things as icons in the west.

But the communist bosses were in a hurry. Lenin himself wrote: 'We have to provide urgent measures to hurry up the sorting process. If we take too long, we won't get anything from Europe or America. You are going very slowly. I want to know what arrangements you are making to hurry things up.' Nevertheless, it took time to discover what they had for sale. Eventually a catalogue was prepared called 'Diamond Reserves' on the basis of which an exhibition was mounted in Moscow at which an English dealer called Norman Weiss created a sensation by buying a considerable part of it for cash. It was the start of what was to become for him something in the nature of a true fairy tale. He became for several years a confidential insider dealer with the Russians. He travelled regularly through Russia, visiting churches, monasteries and mansions and often buying their collections wholesale. He was most helpful in advising them over how to develop a market for such unfamiliar things as icons but what he really longed to get at were some of the artistic treasures still under the control of the Commissariat of Enlightenment.

None of this happened without resistance, of course, especially from the church hierarchy which had not yet been reduced to total submission. Icons and pictures taken from private houses, on the other hand, were often claimed by their émigré owners when the auction houses attempted to sell them. Grabar, whose role in their sale was ambivalent to say the least, advised that more work was needed to be done to create a favourable market for icons amongst western connoisseurs and museums, but perhaps he was playing for time. On the other hand, faced by priests and curators trying to retain their icons, he could be brutal. He did not believe in fighting lost causes and may well have felt that the churches had for too long hoarded too much wealth which could have been used for the benefit of the people. After all, the Trinity Sergiev Lavra monastery in Zagorsk, outside Moscow, alone had yielded 500 diamonds and 150 poods* of silver without sacrificing its essential role. The slogan was 'let church property belong to those who created it'. These treasures were not all sold advantageously. Trotsky wrote: 'It is better to get fifty million roubles in 1923 than wait to get seventy five million the following year'. That is not a good principle for bargaining.

Already by the early twenties, the Western antiquaries were indicating that gems and icons were all very well but what they were really keen to see would be works of art and antiques. As a result, the museum curators began to be put under pressure to prepare their collections for sale, at least those items not considered of 'museum quality' but it was left mainly to them to choose which. In 1925, however, Gokhran set up a special section called Antikvariat to handle the export of art and antiques in a more businesslike way. It was clear to the curators what lay ahead and some went so far as to hide their most cherished treasures.

They still had no intention to give up without a struggle when, in 1927, there was a change in the government's policy. Stalin was now firmly in the saddle and eager to get on with the revolution. The NEP had served its turn, as had all those enterprising comrades and kulaks who had made it succeed. They were about to suffer horrifically. In its place would come the first five year plan. It is probably not a coincidence that Lunacharski was relieved of Narkompros at this time and sent abroad. Grabar, who had developed his own close contacts high up in the party, began to suspect that an official position might soon become more of a liability than an asset. He had resigned from the Tretiakov in 1925 and would soon leave Glavnauka as well. One of the troubles with Stalin was the strong but idiosyncratic views he held about cultural matters. There is a building in Moscow with different window designs on each wall because the architect could not remember which Stalin had preferred and did not dare be wholly wrong. Tradition has it that Shostakhovich was reduced to jelly by Stalin's article denouncing *Lady Macbeth of Mtensk* as not only lacking social realism but any decent tunes he could hum. Anyway, Stalin decided that Russia's heritage from the past was all very well but only of value in so far as it contributed to the success of the Revolution and the establishment of Communism. The country palaces were admonished for not pulling their weight, courses in art history were replaced with the study of social realism in art or by courses for guides organised by a new body calling itself The Society for Proletarian Tourism. The nature of the Curators work changed and there was little they could do to protest. Their problems were as nothing to those of the kulaks. A new English language guide

* One pood equals just over 16 kilos

to Peterhof was produced in 1930. It is too long to quote in full but some extracts will illustrate the new mood as well as anything. It reads like a send-up.

It starts: 'In spite of the malicious calumny of some and the pretended indifference of others, the truth about the Country of the Soviets is becoming known to ever wider circles'. It urges the tourist first of all to visit the marvels of Soviet industrialisation and collective farming, but then acknowledges, more irritably than ruefully, that some people are still not 'indifferent to the past'. For them, 'Soviet historical museums ... present a vivid contrast between old and new Russia. Among these museums, Peterhof occupies the foremost place.' Having discussed the number of serfs who died to build it and the infusion of decadent western ideals in its design, it reassures the visitor that, 'following the revolution, Peterhof has changed radically in appearance and character. From being an exclusive imperial residence, for costly festivals and pompous ceremonies, it has become a place of rest for workers, peasants, soldiers and students from all parts of the Soviet Union.' This last claim was a bit rich but it was true that for masses of Leningraders, a day out in one of the parks was probably the nearest they got to recreation. It was about this time that the curators of Pavlovsk were officially reprimanded in a letter from Glavnauka. The whole tenor of their talk to visitors was wrong, said the letter: 'We modern people do not care about Maria Feodorovna at all. What we want to see is how the serfs lived, the guards and the servants. You should concentrate on their living conditions. The sort of thing people want to know is where the serfs were whipped.' At one time it was planned to convert Peterhof into a big sociological museum to illustrate the struggles of the classes down the years.

Against this background, Gokhran tightened the screws on the curators. Paramount was Russia's need to catch up with the west. The five year plan needed hard currency and from now on artistic treasures were to come under the hammer whatever their museum value. While the Hermitage was in the front line, the country palaces were not far behind. A new body had been set up called the People's Commissariat for Foreign Sales [NKVT] incorporating Antikvariat. Rather than propose items for sale, curators must rather decide what would be a 'necessary minimum' to be kept back if their museum was to remain open. A necessary minimum is hard to define but luckily the world market was not ready to have such a wealth of art treasures dumped on it all at once. Even the new People's Commissariat realised that the matter must be conducted with some skill and spread out over time. Still, it was a period of havoc for the museums but they doggedly remained open despite all the danger in the air. The story is told of one unwise visitor to Pavlovsk who asked where a particular tapestry had gone, only to be led away and disappear himself. Zubov, now in exile, met and upbraided a Soviet sales agent pedalling Russian art treasures in France. He was told: 'The Soviet Union is not just a state but the nucleus of the world wide union of soviet republics. It is not important where the treasures go now. Using the money we get for them, we will bring on world revolution and then we will simply take our treasures back.'

Norman Weiss had long since lost his privileged position. Most of the sales went to four Western collectors. The first in the field was Calust Gulbenkian. He was not a very generous payer but he was valued by the Russians because he dealt with them very secretly. They did not want it to become public knowledge that the great Soviet Union was having to sell off its heirlooms but the mystery of how such marvels were finding their way to Gulbenkian's house in Paris could not be kept secret for ever. There are not so many Rembrandts in the world. Someone was bound to recognise where they had come from and soon other more generous collectors were on their way, led by the American banker Andrew Mellon, or rather by his English agent, Joseph Duveen. Between them they were buying for the gallery Mellon was creating in Washington and money was not a problem. Their main competitor was Armand Hammer who had made it his life's work to straddle the Soviet and American worlds greatly to his own benefit.

The export of treasures peaked in 1934 after which it fell off fairly sharply largely because the slump in the West's economies affected so many collectors' ability to pay. There was one more big buyer to come, however, in the form of the American ambassador in Moscow just before the war. Joseph Davies was a rich lawyer with a fabulously rich wife. His political mission was to try to keep Russia in the anti-fascist alliance and he set about doing everything to ingratiate himself with Stalin and the other leaders. This policy was also extremely helpful for his personal mission which was to collect everything he could lay his hands on which had once belonged to the Romanovs. Suzanne Massie, in her excellent book on Pavlovsk, tells how the wife of an American Ambassador was taken by Mme Molotov down to the store rooms beneath the Kremlin, shown a veritable Aladdin's Cave of marvels and invited to take whatever she fancied. This must have been Mrs Joe Davies. After the war, their house in Washington was more like a museum than a home, and they had to employ a private police force continuously to patrol the grounds. But they were just one wealthy couple. The spoliation had been ruthless and systematic. Seraphima Belaeva, who had by now replaced Makarov at Gatchina, wrote in her diary: 'I lie on my bed and my heart aches'.

The whole business involved a prodigious amount of correspondence which was circulated to the highest level. It involved many people whose role should have been to defend the museums rather than pillage them. The names of Yatmanov, Isakov, Troinitsky [a senior Hermitage curator], Mandelbaum and of Zubov's old friend Professor Schmidt appear regularly in the files as apparently enthusiastic gamekeepers turned poacher. Only one of them, a Hermitage director called Boris Legran, had the courage to come out in the open and publish his disgust at what was happening. Grabar, no longer holding an official position, prudently does not appear in any of the letters but tradition has it that he was busy and quite effective pulling strings behind the scene to save whatever he could. And indeed the correspondence reveals a large gap between what Antikvariat fingered and what it actually sold. It is clear that the curators were fighting a rear guard action, doing what they could to confuse and delay things. The truth was that the men from Antikvariat did not actually know what there was in each palace and the curators were loath to tell them. Their policy was to reveal only the minimum which they hoped would satisfy them but this was dangerous work. Antikvariat took to sending their men as ordinary visitors, buying their tickets and joining the groups who were still being taken on guided tours. They were fairly easy to recognise. One of the Pavlovsk curators, Anatoly Kuchumov, recalled later that they would mutter together and make notes on paper: 'We would know then that we must expect shortly a further demand to provide some more of our treasures for sale.' Some curators are said to have found the courage to hide treasures. But if a great deal was saved by these tactics, a lot was lost also. The modern guidebook to Gatchina claims that when, a few years later, a new inventory was made of the contents of the palace, 120,000 items were found to be missing. This is a staggering amount. It is hard to believe the palace ever contained so much unless they counted every cup and saucer as a separate item.

Undoubtedly falling prices and the tailing off of sales in the mid thirties was an important factor. It is possible also that, by then, the government's attention was being distracted by other developments in Europe. At any rate, in the mid-thirties they called the whole thing off. While they were quite prepared to sell things, the thought that perhaps the Germans might be planning to take them without paying helped to concentrate their minds on other matters.

Chapter 4

GATHERING CLOUDS

The thirties were a difficult period for most Soviet citizens. Most afflicted of all were the peasants, subjected to the brutal collectivisation programme, but it was also hard for anyone associated with the former classes. One of Stalin's more chilling slogans was: 'We have many enemies abroad but even more in our midst'. Writers, professors, curators and people who generally earned their living with their brain were almost automatically suspect. Young idealists were everywhere ready to report an incautious remark or call for struggle meetings after working hours where colleagues they suspected of wrong attitudes or merely disliked were expected to grovel in expiation to save their lives. A curator hiding treasures from Antikvariat or even resisting its demands was running a dangerous risk. The abatement of sales after 1934 was therefore a considerable relief, but in its place came other problems for anyone who cared for Leningrad's historical monuments. Stalin had promulgated the doctrine that anything too closely associated with the Romanovs and their militaristic self-aggrandisement was of no worth and an embarrassment. Keen party members began to look around for things they could destroy to please him. In Leningrad, their eyes lit on such things as the church built to commemorate the land battle of Zusina where the Russians had actually got the better of the Japanese for once, or the monument to the heroic crew of the gun boat *Stereguschiy.** City planners therefore took a delight in removing these wantonly to make way for new proletarian developments. They were planning to remove the angel from the top of the Admiralty column and destroy the Moscow Gate, the huge and much panoplied triumphal arch on the Moskovskiy Prospekt which commemorated Russia's triumph over Turkey. However, before this was done, a meeting was called at the Institute of Architects to rally support for such policies. It was chaired by a rather brutish man called Edelson, who was a better party member than architect. He had spent some time hectoring the meeting but without convincing his audience, when a young man called Nikolai Belekhov spoke up.

Belekhov was born in 1904 and was free of any associations with the wrong sorts of people.

---

* The *Stereguschiy* was part of the Baltic Fleet sent half across the world to confront the Japanese. In the disastrous Battle of the Japanese Sea, the *Stereguschiy* was disabled and surrounded by the Japanese but the crew chose to scuttle their ship and drown, rather than be captured. The Baltic Fleet's voyage was a catalogue of disasters starting with its attack on the British trawlers on the Dogger Bank, mistaking them for Japanese destroyers. It speaks volumes that the *Stereguschiy*'s crew's action was the only thing worth commemorating.

He was a stocky man with an irrepressibly cheerful disposition and a keen intelligence. At the time of this meeting, he was still young but he already understood very well the way Soviet politics worked and the importance of having friends in the right places. He had got to know a lot of influential people including Grabar and through him Malenkov who was already on the fringes of the Politburo. He therefore stood up and took on Edelson, describing his attitude to monuments of artistic value as pure vandalism. There was a stunned silence while Edelson gathered together his thoughts in order to squash this upstart. Surrounded by his heavies, he launched a violent attack on Belekhov accusing him of organising a counter-revolutionary plot. He was an insect that would, he declared, have to be 'rendered harmless'. This was the sort of talk that normally led to the gulag and everyone wondered whether they would ever see Belekhov again. At the very least they expected him to make an abject speech begging forgiveness but he just sat there smiling and the meeting broke up. A week later, it was announced that Edelson had resigned. Nevertheless, the Moscow Gate was dismantled but it was done carefully, so that later, when politics had become rational again, it could be re-erected. He was not always successful, but Belekhov gained a reputation for fearlessness, which many people admired though not always openly.

Nevertheless, it was generally recognised that he was a man to be reckoned with and he was soon afterwards appointed deputy head of a new body called the Inspectorate for the Preservation of Artistic and Historical Monuments, headed by a man called Pobedonostzev. In a way, this was not entirely a new body since it could trace its lineage indirectly back to the Council of Curators set up by Polovtsov but its remit was much wider. It was the Inspectorate that was now responsible for the first steps that were taken to make contingency plans for a war with Germany.

In the meanwhile Lunacharski's work had been bearing fruit. While the propaganda was all about lady tractor drivers and Stakhanovite* bricklayers, better education was uncovering in unexpected places young people of great and diverse talents. The party did not discourage art, provided it was not subversive. Indeed, its propaganda potential was valued but not all young people wanted to prostitute their talents for the party. Several were growing up during these frightening years whose future contribution to the survival of the palaces was going to prove as great, perhaps even greater than that of the first curators. One such was the young inventory taker from Pavlovsk, Anatoly Mikhailovich Kuchumov.

Born in 1912 in a little village on the Volga, he was brought up by his grandmother in a log cabin his father had built. His father had found he could earn more repairing furniture for the gentry in St. Petersburg, while his wife worked in the Fabergé factory. Although the grandmother had no pretensions and was indeed nearly illiterate, the parents' work meant that it was not a typical peasant family. The parents used to send home little luxuries - nice bits of porcelain and reproductions of Romanov portraits. And they owned a much treasured set of china. They sent toys too but Kuchumov preferred to play with the other pretty things. He loved the feel of the bone china. The portraits he proudly arranged as in a gallery. Then one day when he was five, a red soldier forced his way into their house and tore them all down. The revolution had arrived.

* Stakhanov was a coal miner in the thirties who, with some assistance, dug an amazing amount of coal during the course of a single day. From then on, Russian workers were exhorted to try harder in his name.

Everything changed. The Kuchumovs may have been suspected of ideas above their station because Anatoly was now rejected by the local school. This could have been a blessing in disguise. He was a very bright boy and probably made more progress working at home. At any rate, when he was nine, he was accepted by a boarding school in the local town, Mologa. It was a tough life. Every Sunday, he had to walk home 26 kilometres to visit his grandmother - and 26 kilometres back. But the scope of the school was far greater than anything the little village school could offer.

When he was eleven he was sent to a pioneer camp in the grounds of a former aristocratic mansion, now half ruined and boarded up. One day, the boys were taken round it to see for themselves 'how the reptiles used to live'. Though much had been looted, enough had survived to widen Kuchumov's eyes. He had never imagined such beauty, such exquisite craftsmanship. Shortly afterwards, he got permission to live with an aunt, who worked as concierge of the Mologa Museum, where other aristocratic treasures were on display. Seeing how they fascinated the boy, the curator of the museum took him up and started teaching him about art. He thrilled him with stories of his army service, spent as a guard in Tsarskoye Seloe. He guided Kuchumov's reading so well that the pupil soon had a wider grasp of art history than his mentor. Kuchumov was blessed with an extraordinary memory. Later, when he was working as a curator in Pushkin, his staff found he had total recall of every room and its contents. They would play games to test him out, moving objects about to see if he noticed. He always did.

At 19 he joined his parents in what was now called Leningrad. He was entranced by the city, its architecture and above all its museums, but it was 1931 and the collectivisation famine was at its height. There was little hope of a job in the arts. He became a trainee in the electrochemical industry, but managed to enrol in night classes at the Hermitage which entitled him to free run of its library. Many of his tutors were real experts, from tsarist days. Delighted by his enthusiasm and talent, they taught him not just about art but about the secrets of the cabinet makers and the potters, and how to recognise real quality. He took every opportunity to visit the country palaces and one winter's day, wandering in the park in Pushkin, he fell through the ice covering a wet ditch, emerging sodden, freezing and unhappy. Taking sympathy on a regular visitor, the soldiers took him into their guardroom to dry out by their stove. He started to tell them how much he envied their positions, working in such a beautiful place and, the next thing he knew, he was being cross questioned by the palace commandant, who was extremely impressed. A few days later, aged 20, he started work as an inventory taker at Pavlovsk.

From this point, there was no holding him. Within two years, he had become Head Curator of the vast Catherine Palace. Shortly afterwards, although they could not afford the ceremony, he married Anna, a star-struck art history student working there. They had a boy, Felix. The pay was miserable but they were in heaven. In 1937, he was promoted again to become Director of the Alexander Palace while Anna went back to work in the nearby Catherine Palace. The overall head of Pushkin at this time was a man called Vladimir Ladhukin, an administrator, but Kuchumov liked both him and his head guide, Vera Lemus, and the park curator Evgenia Turova. Everything was going well.

These were uneasy days however. Hitler had never disguised his ambition to destroy the Soviet Union and now he seemed firmly in power and busy rearming. Maybe it was time to start contingency planning. Already in 1936 the Leningrad Government had decided to prepare an evacuation plan. It was to be kept secret. Two senior experts from the Hermitage took charge. They decided not to be too ambitious. In the first world war, the frontier had been hundreds of miles away in the middle of Poland but now it was the Narva River, barely 70 miles from Gatchina and a hundred from Leningrad. There would be no time to evacuate much. The two men took it upon themselves to select only what they thought was most precious and unique, picking 4,871 items in all, of which 276 were from the huge Catherine Palace and a pathetic seven from the Alexander Palace. Of course they involved the palace directors in their plans but not the curators, since it was too sensitive. The curators, however, were now charged with the making of new inventories. Once these plans were ready, the palace directors were ordered to lay in sufficient packaging materials and to lock the plans in their safes.

Two years later, the new inventories were ready and revealed just how much had disappeared. They also revealed just what treasures were to be left behind under the existing evacuation plans. During 1939, as a consequence of Stalin's pact with Hitler, Russia had occupied the Baltic states and a large chunk of Poland, pushing back her frontiers to approximately where they had been before the first war. An invader from the south would now have to advance many hundreds of miles to reach Leningrad, giving much more time for the evacuation of treasures. The curators applied for permission to revise and enlarge the plans, but were told that this would require authority from the highest level in Moscow. This was not something that could be obtained in a hurry and, in any case, Stalin had convinced himself that the Nazi danger had been negotiated away. He and Hitler would share the world and not quarrel over it. What Stalin thought, most other people thought too and so nothing more was done about contingency plans. The evacuation plans could not be amended, no more packaging materials ordered nor extra storage arranged in the safe areas to the rear. If war came, the new inventories would help but it would really be up to the curators with their knowledge of their collections and their ingenuity to save what they could. But no-one was expecting a war. After all, Hitler had not yet finished off Britain.

Sunday, June 22nd 1941, was a particularly lovely day which brought the brightly coloured crowds out from the city to saunter round the country parks, in holiday mood, picnicking, playing volley ball or noisy games of hide and seek, dancing to the bands or their own concertinas, or just sauntering through the dappled woods and sunlit glades. The guided tours were doing brisk business in the palaces. This was what Leningraders most enjoyed. The first hint of trouble was a message that Molotov was to speak on the radio at midday. Kuchumov hastily set up a loudspeaker at Alexanderhof and a crowd began to gather buzzing with curiosity. When Molotov started to speak, he did not beat about the bush. 'Early this morning, at four o'clock and without any warning, German troops invaded our country, attacking on a wide front and bombing our cities.' His gravelly voice, usually so flat, trembled with emotion as he described the treachery of the enemy and his faith in Russia and its people. He wound up with a defiant call to victory. The crowd stood in stunned silence trying to take it in.

Vera Lemus, at the Catherine Palace, had had few moments warning of what Molotov was going to say when her son in law came to say goodbye. He had just received a telegram calling him up. With lead in her heart, she watched while the smiling crowds enjoyed a few minutes more in the sunshine but, after midday, it did not take long for the news to start to run through the crowds. As she watched, she could not hear but could see the word spreading, as the picnics were packed up and the mothers rounded up their children. Soon the whole park seemed to be trudging silently towards the station. The halcyon days were over. It was all starting again, the terror, the hardship and the grief that all but the youngest remembered so well.

In the first world war, there had been much hesitation as to whether to evacuate anything but now there was none. The Russians' lack of preparation, Stalin's recent purge of his best generals, the army's subsequent pathetic performance against the Finns, everything pointed towards disaster. And then the violence of the German blitzkrieg, their achievement of total surprise [despite British warnings] and the destruction in the first hours of almost the whole Russian air force on the ground left little need for argument. The Germans seemed to be making a beeline for Leningrad. They were coming. That was the only safe assumption. The only questions were how long would they take and could they be kept out of the city. None of the Pushkin curators felt able to go home that night until they had received their instructions. At 3am, Vera Lemus heard Anna Kuchumova calling her. Ladukhin had called them to a meeting. He told them he had been called up and handed over his responsibilities to the curators. Next he produced the 1936 plan from his safe and told them to put it into effect at once. He then took Anatoly Kuchumov aside and told him that his task was to accompany the first load of treasures to the rear and thereafter to remain there and be responsible for the safety and welfare of whatever else they managed to send him in the time they might be granted. Two days later, someone remembered to declare the museums closed.

It took only those two days for the palaces to put the 1936 plans into effect. They still had plenty of helpers, the suitable crates were waiting ready and it was all on a small scale. All was soon ready and awaiting transport. The planners had undoubtedly been formidable experts but the curators were mystified by some of their choices. They clearly had had only a vague knowledge of what the palaces actually contained. The Germans might be advancing into Russia at a terrifying rate, but they were still hundreds of miles away. It would be several weeks before they could possibly reach the country palaces, if ever they did. Russia was mobilising but, even if the enemy could not be stopped, there must still be time to save a lot.

One of the first men to be called up was Pobedonostzev, the head of the Inspectorate. Belekhov at once stepped into his shoes and it was largely up to him to find the wherewithal the curators would need, the packaging materials, the railway wagons and later the lorries, often ammunition lorries borrowed on their way back from the front for more supplies. While the curators could perform deeds of derring-do, it would avail little without the support he tried to muster for them. His first task was to make sure there were people at each of the country palaces with the knowledge and skills to make the best of the time available. The museum directors were ill qualified for the task because, as administrators, they knew too little about the treasures. Furthermore, being mostly men, they could expect their call-up at any moment. The responsibility therefore soon devolved to the senior curators, mostly women, who turned out to be a redoubtable bunch. The senior was Seraphima Belaeva of Gatchina. She had been trained as an art historian and had joined V. Makarov at Gatchina in twenties. She enjoyed a calm, almost serene character which helped her survive some terrible times. She had suffered greatly to watch the collection at Gatchina being systematically pillaged for sale to the west, but shortly worse was to come. At Pushkin, as well as Vera Lemus, there were Eugenia Turova and Bronislava Volkind. Another woman, Marina Tikhomirova was supposed to be in charge of Peterhof but no-one could find her. There was no time to search and her duties devolved on a junior, Chubova, supported by the head administrator from Oranienbaum, a Mr Rebone.

Nikolai Weiss, the most senior curator at Pavlovsk, was experienced but not cut out to be a man of action. The director, Ivan Mikryukov, was the exact opposite. He had only arrived in the January. As a very young man, he had played a heroic role in the civil war but antiquities were not his speciality. Nevertheless, he had faithfully prepared everything down to the last detail to pack up and despatch the 1936 list, but he had little idea what to do after that. To make matters worse, his relations with the local soviet, never good, came to a head. They had been illegally felling trees in the park and, expressing his honourable outrage, he had fallen foul of their president, a cleaning lady called Ushakova. In a fury, she told him to stop messing about with tsarist baubles and to join the partisans who needed experienced men. Mikryukov carried on working, but Belekhov, whose finger was on so many pulses, realised he would have to send someone to support him. With inspired choice, he selected a young woman called Anna Zelenova.

She was much the same age as Kuchumov but city bred. Her family home was just off the Nevski Prospekt, opposite the Grand Hotel Europa, a very smart address but her father was of humble origin. His job, as locksmith and metalworker gave him entry to all the grand buildings, private and public, in and around the Iskusstv Square. He often used to take his daughter with him and she soon learned to appreciate what beautiful things some other people had. Educated in the Peterschulle, a German language school nearby, she got good grades. She developed a passion for art and art history but, although a good young communist, she was not attracted by the way it was taught by the Society of Proletarian Tourism. So she started to train as an industrial draughtsman while, in the evenings, she attended classes on art at the Herzen Pedagogical Institute. She was quite a good draughtsman but she hated it and, after three years, she one day asked herself why on earth she was doing it. Finding no answer, she decided that even proletarian tourism would be more interesting, and enrolled in the training school for guides, where her passion and knowledge made her stand out. After a short spell as a guide in the Hermitage, she was sent in 1931 to Pavlovsk which overjoyed her, because it was easily her favourite of all the palaces. It was already clear to everyone that she could be much more than just a guide, and she was soon appointed a Research Fellow and then Deputy Director of the Scientific Department. In 1941, she was recalled to become Secretary of the Museum of the History of Leningrad, a big job for a young woman.

Slight, owlishly bespectacled, Anna Zelenova looked like a gentle young teacher. She had a softly rounded face of the type that does not age quickly. She not only was young, she looked even younger, but her bookish exterior hid a steely and passionate nature. When on 6th July, she was asked to go to Pavlovsk to take charge of the evacuation, she at first protested that it was beyond her, but she was not hard to persuade. Once she had accepted, it was with all her heart. She did not even go home to pack a bag but went straight to the station and to Pavlovsk. She did not return to Leningrad until driven there by the German advance. All the rest of her life was devoted to Pavlovsk, the palace and the park. On the same day, the first shipment left Pavlovsk for Gorky as prescribed by the 1936 contingency plan.

With Mikryukov and Weiss, Zelenova set up her command post in the Egyptian Hall, just inside the main entrance. They worked closely as a team until mid-August when Mikryukov's political problems came to a head. At the behest of the local soviet he was dismissed from his post and expelled from the party. He went on working but now Zelenova was left in charge. There was so much to do and, as more and more men were called up, all the time fewer people to do it. Furthermore, as the Germans brushed aside one after another Russian defensive line, there were calls for all able bodied citizens, including the curators and their staffs, to drop everything and help dig trenches and defensive positions for the weary soldiers to occupy if their retreat reached the palaces. The military considered Pushkin and Pavlovsk with their hills and wooded parks to offer promising defensive positions.

The next six weeks were a chaotic time and it is miraculous how much each team achieved. Everything was in short supply. Everything had to be improvised. Everything had to be decided on the run. Packing cases had to be knocked up from whatever timber could be found. Hay had to be cut and cured to augment the scraps of paper and cardboard which was all they had to protect the china, porcelain and crystal. Pictures had to be removed from their stretchers, clipped together and boxed or, if too big, rolled up together, as were the tapestries, and sewn up in oilskin. Samples of wall coverings and upholstery had to be taken for later copying. Not all the lacquered and carved panelling from the walls could be saved, but samples had to be taken from each room. Clearly there was no possibility of taking all the furniture but one chair or table could be taken from every set to provide a model to be copied should the rest be lost. Out of all this unplanned chaos, a sort of order emerged, an incarnation of the combined knowledge and intelligence of these key women.

Agonising decisions had to be made, especially at Pavlovsk where an exquisite unity of style had been preserved virtually unchanged since Maria Feodorovna had created it. In the Catherine Palace, they decided to leave the famous Amber Room. It was so intricate and probably so brittle, that they felt any attempt to move it would surely destroy it anyway. So it was covered with protective cladding and left to the mercy of the Germans. Similarly the parquet floors had to be left, and the ceiling paintings. Only one ceiling painting was detached and shipped out, a Tiepolo in the Chinese Palace in Oranienbaum. This was intercepted on its way to Leningrad by a German patrol and never seen again. It presumably perished in the fire which destroyed Peterhof a day or so later. Ironically, had they left it alone it would have survived because the Germans never bothered to occupy the Chinese Palace. All other ceiling paintings had to be left in situ at the mercy of the Germans and the fortunes of war.

It was soon realised that most of the statues were too heavy to evacuate. One batch from Peterhof's Grand Cascade was sent to Leningrad and spent the war in a railway station but thereafter there was not enough transport. It was decided to hide the rest, mostly buried in the parks. At Peterhof, they rediscovered a tunnel that led from the grotto to the Court of Arms Pavilion and crammed the rest of the statues from the cascades into it. All this was mainly done by women and a few old men, demonstrating the strength of desperation. But some they could not move. The huge statue of Samson, celebrating Peter's great victory over the Swedes at Poltava, was just too heavy as were his two attendant rivers and, in the upper gardens, Neptune and his tritons. Nevertheless most were buried in the parks near but not too near where they stood. Much effort was devoted to disguising the disturbed earth. Luckily in the long summer days, grass grows very fast in Leningrad and by the time the Germans reached the palaces, shells and bombs had disturbed much of the ground anyway. Zelenova, aware of German thoroughness, insisted that statues should all be buried at least three metres deep, and then covered with sand and a board. The huge statue of the three graces in Maria Feodorovna's garden was too heavy to move far from its pedestal so she insisted that its pit be extra deep at five metres. In such a formal garden, it would not be easy to disguise the pit. The classical statues from the library and other indoor positions, were manhandled, or rather woman-handled down to the far end of the cellars where they were bricked in. They distressed the new brickwork as best they could and rebuilt piles of junk around it to look as natural as possible. Belaeva, at Gatchina was unable to move the large statues that flanked the main entrance so she had them sandbagged and then neatly boarded up and painted to try to make them look like a feature of the architecture. She also had to leave the statues of Poetry and Culture looking out over the White Lake

While the curators tried to make rational selections of what to save out of their long inventories, desperate efforts were made to find or make packing materials. Much green wood had to be used and unripe hay. Pictures were removed from their stretchers and used to protect the porcelain. Carpets were rolled round the more fragile furniture. As the cases came ready, they were labelled and left in front of the palaces for the next transport to take them to the station whence they would be shipped to Leningrad and thence to Gorky, where storage had been set aside. There was no time to worry that only enough had been reserved for the original modest evacuation plan.

On 30th August the Germans reached Mga and severed the rail link between Leningrad and the rest of the country. Anything more would have to be stored in Leningrad and the spacious, if damp St Izaak's Cathedral was chosen, whose massive walls could withstand quite a lot of bombs and shells. It was stored there with great secrecy because Irina Benois, one of the great post war restorers, who spent much time visiting her wounded husband in the Astoria, just across the road, had no idea it was there until after the war. Despite Belekhov's efforts, it became steadily more difficult to get transport as the Russian army fell back in front of the German onslaught. Still, the curators kept packing but, sensing that the end was not far off, they also started to take down what they could to the cellars. As the rumble of artillery fire grew steadily louder and Messerschmidts became a daily feature overhead, they redoubled their efforts to board up the windows and protect exposed features with sandbags. Water and sand were put out in every room and coverings spread over the parquet flooring.

Gatchina was the first to fall on the 8th September. Belaeva had just despatched five lorry loads to Leningrad when she was told that she and her colleagues must leave. They set out on foot but, after some kilometres, were able to hitch a lift on an ammunition lorry most of the way back to St. Izaak's. By this time, the Germans had swept across the flat plains and their right wing had reached Lake Ladoga at Schlusselburg, cutting off the city from Russia. They were within artillery range of the city suburbs. On the left there were few obstacles between them and the coast at Peterhof. In the centre, however, the low hills around Pavlovsk, Pushkin and Pulkovo offered the Russians defensive possibilities. They began to form the tip of a Russian salient, vulnerable but from whence a few treasures might yet be rescued. The electricity had long since been cut off. The curators used candles and when they were finished, made makeshift oil lamps with whatever they could find to serve as a wick. Case after case was still being packed and taken out to await the still hoped for lorries.

Exhausted Russian soldiers started to fall back to defensive positions which the citizens had been digging in the park at Pavlovsk. A growing multitude of refugees began to pour into the little town. Zelenova took pity on some and allowed them to rest in the cellars of the palace, scrounging some food for them from an army quartermaster. The army was still resolved to make a stand on this high ground and the HQ of the 168th Division established itself in one of the wings of Pavlovsk. One of its staff officers, a Major Borschev, was later to write his war memoirs with vivid memories of Zelenova. In particular he remembers her storming into his office like a she devil. What, she wanted to know, were those motorbikes doing in Maria Feodorovna's private garden? Sheepishly, he told his men to move them elsewhere.

In the meanwhile, a volunteer regiment of Kirov factory workers took shelter in the basement of the Cameron Gallery at Pushkin. One of its members, the writer Daniel Granin, no soldier, had found to his consternation that the men had elected him to be their officer. It was he, therefore, who was aroused in the night by a dishevelled and furious palace attendant. Propelled by the arm, Granin was being shown evidence how his men were not using tapachkis in the palace, when a hideous scraping sound occurred and a group of soldiers dragged a heavy mortar into the room, leaving great raw furrows in their wake. Beside himself, the custodian hurled himself upon the men who hardly noticed him. Granin grabbed him. "Who are you?" "I'm the custodian of the Cameron Gallery." "Don't you realise there are Germans in the park!" A rattle of fire gun seemed to emphasise the point. "Germans?" shouted the man, waving his arms. "That's your business! Mine is to protect the palace, which your men are destroying!" Granin put out a gentle restraining hand. "Protecting it for whom?" he asked. "For Fritz?" Suddenly the man's eyes widened. He looked about and seemed almost to shrink in size. "For Fritz?" he repeated. "Oh, God! They wouldn't dare! Not when they see it." One of the soldiers burst out laughing. Granin's heart melted. "OK," he said, "go and get some boards and we'll do what we can. It's a pity to spoil the floor." At that moment, bullets started striking the walls of the gallery, ripping into the Doric columns and the busts of the Roman emperors. By morning, the soldiers were on the move again, trudging towards the city. They had discussed whether to take the custodian with them but had decided he would not have come.

That same evening, Vera Lemus was with Turova and Popova, sheltering in the cellars under the Zubov wing of the palace. Miraculously that morning a lorry had arrived but they had had nothing packed. They filled it higgledy-piggledy with gilded furniture and hoped for the best. After that, they had seen no more lorries but had been told that some horse transport was on its way for them. At this point, Lemus became aware that a crowd of terrified refugees was hiding in the cellars and she and one or two others went to try to calm them and to advise them to seek shelter elsewhere. Already there were rumours that the Germans intended to blow up the palace, but they would not leave. When she returned to where she had left the other curators, they found that the horse transport had been and gone without them. They were debating what to do. Where could they go? Some had children with them. At this moment, providentially, a Russian officer entered and they asked him what to do. At least he was decisive. "For God's sake!" he said. "RUN AWAY!" Those that could didn't wait. Rushing about to gather a few last minute papers, they set off on foot for Leningrad, 20 miles away. Surrounded by sounds of gunfire and struggling through the dark, they reached Kupchino, a village on the railway just north of Pushkin, where they halted, too exhausted to continue. They were preparing to conceal themselves in the long grass when they heard sounds of a train approaching. It was going very slowly to allow stragglers to scramble on board. At six o'clock next morning, it reached Vitebsk station in the city and they made their way to St. Izaak's, which would be their home for some time to come.

Zelenova at Pavlovsk was having similar experiences. On the 31st August, Borschev had found her, with Nikolai Weiss sitting on some packing cases in front of the palace. Would they be able to get them away, she asked him. Without much confidence he assured her they would. The division were planning to make a stand. The arrival of the HQ in Pavlovsk attracted the attention of the German bombers and artillery. The park, however, offered good defensive positions against attack from the south and Borschev proved right. A week later, they were still holding the Germans off. But the Germans had fresh units to throw in and gradually the front line was forced back. By 12th September, it was barely a thousand yards from the palace. The emergency had added new impetus to the curators frantically making last minute arrangements. Zelenova remembered that amongst the books in the library were files of all the original plans of the palace. It was a thought they came to bless later. Most of the fighting was now in the town and the front in the park was holding but the Germans had the HQ's range and regularly shelled it. The curators never stopped working but by 15th September they felt they had buried and hidden all that they could. Weiss now wanted to leave but Zelenova would not. There were still crates awaiting transport and it might yet be possible to pack others. Belekhov in Leningrad must know and would surely send transport. On the 16th, the divisional HQ withdrew. In desperation, Zelenova found a drover with a horse and wagon. They had just finished loading the packing cases when a jeep screeched to a halt. A young officer got out. "What are you all doing here? Who are you?" Drawing herself up, Anna explained that she was in charge of the palace. "We are pulling out of the town" "And I want to too if they will only send the vehicles." "Look, lady. There won't be any! You're lucky I came by. Get in! Quick!" She would not. Her responsibility was to a higher authority than him. In desperation, the officer tried once more. "Don't you realise that this is now German territory. For the last time, get in!" But she still wouldn't. He drove off. First she and Weiss went down to the cellars to explain the situation to the refugees. She offered the old and the children places on her wagon. The rest would have to walk, but they would not leave their cover. Luckily, when the Germans arrived, the first sound they heard from the cellars was a baby crying so they forbore to toss in their hand grenades.

Emerging into the daylight again, the wagon was gone but a forester arrived on his motorcycle. Seeing them, he stopped and shouted, "Leave for God's sake! They're not far behind me!" It was time to go. They ran to the Egyptian vestibule where they filled their brief cases with papers concerning the evacuation including the all important map of where the statues were buried. In the gathering dusk, they set off through the woods, taking cover every now then when the fire seemed too close. They lost their way and somehow found themselves re-entering the town of Pushkin. Weiss took charge. He chose the road and steered her parallel to it but through the fields. The further they got, the closer they permitted themselves to approach the road. Suddenly they heard a lorry coming up behind them. Hoping desperately that it was Russian, they flagged it down. It was, but it was full. "I'll only take the girl!" said the driver. She would not leave Weiss. As the lorry drove away, it all got too much for her and she burst into tears. Weiss, much moved, started to comfort her but suddenly a gunfight seemed to break out all round them. It was probably some way off but, for what seemed ages, they cowered in a ditch. Then, as suddenly as it had begun, it stopped. Cautiously they went on their way again. Some hours later, some more trucks were heard. Hardly daring to hope that they were Russian, Weiss concealed Zelenova and flagged them down. Moments later, he was back. His voice brooked no opposition. "Get in!" She did. At 10am next morning she staggered into St. Izaak's.

Chapter 5

THE SIEGE

Leningrad had been cut off on 8th September, over a week before Zelenova finally dragged herself into St. Izaak's, the last to arrive. She found a whole community of curators, living in the crypts beneath their crates and under the kindly eye of the oldest, Seraphima Belaeva. Most of them had nowhere else to go and, while the massive cathedral was virtually bombproof, it was bitterly cold, frozen all winter and with water running down the walls in spring. There was only one little kiosk, formerly the ticket office, where there was a bourzhika stove* and the summer, when vulnerable materials could be dried out, was terribly short. Their immediate task, however, was to survive the first winter of the siege.

The winter of 1941/2 was a story of disaster. There was a bitter fight for the Pulkovo Hills just north of Pushkin. The Germans took them but the Russians drove them off again in a counter-attack and, in the end, after heavy casualties, the Germans desisted. They had other plans. Leningrad's main food reserves were stored in a series of huge wooden warehouses built before the first war and known as the Badaev Warehouses. They were well known to the Germans who attacked them from the air with clinical accuracy on the first night of the siege. All the main warehouses took fire and many other food depots elsewhere in the city were attacked and damaged too. It was so well done that the defenders could only assume that there had been traitors in their midst with torches and signals for the pilots. Whatever the truth, the city was staring starvation in the face.

There have been many good descriptions of what the ordinary people of Leningrad suffered that first winter. One of the most moving is that of the young singer, Galina Vishnevskaya, in her autobiography. It is not our intention to try to compete with it but during our researches for this book, we were handed a school notebook. It contains the diary of a young man, a rather splendid young man. He was in his third year at the Leningrad College of Energy Engineering. It is quite short and we repeat it in full.

---

* A small, often home-made stove rounded like the belly of the bourgeois businessmen caricatured in magazines like *Krokodil* - whence the name.

DIARY
by Vladimir Nikolaevich Mylnikov

25th December 1941.
I have decided to keep a diary and to record what is happening in my life, that of my country and of news from abroad. I got up today at 9.15, put on the samovar and then waited for my Mum to come back from getting some bread. She brought some good news. From now on, we are to get 250 grammes of bread instead of 125. This is the allowance for light workers and dependants. Manual workers get 350gr. Today we got altogether 1,100gr because we are still using father's card.

First I will record briefly what has been happening. Father died on 17th December. We took him to be buried in the Smolensk Cemetery, in the mass grave. We managed to get a coffin in exchange for 500gr of bread, two packs of cigarettes and 15 roubles. We took the coffin on a sledge to the cemetery where the funeral was attended by Aunt Mania, who played a lively part, Uncle Senia, Uncle Sasha, Tania Shokorov, Mum, Lida and me.

Now about the Great Patriotic War. In the last two weeks, our troops have been able to advance in some parts of the front. We have recaptured Rostov-on-Don, Elets, Tikhvin , Kalinin, Klik, Solnechnogorsk and so on. The Germans tried to surround and take Moscow, but they failed. Our troops were able to break through the ring. Every morning I wait impatiently for the news from Soviet Informbureau. Today they said that our army was attacking on the Western, Kalinin and Southern fronts, and taking towns and villages.

After drinking tea, I went to college. There are no lectures at present because so many tutors are too weak and ill but we should start again on 1 April. It was very cold today and we lit the stove.

Yesterday I went to the public baths and had nearly finished washing when they turned the water off. Only women work there now as men can't be spared. We only had some broth for lunch but I was so cold after my bath that I ate it with great pleasure. Actually, a bowl of broth is too little for me but what can we do? The situation is difficult. We also had some tea with bread and sugar. I had three glasses - I had to fill my tummy somehow. I hope that after today things will get better.

Next, I went to the Tolstoy Library and took out two Science and Life magazines and some fiction. I came home by another library where I got three more magazines. So I have got plenty to read.

We have learned that on 7th December, Japan attacked the USA. I think Japan will regret it.

26th December
I woke up very early at six and listened to the latest news. The news from the front is very good! We lit the stove early. Last night, Mum had managed to get some jellied meat which I ate with great pleasure. And then, in college, I managed to get three main courses [horse cutlets] and then, in the canteen, two bowls of soup. The canteen soup is terrible. It smells smoky because they use rancid butter. Mum's broth is a hundred times better.

Nothing special happened today.

27th December [Saturday]
There was good news from the front. Our troops have recaptured Naro-Fominsk and another town.

In the morning I went to the wood depot to find out about wood supplies. On the way, visited the cemetery to see if they had buried father's coffin but they still have not. What I saw there was a nightmare. So many corpses are being brought in, many without coffins. Mum said that about 3,000 people are dying every day. Apparently it's true. Later I went to the Goloushkins to try to get warm. It is very cold today, about minus 20. We and Uncle Sasha are making a bourzhika stove

Mum got some rye flour and we made porridge which I ate hungrily, without butter but with some sugar on top. Poor Mum is always busy with the housekeeping, worrying about food. She gets very tired and the bread gives her heartburn. We had some tea and bread with mustard and salt. How much I appreciate bread now! Many people have told me that we will get more bread in the new year. That would be wonderful! I am longing to see the new food cards. What will the new year bring us? What presents?

28th December [Sunday]
I listened to the news which was very good. The Soviet Army has taken four more towns and many villages. On the Leningrad front we have a very good general, Major-General Feduninsky. He has beaten the Germans at Volkhov.

We lit the stove and cooked some porridge for breakfast and some soup with meatballs for lunch. Lida went to borrow some fat from the Goloushkins. Mum works from 11am to 3pm. There's been no electric light for over two weeks. With everyone out, I felt like doing some housework. I cleaned everything up, disposed of the ashes and the dirty water, swept the floor and so on.

I got annoyed with Lida. When she came back with the fat from the Goloushkins, she started shouting at me because I hadn't found a bathhouse for her that was open. I tried to explain that it was too early but she just slammed the door and went off. It's always like that with her. I try to be polite but she always makes a scene.

Today we were able to exchange our mincing machine for a plate of jellied meat. Also, Mum stood in the bread queue for someone so we will have a full lunch and supper. It is now 2pm. Mum will come soon but I feel hungry. Shall I try the soup which is on the stove - just to see if it is ready or not?

Everything was alright. Mum swore a bit but soon calmed down.

29th December
Our troops still keep going forward. In the morning I went to try to find an open bathhouse for Mum and Lida but I failed. Mum bought some jellied meat. It is very cold.

30th December
Our troops keep advancing and have taken two more towns.

In the morning I went to college to get a new food card - but it is the same. I saw Mikhailov and Starostin there. They said they were going to study. We'll see!

31st December
The last day of 1941. The wireless brought good news. Our troops have reached Feodosia, Kerch and two other towns. What a nice new year present! I celebrated the new year in bed. They broadcast a very good concert which went on till 2am. The bread ration is still the same - 200gr.

1 January 1942
HAPPY NEW YEAR!

1942 will see the complete defeat of the Nazi army. Our reserves are fighting fiercely. We will show the Nazis what the Soviet people can do. Our troops have taken Kaluga and an important railway junction.

In the morning we lit the stove and cooked rye porridge. Mum has got us rye for the next ten days. Then Marusia came. She is swollen with starvation. We gave her half a glass of flour. I just can't understand why she won't work. She could send her child to a kindergarten and go to work. Then she'd get 350gr of bread.

The Jews too have begun to starve. It serves them right! It shouldn't only be the Russians that suffer.

I went to Goloushkin to give him a sheet of iron. The stove is almost ready. It just needs a few details and a second bottom. I should have taken him a chimney and some more iron but it was already dark so I decided to do that tomorrow. Mum wanted to visit the Paullekovs and the Koroliovs but didn't because she wanted to get registered with the shop. But she didn't get to the shop either because it got dark.

We had porridge for lunch. This was made from a different sort of grain - containing malt and not so sticky. But still - it was porridge. We can't be fussy about food now, so long as it fills the stomach.

I am going to put the samovar on and we'll have tea with bread and mustard.

I got a letter from Smoliakov saying he was in Leningrad, staying somewhere near the Gigant Cinema. It said he would be in Leningrad for a week but it was posted on 15th December. I only got it today and I don't know what to do. He gives no address so I don't know where to write.

2 January
I woke up at 6am wanting to hear the news from Moscow. The reception was very bad. Our troops have captured another town but I could not make out its name.

After breakfast I went to college where I learned that there were still to be no lectures, only tutorials. We are to be examined according to the courses we have been able to do. On Monday, we will be given a schedule of tutorials and I will study at home. We'll see how it will work. I saw Sasha Ioffe and Starostin at the college. The stoves there are lit so there are lots of people. All the rooms were available for use.

After college I went to see Goloushkin but he was cross because I hadn't brought everything yesterday. He hadn't finished the bourzhika and was in a hurry. His holiday is over and he had to go to the factory.

We had rye porridge for lunch and stoked up the stove. Yesterday, Mum managed to get two very good bits of wood - dry and thick and long. This morning started very cold - minus 30 degrees - but later it warmed up to minus 23.

Mum told me there had been an air raid warning but I had not heard it. I was very surprised for we haven't had any raids for 15 to 20 days.

The wireless works very badly. Yesterday it would not work from 6pm till morning and it is still not working properly. We still have no electric light and the trams are not running. Destruction is everywhere and in everything.

3 January
So far I've been very regular with my diary but I've no idea what it's going to be like. Sometimes I'm not in the mood to write, especially when I'm crouching by the stove and trying to write by the light of the burning wood.

I woke at six as usual but Mum had already gone out to get some bread. She didn't get any. She queued for three hours but they hadn't brought enough bread to the shop. We ate some porridge and drank some boiled water. We had porridge for lunch too but we got some bread in the evening and had a good supper.

The news from the front is good.

4 January
Nothing much happened today. We had meat broth and porridge for lunch! Such luxury! Then Mum divided a bit of meat into five parts so that we'll have some each day for five days. We light the stove every day but the draughts carry its warmth away.

5 January
Our troops pursue the Nazis. It is bitterly cold outside. I am in no mood to go out. I read magazines. I did go to the library but found it closed. I could not see why. Then I went to the solicitor.

6 January
The situation at the front is about the same but the situation over food is very difficult. I went to the college and got the schedule for tutorials.

7 January
Today we have had almost nothing to eat. The grain is finished and all we have for tomorrow is the rest of the broth and an old piece of meat.

There is bitter fighting at the front but our troops took another town and a few villages.

Yesterday, I had to go to the registry for call-up but all went well. All they want is a certificate to prove that I am a student. That's no problem.

In the morning I went to the solicitor at 13 Skorokhodov St. and gave him the necessary documents. I visited Korinov on the way. In the end, his father died. Korinov was making a bourzhuika and gave me a piece of iron. His flat is dreadful - bitterly cold! I came home exhausted and cold, which was hardly surprising, having walked so far on such miserable rations.

After lunch, I fell into a deep sleep. I slept until 9.0pm and afterwards felt better.

Mum ...[illegible few words]... I understand her situation.

8 January
Our troops have taken another town. I like to hear such news. In the morning, Mum bought some 11-rouble wine, poor stuff but helpful in the absence of decent food.

I went to college. There was a tutorial on mechanical engineering run by Melnitsky. I also collected the certificate from the solicitors for the military.

What didn't we have for tea! There was glycerine, plus caramel from my father's medicine, and the wine. But what can we do? We must get used to our new circumstances. Today we ate the last of the soup and don't know what we'll eat tomorrow. I have filled in the funeral certificate for Aunt Irina. Mum and Lida have gone off to visit Maria Mikhailovna and her family. The street is full of swollen people and a lot of coffins being taken to the cemetery.

I heard that Gera Tumshevich has died. That's sad. He was a nice chap.

I feel much better after a bit of wine but still very weak.

The diary ends there. He died within two weeks. He was a komsomol* member and an idealist.

In the autumn of 1941, the civilian bread ration was reduced to 125 grammes a day for office workers, dependants and children. Manual workers got 250 grammes and even front-line soldiers only 500. At times when bread was short, substitutes like animal glue were offered instead. The black market continued to operate, but only for those who had something to barter. Some would dig in the rubble of the burnt down food warehouses, hoping to find earth enriched with melted sugar. A trickle of supplies could be ferried across Lake Ladoga and later, when it froze, brought by truck, but in that first winter, it was never near to what the city needed and priority went to the soldiers at the front. Confident that the city must fall, the Germans dug in and contented themselves with a steady bombardment to add to the people's other miseries.

The scene in Leningrad was not always as edifying as Mylnikov's diary. To add to everything, it was a bitterly cold winter. The first to go were the very young and the old, but soon exhausted citizens, struggling home through the snow, could be seen to pause for a rest and not move again. Next morning, their stiffened bodies would be found powdered by new snow and sometimes minus their buttocks. Men and women died at work and one evening an actor died on stage in the Pushkin Theatre. They dragged the body off and the show went on. Many families lacked the resources and, even more so, the energy to do anything about the disposal of their dead, sometimes simply tipping them out of the window if it was beyond their strength to carry them downstairs. The authorities, preoccupied with defence, could do little more than send round carts to clear the streets. Piles of bodies accumulated in the cemeteries to be buried in mass graves when the effort could be spared or warmer weather made it urgent.

Not everybody's morals were equal to the situation. That winter, the celebrated artist and restorer Anastasia Vasilieva was a teenage girl with her family, sharing a floor in a once fine mansion

* Komsomols were high school students who were on the path to becoming full-fledged members of the Communist Party.

with several other tenants, one of whom was an emaciated young mother with a little boy born in October. The baby was obviously sinking and, in desperation, she dragged herself off to the hospital to seek aid. She left the boy with other neighbours who at once put a large pan of water on to boil. But nothing is private and Vasilieva's mother, seeing the pan and suspecting what was in hand, seized away the baby. "But she will never come back!" complained the neighbours, "and it is such a clean little body." The mother did return but empty handed. Her son died two days later and was decently buried.

During that first winter, cannibalism became quite widespread - even a trade. Suspiciously well-fed men were offering sausages for sale on the black market. The streets could be dangerous especially at night, for children and for soldiers returning for a short break from the front. Soldiers were better fed. It was a terrible time.

Belekhov's first priority was to do what could be done to protect the city's monuments from the German bombardment. Some, like the statues in the Summer Gardens, could easily be buried. Others like the horses on the Anichkov Bridge had to be dragged some way to be buried in the courtyard of the Anichkov Palace. Some could not be moved at all. The great equestrian statue of Peter the Great was smothered in sandbags and then boarded up. All the golden domes and spires which offered the German bomber pilots such inviting targets had to be camouflaged. This was not easy. Belekhov recruited a band of mountaineers including a young man called Michael Bobrov. He recalls that to reach and attach a climbing rope to the narrow Admiralty spire, they had to float a man up under a gas bag hoping that the wind would not arise until he had managed to lasso the spike. Bobrov was an extraordinary man. Too young for the army, he had already been wounded with the partisans before Belekhov located him recovering in hospital. After the camouflaging was done, he returned and spent the rest of the war with the partisans, surviving to become a famous athlete after it was over. Long after the war, at the age of 76, he joined an expedition which walked to the North pole and back.

During 1942, 513,529 citizens died, the rate reaching a peak in February 1942 of 10,000 per day. The effects of the great hunger remained with many all their subsequent lives and continued to carry people off in large numbers all through the rest of that year. In a macabre way, the loss of life brought some relief. There was no more food available but fewer mouths to feed. On 26th December 1941, it was already possible to raise the food ration from 125 to 250 grammes per day which seemed princely for a short time. Furthermore, with the front stable, the authorities were able to divert their attention more to the plight of the citizens. Many, especially children were now evacuated across Lake Ladoga. Emergency hospitals were set up to help those too weak to help themselves. As soon as Belekhov had done what he could for his monuments, he turned his attention to his curators and museum workers. Appalled by the gaps in the roll call, he realised that if he did not do something soon, he would have no experts left to cope with the damage if and when this terrible siege should ever end. He organised a special lunch daily at the Architects Club for those who could still get there and a sanatorium in the Astoria Hotel for those who could not. He tried to find healthy accommodation for those still squatting in St. Izaak's. This was not too difficult. So many people had died or left that there were plenty of empty apartments. Housing had never been so good since the revolution. When he had done all this and felt convinced that he had done everything for his people and his monuments that he possibly could, he fell desperately ill himself. He too had been starving. He recovered but never completely.

During the first winter of the siege, the conditions for the curators in St. Izaak's had been appalling. Several of them had nowhere else to go and had to live, with their children, in the cold damp crypt, deep underground with only one small stove for comfort. It was very crowded. There were three from Pushkin -Vera Lemus, Tamara Popova and Eugenia Turova with her five year old son Aliosha - and two from Gatchina - Seraphima Belaeva and Irina Yanchenko, with her two children - while from Pavlovsk there was Zelenova with Nikolai Weiss and his two children. His wife slept in the hospital where she worked as a nurse. Although Seraphima Belaeva was the mother superior of this little convent, it was Vera Lemus who kept them amused with her stories and jokes. From the beginning they adopted a number of rules. One was that no-one was allowed to talk about food. By the spring, however, it was being discovered that there was no shortage of empty apartments. One by one, they all found somewhere better to live and moved out. They converted the crypt into their office but spent as little time in it as possible. In any case, in the spring of 1942, a bomb burst the water main under the cathedral and flooded the crypt. They all had to rush down and rescue their boxes and papers from the rising waters. Anyway, life was far preferable on the ground floor. There was the wooden ticket kiosk by one of the columns where the one bourzhuika was located around which they huddled and did their paper work in the relatively clean and dry air. It was only relatively dry. St. Izaak's is a dark, dank building in which condensation streams in rivulets down the walls, especially in summer.

The curators agreed that, in theory, each would look after their own packing cases but in practice so much of what they needed to do was beyond their strength that they finished by mucking in. Furthermore, there was no-one to look after the Peterhof cases. No-one knew where Tikhomirova was. They were left to hope that she was safe in the Oranienbaum enclave, on the other side of the Germans.

Belaeva, Zelenova and Turova spent most of their days struggling to protect their treasures from the worst of the conditions in the cathedral. Its floor was covered with cases, stacked two or three deep. During the winter they tried to take stock of just what they had and, naturally found that the silks, canvasses and veneered woods that were most vulnerable to the damp were always at the bottom of the pile. Furthermore, when they opened the cathedral doors in the spring, they discovered that these corridors of packing cases provoked a turbulence with the wind howling between them and threatening to damage the cathedral's paintings and mosaics. As a result and despite their enfeebled state, they had to set about to lower their stacks and at the same time to try to achieve access to the most vulnerable items. In fact, the damp was so penetrating that not only were the materials and veneers suffering but even the statues. To dry anything out, which was only possible during the short summer, it had to catch the fleeting sun on the southern colonnade. It faced towards the sun but also towards the German artillery which had the habit of bombarding between 11 and 3 each day. The citizens soon learned to walk on the south side of every street because it protected them better from the slanting trajectories of the shells. But the curators had to let their drying treasures take their chance. They themselves, at least, could quickly dodge inside the cathedral if a bombardment started. German aeroplanes were less predictable. One day, Belaeva and Zelenova had just managed to manhandle a heavy plaster statue of Perseus onto the colonnade when they looked up to see a Messerschmidt diving straight at them. They ran for cover and luckily the statue was not hit but perhaps other Messerschmidts would follow. Frantically they struggled to get Perseus back under cover, but the plane was alone. Still, the incident convinced them that they must somehow find help. They had a stroke of inspiration. They went to the military prison and arranged to borrow some of its inmates, who came daily to help them manhandle their crates. This the soldiers did with alacrity. It was far better than their punishment cells and their help just arrived in time, for the starving curators were at the end of their tether. It was a turning point but Belekhov had an even better idea. He had agreed with Professor Kwerfeld that the Hermitage should set aside some reasonably dry storage for their most vulnerable loads. By the end of 1942, the worst of their problems were over.

In the meanwhile, Kuchumov with his long trainload of crates and museum workers was not faring much better. On arrival at Gorky, they found that all the suitable storage had already been taken by earlier arrivals from Moscow and the Hermitage. After some delay, they were offered a church into which they just managed to squeeze their cargo but most of the 16 workers and their families were sent to billets in a village across the river, a complicated journey away. Things had hardly settled down when Kuchumov smelled and then saw signs of rot in some of the cases. Against all orders, he would somehow have to get them out, open them up, remove the rotting hay which was presumably the problem, dry everything out and repack them. Happily, his hosts had plenty of wood shavings to offer him but the work involved stretched his reduced team to the limit. Whatever the difficulties, Kuchumov was not the man to compromise or take short cuts, but the next problem was one he could not solve.

Gorky stands on the junction of two great rivers, the Volga and the Kema, and its significance is that its bridges across them link Russia to Siberia. It was now in bomber range of the Germans trying to surround Moscow and it was not long before German planes were overhead. Kuchumov's job was to evacuate the treasures to a safe place and he now had to exert all his passion and personality to persuade the authorities to let him move on. Despite the shortages of rolling stock and the lines clogged with industrial and military traffic, he was eventually allowed some space on a train moving eastwards to Tomsk. Out came everything again to be reloaded and a signal was sent to the families across the river to rejoin as soon as possible. As the time approached to when the train must leave, Kuchumov wrestled with the question of whether to abandon them or not but at the last minute they arrived. The train set off, inching across the long bridge at just the moment when the Germans launched a severe air raid on it. The crossing seemed to go on for hours but eventually, miraculously unharmed, they reached the thick forests on the other side. They had not gone much further when they were told that their train would not go straight through to Tomsk. It was diverted down a spur which led to a sawmill and there it stopped, in deep snow. They had very little food and had to go scrounging from the local villagers whom they found to be poor but wonderfully generous, sharing with these strangers from the city their meagre winter reserves. For a fortnight, they employed their time stocking up the train with fuel some of which was rather

Between the Wars

Workers in one of the Tsar's palaces and (below)
the Menshikov Palace 1931

1944 Soviet troops re-entering **Catherinehof** (right),

Pavlovsk burning (below)

Ruins of the **Catherinehof**

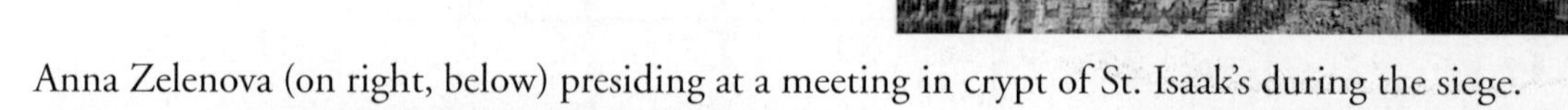

Anna Zelenova (on right, below) presiding at a meeting in crypt of St. Isaak's during the siege.

Alexanderhof (1930s, left) and in 1944 (below) with one portal destroyed and an SS cemetery in the former garden.

Catherine Palace Great Hall 1944 (below) and (right) lowering new roof section in place.

Subotniks clearing up the mess,
Peterhof (above) 1945.

Naval cadets at **Peterhof** (below)

Students registering fragments of plasterwork at **Pavlovsk** (right)

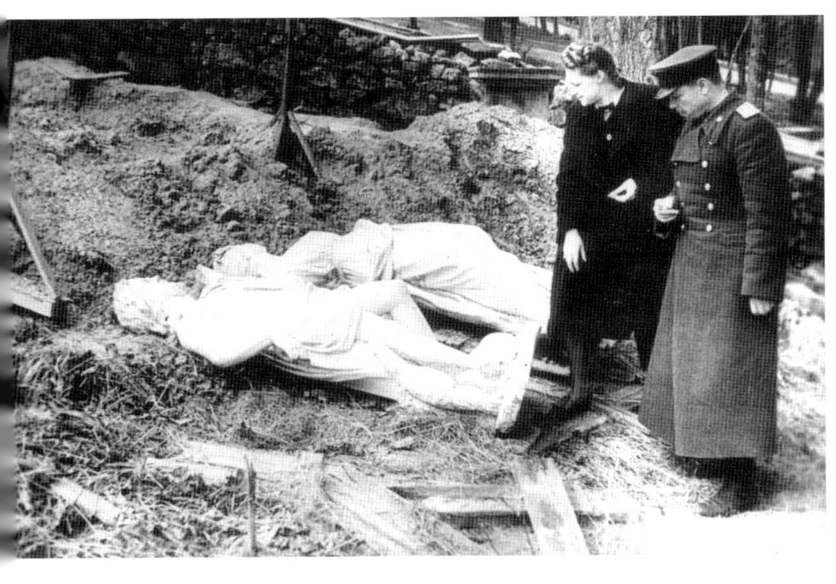

Restoring the statues and fountains: Adam and Eve (above), **Pushkin** (right), women repairing the cascade at **Peterhof** (below left) and statues hidden in the **Pavlovsk** cellars (below right)

Artists at work:
Leonid Lubimov and team (top left); Evgenia Kazanskaya with student (above right); Feodor Oleinik (left) at Pavlovsk; Lilia Shvedskaya with her Ossetian girl (above); Anatoly Treskin (below left); Constantin Kochuev (below, right)

Key Players:
Anatoly Kuchimov at Gatchina (top left);
Alexander Kedrinsky (top right); Anastasia Vasilieva with
Kruschev (below right); Anatoly Lunacharski (black homburg
hat, below); Anna Zelanova at Pavlovsk (bottom right).

More Key Players:
Nadezhda Ode (above left);
Valentin Zubov (above centre);
Nikolai Belekhov (above right);
Boris Lebedov and Ivan Alexeev (left);
Valeria Belanina (below left);
Galina Khodasevich (below centre);
Irina Benois (below, rightt);

green but, in midwinter, better than nothing. It nearly was their undoing however because, used in the engine's furnace, it produced a prodigious display of sparks some of which settled on the partly wooden roof of their accommodation wagon. Soon it was filling with smoke and panic. They scrambled forwards and tried to signal to the driver to stop but he mistook their meaning. In desperation, they climbed onto the roof and started shoving snow with their hands onto the burning timbers, at last calming them to a smoulder. In this state, they were able to reach the junction with the main line where the train had to stop anyway.

After another fortnight on the train, they got to Tomsk, where they were told that there was no proper storage space left. They would have to use a ruined church with a damaged roof and no windows. Kuchumov put his foot down. He had not come all this way to see his treasures destroyed by the elements. Eventually after much bad tempered argument and telephoning, NovoSimbirsk was persuaded to let them use its large modern theatre. At the last minute, the railwaymen lost their patience and refused to go any further unless they were paid extra. Kuchumov had hardly any money left so he had to use all his powers of persuasion. He succeeded and back they went to NovoSimbirsk which they finally reached about two months after leaving Gorky. And even then, it was not NovoSimbirsk proper that they reached but a wayside station some distance short of the city. Here, they were told, the train was stopping and they must unload into the deep snow. Kuchumov reluctantly agreed but insisted that something should be brought to protect the crates from further falls of snow. They brought him the theatre's stage scenery which was draped over the cases. They were also given the use of some horse drawn sledges on which to transport the cases to the theatre. It was an exhausted party that finally reached what was to be their wartime home, a large room in the cellars under the stage. With 16 families including children, it was a bit cramped, but at least it was drier than the crypt of St. Izaak's.

In the autumn of 1942, a woman who had worked as a junior curator at Pavlovsk before the war was lying in hospital in Leningrad recovering from dystrophy, when she thought she recognised the unconscious woman in the next bed. Emaciated as she was, she looked like Marina Tikhomirova, the missing curator from Peterhof. A day or so later, Tikhomirova regained consciousness and they got to talking. She had known nothing of the storage in St. Izaak's but was delighted to hear that her friends were there. When she got better, she went straight to the central office of the Museum authority where the first person she met was Zelenova. Zelenova was delighted. They had all thought she must be dead! She deluged her with questions but Tikhomirova was reticent and Zelenova knew better than to press her. But press her she did to rejoin them at St. Izaak's. Chubova, who had stood in for Tikhomirova during the evacuation, was really from Oranienbaum, and was now working in the Hermitage. There was no-one taking proper care of the cases from Peterhof that were in the cathedral. Tikhomirova said she must tidy up what she had been doing but would willingly rejoin them in a few weeks.

The mystery of her missing months remained, even when she wrote her wartime memories. It was only on her deathbed that she dictated the true story. On the day the Germans attacked, she happened to be in Leningrad and had apparently received a message from the Museum Administration to remain in the city and await further instructions. When none came, she went to the offices of the Inspectorate but found them empty. She concluded that they must have already been evacuated and for a few days wondered what to do. It does not seem to have occurred to her to return to Peterhof, but, wanting to do her bit, she enrolled at the Ministry of Telegraphy and for some time worked there. Then, in 1942, she started teaching in a school but, after a few months, she had collapsed from exhaustion and malnutrition and had woken in hospital. It was a very odd story indeed. No wonder she kept quiet about it. However, the team in St. Izaak's was now complete again; Belaeva, Turova, Zelenova and Tikhomirova, four formidable women.

By 1943, hope was beginning to rise in the hearts of those still remaining in Leningrad. Schlusselburg was retaken in January and a narrow corridor opened joining Leningrad to the rest of Russia. A railway was built and trains ran the gauntlet of the German guns to bring supplies and reinforcements to the city. There came a marvellous day when fresh troops paraded through the city on their way to the front. The siege was far from over but the Leningraders began to feel they were winning. Concerts were being organised although there were no flautists left in the city. On the 7th November, all the bunting came out to celebrate the day of the Revolution.

Belekhov, who had never been anything but full of hope, now summoned the curators to help him with other things. During the worst days, he had divided up the city into twelve districts, each with an architect, or at least a responsible person in charge on behalf of the Inspectorate. Their main task was to keep an eye on all the historic monuments and sites in their districts and obtain help if needed. But also, they were to work with private people who owned worthwhile things. It had long been a regulation that such possessions should be registered but now, as they felt their strength ebbing away, private owners had been getting more and more concerned as to what would happen if they were no longer able to look after them themselves. Life was bad enough without this added burden of worry. Belekhov had a shrewd idea as to who might be in such straits and where, so he enrolled the curators to go on visits to see how the land lay. It was painful work. Some flats were occupied only by frozen bodies, others by emaciated creatures huddled in blankets. Still others had been evacuated and were empty or had strangers squatting in them. No-one resisted the idea that everything valuable should be collected up and stored centrally. It all had to be correctly done and a detailed list made of everything taken into care. The curators always took a policeman with them as witness that they had not stolen anything. Zelenova, in one flat in which she had spent a particularly long time making her inventory, turned at last to the policeman sitting patiently in the corner only to find that he was dead. These collections were carefully recorded, stored and kept until the end of the war but by no means all reclaimed. They went some way to replace items stolen by the Germans from the country palaces.

Belekhov had other duties for the curators. They spent much time giving lectures and talks about the city, its history and its cultural importance. These would often be given in the battle zone. The people and the soldiers at the front had had to make such terrible sacrifices for it, they needed to be reassured that it was worth it and why. Tikhomirova, who was sparky and very pretty was the star. Zelenova gave some too but spent more time working with an academician called Rakov to create a Museum of the Siege of Leningrad. Much later another museum was made underneath the monument to the Defence of Leningrad on the way to Pulkovo but the one

Zelenova made was quite different. It did not hide the sufferings of the city. It was of course full of military things but it did not glorify them. There were letters and tragic human memorabilia. There was a day's bread ration, its equivalent in animal glue and a lump of sugary earth from under the Badaev Warehouse. It was developed bit by bit, while things were still fresh in peoples' minds and it was not finished until after the siege was broken and they brought in a smashed Tiger tank and an 88mm gun to adorn its entrance. It was and is again today a very moving museum, too seldom visited.

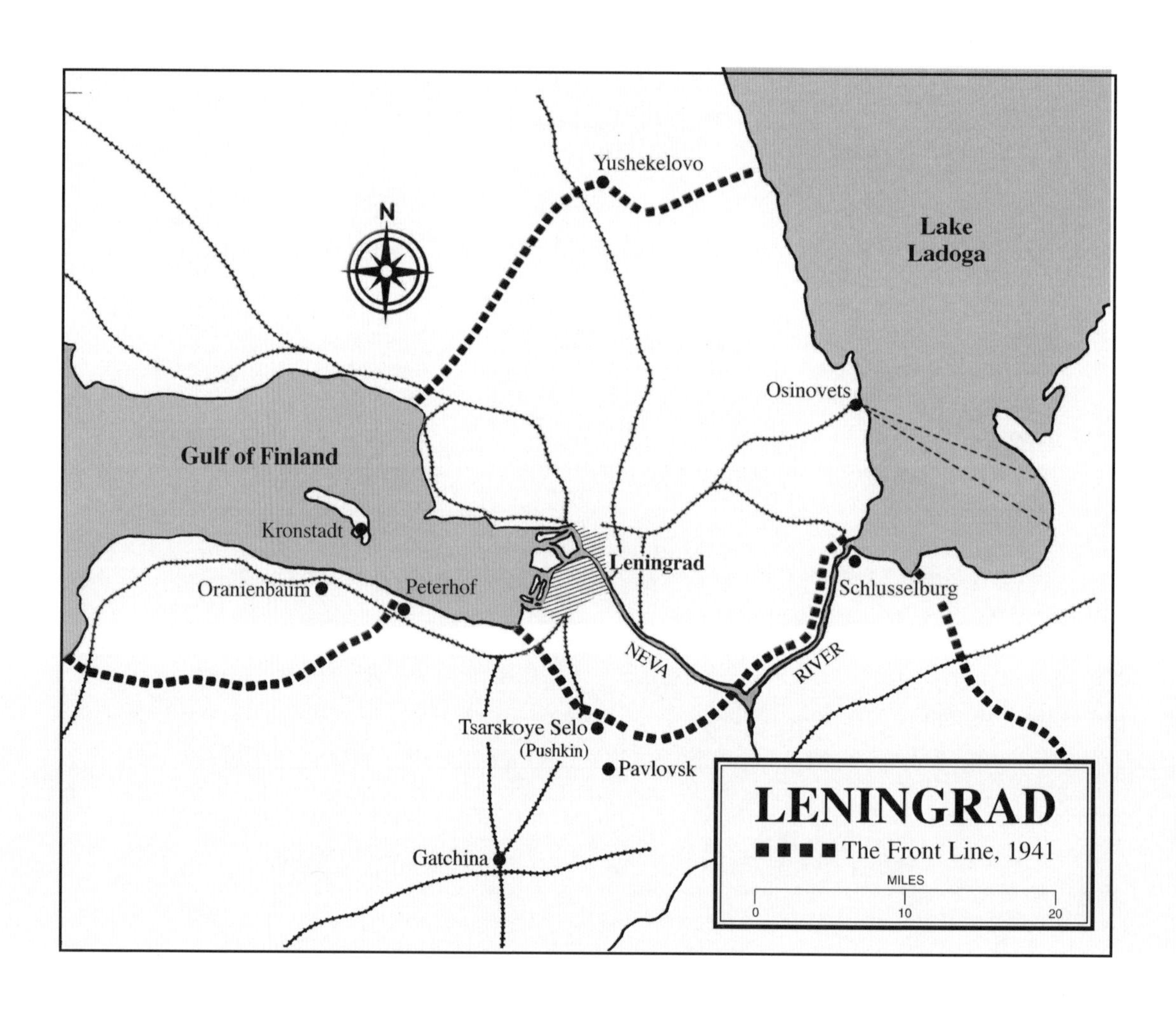
Yushekelovo
N
Lake
Ladoga
Osinovets
Gulf of Finland
Kronstadt
Leningrad
Oranienbaum
Peterhof
Schlusselburg
NEVA
RIVER
Tsarskoye Selo
(Pushkin)
Pavlovsk
Gatchina
LENINGRAD
The Front Line, 1941
MILES
0
10
20

Chapter 6

THE BREAKOUT

The Germans misunderstood Leningrad. They evidently thought that, like most normal cities, when the inhabitants realised that the game was up they would give in, especially, indeed, because these were only despised Slavs. Perhaps if the declared aim had been the destruction of communism, they might have done so for there were many people in Leningrad who had suffered horribly since the revolution. But the Germans aim was quite explicit. It was the destruction of the Russian people and, since they could not hope to kill them all, the destruction of their culture, their history and their memory so that it would be difficult for them ever to regroup again as a nation-race. They would remain for ever, or at least as long as the thousand year Reich, merely *untermensch*, serfs.

This policy informed everything the Germans did. When the Germans overran western Europe, they set about looting its artistic treasures, but they did it almost with delicacy. They created an organisation called the Kunstkommission, under a particularly loathsome man called Alfred Rosenburg, charged with the collection of the choicest works of art. They were not looting, they said, but merely taking the most precious things into 'safe keeping' in Germany. Meanwhile, Hitler was dreaming of establishing a museum to end all museums in his birthplace Linz once the war was over, and several of his henchmen were making collections of what he did not want for it. Scrupulous records were kept of everything the Kunstkommission did in the west but not so in the east. In Russia, its policy was to grab everything that seemed desirable and movable, sorting it out later into what was of western origin and worth keeping, while throwing away whatever was Russian and therefore degenerate and valueless except for any raw materials which could be extracted. If individual soldiers fancied anything left over, looting was not discouraged. Implicit in this policy was that anything that could not be moved, should be destroyed rather than left for the Russians although, of course, such a circumstance was not to be imagined. Hitler's order to his generals, however, had been 'to erase Leningrad from the face of the earth'.

Although some of Leningrad's inhabitants might be feeling disillusioned with the benefits of communism under Stalin, the Germans' behaviour in Russia gave them every incentive to keep them out of their city. It would be unjust to suggest, however, that it was simply fear that inspired them. The very creation of St. Petersburg had been an extraordinary affirmation of human will power. To build a capital on a freezing swamp on the very edge of his empire, only recently captured from the Swedes, had been nothing if not such an affirmation. So was the sustained effort that followed to create a Russian city and culture equal to anything that had been achieved in the west. So much had been sacrificed by so many to do so. Leningraders were intensely proud of Pit'r as they still called their city, no matter what name the politicians might give it. They shared some of that will power that had inspired Peter and they believed that if the city fell, something would be lost of enormous value and forever. They therefore did not, as the Germans expected, behave rationally.

But the Germans had miscalculated in another way. Hitler had wished to settle the Balkans before launching Operation Barbarossa, his attack on Russia. This had been accomplished but it had taken longer than he expected. The Yugoslavs had refused to give in and a quixotic British attempt to defend Greece had cost time. Barbarossa therefore started late. Launched in mid-summer, they had reached the outskirts of Leningrad in ten weeks, as planned, but if they were going to have to take the city street by street, their drive on Moscow would be fatally delayed. They needed to switch most of their forces to that front if they were to take it before Generals January and February came to aid the Russians. Perhaps, in the context of the siege, those same Generals would change sides and, with General Starvation, bring about the fall of Leningrad without any more waste of resources. Well, they were wrong. Leningrad preferred to freeze and starve.

Despite the horrendous conditions and the terrible casualties, it was not, for the inhabitants, a time of unalloyed misery. In some ways it brought them relief. Recent memories of the black NKVD cars and of the fear, when an unwise joke or even laughing at one could result in an early morning knock on the door, were now overlaid by new, more pressing problems. And with these problems came new feelings of comradeship, trust and unity in suffering. Even the rulers seemed to become more affable. And as an initial stubborn refusal to be beaten began to turn to hope and then even to belief in victory, a glow of pride and patriotism suffused their hearts. On 9th August 1942, the 14 surviving members of the Leningrad Symphony Orchestra came together, reinforced by some army musicians, and played for the first time Shostakovich's 7th *Leningrad Symphony*, broadcasting its lament, its defiance and its pride to the whole nation from the beleaguered city. Although he had tried to join, Shostakovich had been rejected by the army because of his eyesight, but he had shared in the digging of the trenches and in the privations of the first winter. He was eventually ordered to the rear by the city authorities.

With this feeling of shared suffering was born a hope that, once it was all over, things would be better than before. After all they had gone through and all they had achieved, there could surely be no going back to all the fears and hatreds of the pre-war terror. Belekhov, once he had recovered from dystrophy, soon regained his own natural optimism. Like Churchill, he saw no point in being anything else. But he saw also that the end of the siege would bring new challenges and problems for which the city was poorly prepared. He could see all round him the results of the sustained battering it had received. No less than 678 of his listed architectural monuments had been damaged and some, like the charming Elagin Palace, more or less destroyed. He knew that the Great Palace at Peterhof had been terribly burned because a German had been captured with a newspaper cutting in his pocket containing pictures and an article. Pilots were reporting that the Catherine Palace also had suffered damage. There would be a huge job to be done if these national heirlooms were to be saved.

His pre-war resources of artists and craftsmen had been related to the ongoing job of maintenance. Most were old and many had not survived despite the measures he had taken. In 1943, therefore, long before the siege was raised, let alone the war ended, he started to organise for special schools to be set up to develop all the skills needed for restoration work. It is not to be thought that, even in the extraordinary circumstances of the war, someone in Belekhov's position could make something of this importance happen. Belekhov, however, was politically resourceful and obtained the approval not only of the Leningrad authorities but of Stalin himself.

The first school opened in November 1943. It was in the Peterschulle, Zelenova's old school. Two more opened early in 1944, one in the nearby Catholic church on the Nevski Prospekt and the other near the Mariinski Theatre. About a hundred talented pupils joined the first course, some from Leningrad but many brought back from their places of evacuation. There had been a search amongst the evacuated children for candidates. They had to be over 15, able to draw and with good records as komsomols. Tragically, a few days after it opened, the Peterschulle was hit by a German shell and several children killed. The schools were popular however if only because both students and teachers were classified as workers and therefore got better rations, while the pupils were given warm army uniforms. Tchaikovsky's theory that most people are talented became widely believed in Leningrad. There was quite a queue.

Although the Russians had broken the German ring in early 1943, they lacked the strength to drive them away and the Germans were under the strictest orders not to retreat. The siege was therefore not yet over. Indeed, during 1943, the Germans stepped up their rate of bombardment, perhaps out of pique and for a while, they tried strenuously to regain Schlusselburg but without success. For most of the year, the two armies were content to glare at each other across no man's land.

Then, on 17th January 1944, Leningraders awoke to the roar of hundreds of guns. They realised at once that this was something different. Vera Imber wrote in her diary: 'Today the people are wearing special faces'. The Russians attacked both German wings from both sides. The Germans put up a spirited defence but ten days later, they broke and fled. The siege was over. On 27th January the Russian guns roared again, joining in 24 salvoes to celebrate. The 'Stalin's organs' hurled their rockets harmlessly into the sky. The war would continue for another year but in Leningrad, it was time to pick up the pieces and start to put them together again.

Of the 2,700,00 inhabitants of Leningrad at the start of the siege, only 730,000 remained. The rest had not all died or been killed, of course, but a great many had. The total number is not known.

Chapter 7

WHAT CAN WE DO?

On the first of February, four days after that great victory salvo, a small bus was arranged for the curators to go and visit their museums. As a journalist with a poetic flair, Vera Imber went along to cover the event. They were apprehensive but could not entirely suppress their jubilation and excitement at the prospect of seeing their palaces again. There would not be time to visit Peterhof and anyway, everyone knew what had happened to it, but Tikhomirova insisted on coming and, where the roads parted, she dismounted and started to walk. Soon she got a lift on a tank to Strelna where she was picked up by a lorry load of cheerful sailors. "See you when the fountains play again!" they shouted as they dropped her near the Great Palace. From there, she could see that the building was dreadfully damaged, that there was nothing behind the open windows. She had to pick her way carefully towards it along paths marked as mine free, passing the anti-tank ditch which had been dug through the centre of the upper garden. She noted that Neptune and his tritons had disappeared but she desperately wanted to see the other side, the seaward side, where the main fountains and cascades were. When she got there, she was dumbfounded. Nothing familiar remained. The canal that had led from the cascades to the sea had become another anti-tank ditch and each side of it was an unrecognisable waste land of broken trees, mud, wreckage and rags, criss-crossed with trenches and barbed wire. A few hooded crows were flapping about the dirty snow in search of something edible. Her heart stood still. How could it ever be restored? Guided through the minefields, she was able to view Marli, the Hermitage and Monplesir. At least Monplesir looked relatively undamaged, but it was with a heavy heart that she started back.

The others had by this time reached Gatchina. Driving up to the edge of the parade ground, Belaeva's hopes rose. The facade of the palace seemed to be intact. She could even see the casements in which she had hidden the two statues and they seemed to be untouched. With rising excitement, they crossed the square and pushed open the great entrance door. Behind it there was nothing but smoking wreckage. Then they saw the graffiti on the wall. 'We were here,' it said. 'We will not come back. When Ivan comes, he will find nothing.' It was even signed 'Richard Wurf, Stettin, Uhlandstrasse 2'.

There was no time to hang about. The days in February are short and there were two more palaces to see. Arriving at Pavlovsk, they found they could not approach the palace. The bridge over the Slavyanka had been blown and the bus could go no further. As they stood on the bank, they could see a sinister wisp of smoke rising from where the cupola had been. It was too far to see what damage had been done and some were turning back to regain the bus, but Zelenova could not restrain herself. Running down the bank, she managed to leap from one tumbled stone to another. Hearing them calling for her to come back, she was hesitating to make the last jump to the far bank when she found a man beside her. Wading ahead, he offered her a steadying hand and they ran on to the palace. There were sooty streaks above most of the windows and she could now see that the wall of one of the wings had collapsed. Clambering over debris and ashes and pushing past the sign *Achtung Minen*, they managed to open the door into the Egyptian Vestibule. It was a scene of chaos. As she stood momentarily to get her bearings, a drop of molten lead plopped onto her camera and froze. She kept it as a souvenir. The stairs into the main building were covered in debris but negotiable and they clambered up. Everywhere was smouldering chaos. She was barely able to recognise what she was looking at, or appreciate the full extent of her loss. The man was still with her. "We must go or they'll leave without us," she said. "Hardly," he said. "I'm the driver. But still. Come back with me." White-faced, she let herself be led back. She could not yet fully comprehend what had happened to her beloved palace except that the Germans must have set the fire as a parting gesture of spite. Anger began to dilute her sorrow.

Finally, they reached Pushkin. From a distance the Alexander Palace looked battered but intact as, on first sight, did the Catherine Palace. The walls still stood but soon they saw that there was nothing behind them. They climbed inside but the soldiers warned them that there were still eleven huge bombs in the cellars, defused but who knew how stable. But they could see that one end of the palace had collapsed. Returning through the gathering gloom, they saw through the blasted trees, the silhouette of the Hermitage Pavilion. "Look," said Turova. "At least they've left us one ruin."

It was a silent group of curators that drove back through the wreckage of war to Leningrad. For all of them, this was their darkest moment but it did not last forever. That same spirit that had supported them through the siege was not to be swept away so easily. A few days later, Zelenova hitched a lift back to Pavlovsk and was standing once again on the bank of the Slavyanka, not even trying to stem her tears. She had thought she was alone when a quiet voice beside her said, "Don't grieve. Fear has a hundred eyes - but your hands will do it." It was a woman who had come to try to find where her son had been buried. He had been killed somewhere in the park only a few days before. Zelenova felt ashamed so to have given way to her grief. She would not do it again.

On the eighteenth of February, Belekhov called a meeting at the Architects Club, which, ironically, now occupied the former town house of Polovtsov. The curators were invited, senior members of the Inspectorate and a few architects from the city. He opened by saying he was preparing a report about the condition of the country palaces. "Its aim is to inform architects and others about their barbaric destruction. And we must also discuss today how to conserve what is left from deteriorating further. The ruins are new and there are still some remains of their former decoration but we all have seen what happened after the Elagin Palace was hit. The rain and the frost soon destroyed whatever was left. What can then be done to reconstruct and restore the palaces, what their future destiny will be, we can only consider after further visits."

"We must report on their state and there is one thing I want to say now. We architects and curators of Leningrad are the only people who know the true extent of this barbaric destruction of our national heritage. It is up to us to make it known to the governments and architects both of our own and of friendly countries. The ransacking and destruction of the Leningrad country palaces is the most terrible tragedy that we have suffered in this terrible war - our palaces which were the pride of the Russian people. So far the people do not understand the scale of the tragedy, but we, the professionals who know the value of what has been destroyed, we must not rest in making the world understand. If in the last war, the cathedral of Rheims had been destroyed by German barbarism, would not the world have held the Germans in everlasting disgrace?"

He then took the meeting on a mental tour of the palaces as he had seen them. Starting with Peterhof, he described the havoc in the park. It would take a hundred years to achieve its former glory but Monplesir looked as though it could be saved. The leading Russian troops had defused the demolition charges in time though its structure had been weakened by the firing of the guns and the vandalism of their crews. It would need to be shored up before worse happened. The Catherine Block alongside, however, had been gutted by fire. The Hermitage Pavilion, apart from a gun embrasure in one wall, seemed to be intact externally but they had wrecked the delicate eighteenth century mechanism by which the dining table had been raised and lowered. They had blown up Marli, however, in the face of the advancing Russians and it was in a terrible state. Far the worst of all was the Grand Palace. Although roofless, its outer walls were fairly intact but within all was destruction, reduced to mud by two winters. Perhaps under it some recognisable remains might yet be found. The walls were restorable - but what would be the point of that? Saddest of all were the beautiful water gardens, once comparable to Versailles. They were unrecognisable. The Samson statue, and several others, had disappeared and the water supply had been systematically sabotaged. Finally, all the dachas, pavilions and small palaces in the eastern park had been near the front line and grievously damaged. Only the Cottage Palace, which had been used by the Germans as a hospital, seemed definitely restorable, although it was much vandalised within.

Turning to Pushkin, he said that the park was not so devastated as Peterhof's although none of the pavilions and monuments had escaped damage, while, as they all knew, the Chinese Theatre had been burnt down right at the beginning of the war. The Catherine palace presented a terrible scene. The great hall, the picture gallery and the gala staircase had all collapsed, though miraculously some of the baroque decoration on one side of the great hall seemed to be fairly intact. The Amber Room had been stripped and the gala rooms gutted by a fire. Unfortunately, a new fire had broken out again after the palace was liberated which had made matters worse. A most terrible sight was Rastrelli's vista of golden doorways, now reduced to raw bricks laden with snow. Cameron's classic suite of rooms was not destroyed but had been much vandalised. Externally, the Alexanderhof seemed to have escaped direct hits except for one portico but inside it had been appallingly vandalised.

As to Pavlovsk, the favourite palace of so many of them, the outer walls were intact but the roof had collapsed and the inside totally gutted by fire. Some of the decoration and some frescos could still be saved if they moved quickly. The park had been devastated. Most of the trees had been reduced to stumps and those monuments that had not been wrecked, had been disfigured with Spanish graffiti, disproving the claim of the Spanish government that they had sent no troops to Russia. The Rose Pavilion, in which Alexander I celebrated Russia's great victory over Napoleon, had disappeared. The park would be hugely difficult to restore but there perhaps was hope for the palace since its outer walls were intact.

Finally at Gatchina, the main block and Arsenal wing had been consumed by fire but the kitchen wing was reasonably alright. It was clear that the fire had been deliberately started in no less than three different places, not long before the Russian troops arrived. The mess inside was indescribable and would take ages to sort out. All the bridges in the park had been blown up but most of the pavilions seemed intact except for the Birch Pavilion which had completely disappeared.

"Summing up," he said, "we all know what will happen if we do not move fast to preserve and protect what is left. Only when we have conserved whatever there is to conserve can we start to consider what will be the future destiny of these ruined palaces." Then he asked for the reports of the head curators.

Tikhomirova was the first to speak. Her first sight of the ruins of Peterhof, she said, had filled her with despair but now she had recovered some heart. She felt the rubble might hold much that was valuable and perhaps in the cellars below, some of the furniture they had taken down could have survived. Monplesir needed urgent attention but she was sure it could and must be restored, if only to house the many personal effects of Peter the Great which had been saved. The Catherine Block was gutted. Inside, they had found Shubin's plaster statue of the empress. It had fallen but seemed to be alright but when they touched it, it had crumbled into dust. It was a warning. The Hermitage Pavilion could certainly be restored but perhaps not its machinery. Marli filled her with despair. Finally, she was sure that the fountains could be repaired and there seemed good hope of finding most of the buried statues. A search for Samson, Neptune and the other missing statues should be made at once. The Germans could hardly hide them. But the park would take decades to restore.

Turova confirmed much of what Belekhov had said about Pushkin but wanted to add a few points. First, she had to acknowledge a problem that during the evacuation, no proper record had been made of what statues had been buried and where. Finding them, if they were still there, could be a problem. She wondered whether there was any hope of obtaining the help of soldiers and maybe also ordinary citizens, to search through the rubble and in the park. She agreed that it was important to locate and save every scrap of evidence as to how it had been, even fragments of charred silk from the walls. She felt also that there was probably a lot of furniture from the palace in the neighbourhood in houses where the German soldiers had made their billets. In fact, she had already seen evidence of this.

Zelenova, who spoke next about Pavlovsk, was more upbeat. Although the roof had collapsed, much of the internal decorative work was still intact. She felt she already had enough of the contents saved to make a museum and, like Turova, she was convinced that there was much more to be recovered from the neighbourhood. She had seen the grand piano sitting outside a German dugout with Beethoven's music still on its stand. For her, as for the others, the priority now must be to conserve and carefully record every remaining piece of internal decoration. Because they would be working against time, she thought it would be wise to have everything recorded as it was by an artist. In her opinion, however, the palace could be restored but would they ever see the park again? Trees grew so slowly. Belaeva told the same story but emphasised Tikhomirova's warning that some of the plaster decorations scorched by the fire were extremely fragile. A method for consolidating them was urgently needed, before they could be handled.

Belekhov sought the views of the others present. Lekschein, who had been with Kuchumov in Siberia for most of the siege had no stars in his eyes. "Let us be honest," he said, "we're talking about ruins. Do not let us underestimate the task of restoration, even should the government agree to it. What would it cost? Who is qualified to do it? How could the palaces be furnished? How many years will it take?"

Professor Udalenkov pleaded that it was far too soon even to discuss restoration. Professor Peliavsky said there should be a commission of investigation set up. In this way, the meeting ended in an inconclusive way. Some people evidently thought that the faith of the curators, and possibly of Belekhov too, was more romantic that practical. Belekhov wound it up in a way that avoided tackling any of the difficult issues. They could all agree on the urgency of the conservation work. In addition he said, two reports would be prepared. One would be prepared as evidence for use after the war at any trial of war criminals. The other would be to set before the Leningrad Council and possibly the Politburo the alternatives facing the architects of Leningrad regarding the future of the palaces. In the meanwhile, he would obtain the services of celebrated photographers, like Velichkov and Trakhtenberg, to make a detailed record of the state of the palaces as they had found them. Once done, he emphasised, a start must be made on the conservation of what was left.

Shortly afterwards, a delegation came from Moscow to see for themselves. It was led by an eminent professor, Schusov, who had known the palaces well before the war. They were awe-struck by the scale of the destruction, but, even so, Schusov declared that they could and must be restored. "If we," he said, "who knew and remember these palaces in all their glory do not restore them, the next generation will never be able to." This was encouraging. At least they would have well-connected champions in Moscow for what they wanted to do. It was already becoming clear, however, that they would not have the wholehearted political support of the party leaders in Leningrad. There was much talk of pulling down what remained and building holiday apartments for workers. Zhdanov, the Politburo member who had led Leningrad throughout the siege, first asked for an estimate of the cost. When someone suggested 20 million roubles he replied, "How can you ask so much? Our country is in ruins, many people are living in earthen huts. Why are palaces and fountains necessary? We must establish priorities. We can only allocate a much smaller amount." Still, with even this tepid support they could make a start. In the meanwhile, Belekhov was not without his own contacts.

His first priority was to send to Moscow a dossier, with Velichkov's photographs, for use at the proposed Nuremburg trial of the Nazi leaders. Using the same pictures, he then sent a well-presented case asking for support for the restoration of the palaces, in principle. Luckily, someone in the secretariat in the Kremlin saw it and sent it back. First of all, it was too luxurious, bound in vellum - not at all the application of a poor man counting every penny. Secondly, they had used Velichkov's photos taken to maximise the impression of destruction. If they were to hope for Stalin's support, they should send pictures of how much there was left for them to work on. Gratefully, they re-engaged Velichkov and re-planned their submission, binding it in cheap cardboard. It worked. Zhdanov got a message to say that Stalin wanted the fountains restored.

In March, Belekhov called another larger meeting of all concerned in the Architect's Club. Zhdanov's decision was clearly very encouraging but it was limited. They must not assume that it amounted to a decision to restore all the palaces. In any case, first they, the professionals, needed to make up their minds whether it would be possible to restore them anyway. The sentiments expressed in this meeting, which continued for two days, were even more divided than before. Two reports were read out, one by Udalenkov and one by Makarov, Zubov's successor at Gatchina. Udalenkov believed that there was enough left in each palace to recreate a museum, but no longer a whole furnished palace as before the war. Perhaps each museum could be given a theme. Peterhof should contain a collection to the memory of Peter the Great and Pushkin to Elizabeth. Pavlovsk could celebrate the classical period while Gatchina might be dedicated to the history of the Russian army. He did not see why other parts and the parks could not used as workers' rest homes and children's' playgrounds. The two aims were not incompatible. Makarov did not disagree but others did.

In the wake of Stalin's concession, restoration might be a popular idea in March, but who knew whether it would be in April. Many were anxious not to find themselves standing on the wrong square when the dice stopped rolling. Some also were nervous of the idea of collaborating with the all powerful military in Gatchina, who might steamroller the curators. Others wanted to put it on record that they thought rest homes for workers were very important. Someone proposed that Pavlovsk might become a rest home for architects.

On the second day, several took the opportunity to air their aesthetic opinions. Some suggested that they now had an opportunity to resolve the conflict between the baroque and classical parts of the Catherine Palace. Why not pull down the Zubov Block? Others wanted to strip out the heavy art nouveau decoration from the Alexanderhof. It had been desecrated by the Germans and it was poor stuff anyway. Better to rediscover Quarenghi's classic designs hidden beneath. Most agreed that where something had completely disappeared, like the Chinese Theatre at Pushkin or the Rose Pavilion at Pavlovsk, no attempt should be made to recreate it. Zelenova, herself, pointed out that, before Maria Feodorovna built the Rose Pavilion, there had been playing fields. Why not again? Someone made the point that parts of the Catherine Palace as they had been before the war were not themselves original. Early in the nineteenth century, some of Rastrelli's work had already been destroyed by a fire and restored. What had been copied once could be copied again. All agreed however that parts had been so utterly destroyed that they could not be restored, only reconstructed. All the curators by this time felt it important to offer at least a part of their palaces to be used for socially correct purposes. Only one man, a Professor Farmakovsky, pointed out that before the war, the public had been prepared to pay amply for the cost of maintenance and ongoing restoration work by their visits. Investment in restoration would bring a financial as well as a cultural dividend which rest houses would not. Others felt this to be politically wrong, even unwise. Several expressed great doubts about any attempt to replicate what had been so thoroughly destroyed but a delegate from the city archive advised them that there were records and designs there which had survived and which could be the basis of a reconstruction. Only one, a man called Manikov, observed dryly that no-one knew yet what they were talking about. First, he said, protect the ruins and then start to measure and study just what their reconstruction would involve. Only then would rational decisions be possible. It was left to Kuchumov, who had recently returned from the east, to propose something practical. Let the Alexanderhof, he asked, be used to store the evacuated treasures. It was still structurally sound and the inhabitants of NovoSimbirsk wanted their theatre back. This was agreed but he was advised by several on no account to let his treasures be unloaded on their way through Leningrad - better still, bypass the city altogether.

Belekhov did not really try to sum up this wandering discussion. He felt that Monplesir and the Hermitage Pavilion at Peterhof should be restored but not Marli. Of the main palaces, Pavlovsk offered the best prospect of success, if only because it was the most newly damaged and the weather had not had time to aggravate what the fire had done. On the other hand, Gatchina's would be the simplest roof to replace so perhaps it should have priority but it was such a huge building. He did not like the idea of making it into a military museum, but agreed that they should seriously consider the various suggestions made for putting bits of each palace to proletarian use. In the meanwhile, the Alexanderhof should be used as a store and a determined search mounted for palace property stolen by the Germans, not just in the vicinity of the palaces but in the wake of the advancing Russian armies. Kuchumov was the natural choice for such a task. Otherwise, Belekhov avoided anything resembling a decision, realising that they had got from the authorities as much as they could expect at this stage. Their hands would be full for the foreseeable future clearing up the mess and conserving what was worth conserving. After all, the parks were not yet clear of mines. Furthermore, the repair of damaged buildings and monuments within the city would use all their resources of skilled manpower and materials for some time to come.

Belekhov called many more similar meetings during the following years. During the course of these, they avoided precipitating any decision of principal as to whether the palaces would be restored but formulated requests for money to take on the simple, urgent things. It cost money to sort through the rubble and to conserve the relics. It cost money to clear the parks and uproot and replant the thousands of trees which had been destroyed. It cost even more money to repair the fountains and to restore Monplesir but these were projects on a scale which Leningrad, with Moscow's support, could finance and which the available skilled people could cope with. The first graduates from the Restorer Schools would not be available before 1946, at the earliest. He did not feel the time was ripe to push for a major decision that would involve the highest in the land.

In the meanwhile, however, he shared the growing determination of his architects and curators to restore but most academicians and professors took a contrary view. At a meeting in April 1945, an extremely depressing report was tabled recording the views expressed at a recent international meeting in London. It seemed that the rest of the world regarded the palaces as a lost cause and Professor Ol, who was in the chair, actually called upon everyone to stand for a minute's silence in requiem for them. At this moment, an architect called Oleinik entered. He had just arrived back from the front and discovering how the discussion had been going, he strode up to Professor Ol and demanded to be given the floor. Stretching out his hands, he said, "What are these for?" Tapping his head, he said, "What is this for? What are heads and hands for? To let ourselves become poorer? We who have brought peace and life again to so many of our cities. Have we not been fighting to get back all the Nazis took from us? I do not believe our people will forgive us if we leave Pushkin, Pavlovsk and Peterhof as ruined monuments to the fascists' occupation of our land! Something of beauty was created in our land and the loss of such beauty is a loss for all mankind. We must create them again. Our beautiful palaces are wounded. They are waiting for us, specifically for us who know them to the last detail. While I was lying in the trenches, I used to draw from memory what we are talking about. That was in battle. Don't we have here in Leningrad hundreds of excellent architectural designs? Am I the only one who knows the exact measurements of the ruined cupola of Pavlovsk? Don't we have thousands of photographs? And what survived is still alive - wounded but alive! Only we must not lose anything or let it perish. Save it now and not wait for the end of the war. Let us roll up our sleeves, work and save that which is whole, restore that which suffered and return to mankind throughout the world that which will make mankind the richer. It is not the first time we Russians have done this. Let us restore and recreate what has been lost."

Zelenova was convinced that this speech marked some sort of turning point.

Chapter 8

CLEARING UP THE MESS

Before much else could be done, the palaces and parks had to be made safe. The worst of the mine problem was at Peterhof and Pavlovsk. Eventually, they had to lift 72,000 mines, booby traps and unexploded shells from the park at Peterhof. The total number at Pavlovsk was not recorded but there were 240 in the cellars of the palace alone and the huge size of the park made the task daunting. Furthermore, the departing Germans had amused themselves thinking up the most ingenious booby traps, leaving behind, as if in their hurry, desirable things like a pair of new boots, a crate of beer or a child's toy, concealing the wire to the charge below. Other booby traps were not so cunningly concealed but placed in awkward places which made them dangerous to defuse but destructive to explode. One such had been left in one of the fountains of the Chequerboard Cascade at Peterhof. The young engineer officer from Kirghizstan did not like the look of it at all and wanted to blow it up but the curators pleaded with him not to do so. "Is it that important?" he asked. They nodded. "Very well," he sighed, "if we have to, we will save it." While everyone else stood well back, he climbed up to where it was. It took him a long time to unravel its mechanism but he succeeded. He was white and shaking when he rejoined the others.

Most of the minesweeping at Peterhof was done by a naval unit from Kronstadt supported by some army engineers under a Major Ivanov. Another army unit was allocated to Pavlovsk. Awed by the size of the park they had to clear, they were predicting that it would take them many months when, according to Suzanne Massie, some local girls started coming to offer their help. Using their bare feet, they said they could locate the mines for the engineers to lift. Forming themselves into brigades, Massie describes them singing on their way to work but all too often returning at the end of the day with a dead or wounded comrade on a stretcher. It took about three months to get the parks reasonably free of mines though accidents continued to happen for a long time afterwards. Indeed, it is quite probable that there may still be a few mines lurking in the parks, but it is a long time since any went off and so they are presumably now defunct.

Long before the parks were declared safe, work had started on the palace interiors to sort out the mess and to prop up the walls. Turova got her soldiers for Pushkin, a battalion of air raid girls who had spent the siege digging out victims of the bombs and shoring up damaged buildings. This had been ideal experience for the work in hand except that it was too much to expect these girls to be sensitive to the many fragments of artistic value lying amongst the wreckage. Therefore

Belekhov decided that at this stage no better training could be provided for his Restoration School students than for them to sift through the rubble. Nearly all the restorers looked back later on this period as one of great joy and camaraderie. Whole classes would take the train and spend their day under their teacher, learning and helping and thoroughly enjoying themselves.

Zelenova, in the meanwhile, had been using her own initiative. She was in Leningrad one day to discuss how to stabilise fragments of plasterwork, when she met an old friend on the tram. He was a sculptor called Taurit who had done some conservation work at Pavlovsk before the war. Overjoyed, she said he must come at once to join her but he pointed out he was still in uniform. He was in a unit that had been detached to repair the airport. This was enough for Zelenova. Within an hour she was at its headquarters, arguing and cajoling her way through all the outer offices until she reached the sanctum of its commander. She had expected a gruff old colonel but here was a rather supercilious young captain called Sapgir. Having shaken her hand and discovered her business, he rang for his secretary to escort her out. The secretary, whom Zelenova had already charmed, pleaded with him to hear her out, so he did. She was asking for no less than a detachment of his unit to come to Pavlovsk with scaffolding and anything else necessary to secure the safety of the building and to help the restorers reach and dismantle the plaster decorations which kept falling off the walls.

"I can only do what I have been ordered to do," he said coldly.

"So you won't help?"

"No."

"To whom then can I take my case?"

"I am a soldier," he said, irritatingly. "You know who is the supreme commander."

With that he prepared to leave, but in the doorway he softened and turned. "Try Tikhanovsky," he said. "He is my superior. You must convince him that you need me more than he does."

He did not expect ever to meet this strange, ardent young woman again but Zelenova was nothing if not resourceful. Furthermore, it seems likely that during the siege, she had somehow got to know Marshal Voroshilov who had commanded the defences. Anyway, she got busy trying to reach Tikhanovsky and must have succeeded, for a week later, she was back in Sapgir's office with an order detailing him, as a matter of exception, take his unit to Pavlovsk to begin work saving the internal decoration of the palace. In the event, he was to remain there for two years by the end of which, he too had fallen under Zelenova's spell. It was, he wrote later, something about her face and the way her radiant soul was reflected in it.

But it was one thing to sift through the rubble and select any fragment that looked useful. As archaeologists well know, if a find is not thoroughly documented as to its exact position in the dig, half its value will be lost. So it was with the shards of decoration which lay on the ground or, indeed, which were still clinging to the walls. A system had to be developed by which these could be logged and located and then placed in a coherent order in some safe storage. Zelenova's orderly German education was a great help in enabling her to address this problem but she was much indebted to the help of an assistant called Natalya Gromova who was early on sent to join her team. Gromova was a senior museum researcher and between them they devised a code which would enable them to trace the exact location from which every fragment had come. Since eventually 40,000 such fragments were collected at Pavlovsk alone, this was an extraordinary feat, which the other curators hastened to copy. Indeed, when a description of the system was published by the Department of Culture in Leningrad, it became widely used by restorers from other countries. It involved mapping each wall, each surface, to show where everything had been and it did not only cover pieces of decoration. Any other information which might be of value later, was obtained and recorded while there was still time. The general destruction, for instance, had burnt away patches of paint enabling the restorers to trace backwards every application of new paint to the very earliest colour chosen by Maria Feodorovna and her husband Paul. 'The Method' as it came to be called was nothing if not comprehensive.

The business of saving useful fragments and removing the rest was clearly going to take a long time. High priority was therefore given to rigging up temporary shelter or, if possible, a temporary roof to protect the material in the meanwhile, anything to keep out the rain and the snow. The whole job took several years from when it was started in the summer of 1944. It was meticulously carried out in the faith that it was but a preliminary to the restoration of the palaces. However, there would be many twists and turns, many rising hopes and reversals of fortune, before the restorers could really feel that they had the necessary support behind them.

As soon as the mines were gone, a second huge task could be started, the clearing of the parks. Once again, Pushkin and Gatchina were relatively less affected although every one of the decorative bridges in the park at Gatchina had been blown and parts of the park at Pushkin around the Hermitage were in a terrible state, but these were a minor problems compared with what had happened at both Peterhof and Pavlovsk. These had been seen by the Germans as good defensive positions and prepared as such, with anti-tank ditches, barbed wire entanglements, trenches, small townships of dugouts and vistas of shattered trees, cleared to provide good fields of fire. And, of course, everywhere was the debris of war - wrecked machinery, personal effects, bits of uniform and rags and, in many a dugout, treasures from the palaces. These had not all been taken for the pleasure of them or with the intention to loot. At Monplesir, for instance, although the German gunners had used the most precious lacquer panels for firewood, two had survived, one being used to bridge a trench, the other as the wall of a latrine.

So, even in the parks, care was needed in sorting through the mess lest something valuable be overlooked. The main problem, however, was the sheer enormity of the task. The professionals were feeling daunted but they underestimated the enthusiasm of the people. As soon as the parks were reasonably clear of mines and the trains were once again operating, volunteers began to arrive from the city offering to help. It was not long before they arriving in huge waves, especially at weekends. Sometimes whole factories would come. They were called Subbotniks if they came on Saturdays and Voskresniks on Sundays. It was easiest for them to reach Peterhof where it was not unusual for up to 2,000 to come out for the day to do something useful and work off some of their anger against the Germans who had sought to deprive them of their inheritance. The whole thing took some organising. There were often not enough tools for the multitude but there was always enough work and people were prepared to use their bare hands.

At first the curators had tried labour-saving experiments. To hasten the re-establishment of the avenue of a thousand lime trees that leads from the Alexandria Park to Marli, they tried blowing up the stumps on one side and simply planting saplings beside the stumps on the other. Both ideas failed. The only thing they learnt was that there was no short cut. Each stump had to be dug out and each new sapling planted in its place. 70,000 new trees were eventually planted in the park at Pavlovsk. In addition, they had to fill in the dugouts and trenches, remove all the debris of war, clean out the canals and the ponds, and, not least, join in the search for the buried statues.

Thus, by means of this extraordinary popular effort, on 17th June 1945, barely a month after the end of the war, it was possible to reopen the Lower Park at Peterhof to the public. Of course, it still looked like a shorn lamb and the fountains were mute, but it was possible to recognise the former geometry of the park. The avenues were there, the side alleys, the junction points and the places where the fountains and statues had been and would no doubt soon be again. It was a day of great joy and celebration. And there was a huge portrait of Stalin decorating the wall of the palace. The Pushkin and Pavlovsk parks followed later that year.

Chapter 9

THE TREASURE HUNT

During the first days after the German withdrawal, the curators all shared the same frustration. They could view their ruins but only from the mine swept pathways. They could report bravely on what they saw. They could worry about the conservation of whatever might be left, but until they could get at it and get some help, they were impotent. What else could they do? Well, what they could do was to try to retrieve any treasures that the occupying Germans might have taken for their own use and comfort and thus inadvertently saved from the fire. There was no time to be lost, for such treasures might not stay put for long.

Each curator approached the problem in her own style. Belaeva was the eldest and perhaps the wisest. Instead of rushing about, she decided to invoke the help of the remaining townspeople. Sitting down to compare her pre-war inventory with the list of items evacuated, she deduced just how much was missing. She did not know whether it had been taken away by the Germans or burnt in the fire but she made a shrewd guess as to the sorts of things their soldiers might have taken to improve their quarters. She made a list of things to search for, which she circulated to the few survivors who had spent the war in Gatchina village. Her appeal was amply repaid. The locals knew where the Germans had been billeted and where they had dug their dugouts and had often actually seen things being carted away. They were soon scouring the district for her with considerable success.

Zelenova, more passionate but, for once, less organised, simply set off to Pavlovsk village pulling a sledge behind her on which to pile anything she found. Having been in the front line, Pavlovsk was nearly deserted with but a handful of survivors flitting about the ruins. One of the first people she met was an old friend, Ushakova, the pre-war mayoress, who had come back to try to prepare for returning refugees. "Hallo, mayor without a town," she said. "Hallo, curator without a museum," replied the other. The mayor would much have liked to help but was preoccupied at that moment with the water supply. Was it safe to drink? How could she get it tested? Zelenova was not one to mess about. Taking a long drink she promised to let her friend know how she felt next day. She had to carry on on her own working her way methodically through what had once been streets. It was not long before she began to fill her sledge but it was a heavy physical task for a rather frail woman with a game leg. Perhaps it helped her to dissipate some of the anguish and anger churning within her. Such people as she did meet were always helpful but mostly she had to do it herself. Still, even she had to admit defeat when confronted by the grand piano.

Nevertheless, she threw herself into her task so recklessly that one night she collapsed and was lucky to be found by a villager before she froze to death.

Between them, the curators were thus able to retrieve a good deal of stuff before the weather ruined it or someone else helped themselves. Most of it was small-scale stuff, chairs or porcelain, but sometimes the officers had provided themselves with messes furnished in the height of eighteenth century fashion, with antiques, fine panelling, valuable pictures and tapestries. Tikhomirova found one such where they had, before leaving, cut out a swastika from the centre of the tapestry. She also found the two surviving eighteenth century lacquered panels from Monplesir. Some Germans had taken to heart Field Marshal von Reichenau's order of the day instructing them that 'in the East, art objects have no value'. They had warmed themselves with precious parquet flooring.

In March 1944, Kuchumov returned from Siberia. His first task was to prepare the Alexanderhof for the storage of the treasures he had been cherishing in Siberia plus what was in St. Izaak's or elsewhere in Leningrad or which was being recovered by the curators in their searches. The building was still structurally sound, but the interior was a revolting mess of wanton vandalism, filth and graffiti. Nothing of any value remained in it and its decorations and fittings had been deliberately ruined, apparently shot to pieces for fun. Its beautiful fireplaces had been smashed with heavy hammers. It took eight large lorries just to remove all the empty bottles. Judging by the graffiti, it had been occupied at some stage by the Spanish Blue Division, but later it had served as Gestapo Headquarters. Whenever he had moments to spare however, Kuchumov joined the curators in their searches and proved to be extraordinarily serendipitous. Searching in a nearby village called Antropshino, he not only found some chairs and statues but, rolled up in the attic of a farmhouse, the famous contemporary portrait of Peter the Great by Tannauer. It had been grossly mutilated and some of the bayonet scars are visible to this day but it was quite irreplaceable. In the same attic was a portrait of Paul I.

All this time, however, he was longing to get the Alexanderhof ready, so that he could set off in pursuit of the retreating Germans. He was sure that apart from the organised thefts of the Kunstkommission, there would be much that had been stolen by individuals who might, under the pressure of events, be dumping them anywhere in their haste to escape. Speed was of the essence. The closer he was to the action, the more he felt he would find. Furthermore, there were rumours that huge hoards had been taken to places like the castle at Koenigsberg for temporary storage and sorting. He was terrified that if he was too far behind, it would be gone. Once the space in the Alexanderhof was ready and without waiting for the trains from Siberia to arrive, he was granted permission to set off on his search. He was warned that he could not expect much practical help. There was still a war to be fought. He took with him one companion, an architect friend of his youth called Veselovsky. They had no transport and had to hitch lifts but there were many supply vehicles following in the wake of the advancing army. All they had was a search warrant, some inventories and Kuchumov's prodigious memory. He got someone to type out a letter on official paper, verifying that they were 'working officially to find museum valuables stolen by the German Fascists from the country palaces around Leningrad.' It asked all concerned to help them.

The scale of the looting by the Kunstkommission had been awesome. Shortly before the end of the war, its head, Rosenberg, claimed that he had so far shipped 1,418,000 freight loads of valuables out of Russia plus a further 427,000 tons shipped by sea. These shipments, of course, came from all parts of occupied Russia but the figures were scarcely imaginable, and they did not include the work of amateur thieves, filling their lorries and their knapsacks from what was left over. Everything was taken wholesale to be sorted out later, not only to allocate who should get what but also to disentangle the valuable works of western artists from the degenerate Russian stuff, which could be destroyed. Kuchumov was not, of course, aware of these statistics when he set out but he knew that the curators had only been able to evacuate about a third of the treasures their palaces had contained. He had seen for himself that virtually nothing remained in them but shards and charred fragments amongst the ashes. What the curators had been retrieving locally was but a drop in the ocean. Herr Wurf of Uhlandstrasse, with his graffiti '*Wenn Ivan kommt, ist alles leer*', had not been exaggerating.

So the two men set off in high hopes of finding something, working methodically outwards from the localities of the palaces, initially through the neighbouring occupied villages but then following the general path of the retreating enemy. They were much helped by the constant traffic of army supply lorries offering them a lift forwards and also a means of sending back their finds. It was not long before their search was rewarded. Kuchumov's serendipity was matched only by his equally extraordinary ability not only to recognise the quality of a chair leg sticking out from a rubbish heap, but to know at once from which room in which palace it had come. Hitching a lift in Estonia, he spotted just such a pile of rubbish by the road. Insisting that the driver stop and back up, they discovered a small slagheap of marble busts, fragments of ceiling paintings and some four hundred books from Pushkin, dumped by a German, who had decided that his life was more important than his loot. Wandering on foot through Baltic villages, Kuchumov would peer through the ground floor windows of the cottages and see all sorts of things the Germans had discarded. Eating one evening in a small hostelry, he went into the kitchen to complain of the slow service. At once he saw two large wardrobes from Gatchina standing against the wall. Turning to remonstrate, he found the cook sitting on a 17th century Venetian chair, while kneading dough in an eighteenth century Japanese bowl. The Germans in their flight had been scattering treasures like confetti. The Baltic villagers were as helpful as he could have expected, given that he could not speak their language. They tried to guide his search and did not resist him even when he pointed out that they themselves were sitting on chairs from this or that palace. They had thought they had belonged to the Germans. Often abandoned German locations had been taken over by Russian units who could be quite suspicious of this stranger eyeing their furniture. Was he a spy? They were not always impressed with his rather rough documents but he was usually able to prove his credentials by showing them the museum mark on the table around which they were sitting. At times he was only a day or so behind the departing Germans.

He and Veselovsky soon divided their job. Having collected a load, Veselovsky would remain with it to organise its return to the storage in the Alexanderhof. If he could not find a returning ammunition truck, he would sit by his load on a station platform until a train with an empty wagon would consent to take it. Gradually their activities became known throughout the army. Drivers would recognise them and willingly help, not only to give them a lift to where they wanted to go but often to help them collect together their finds and take them to some relatively safe location where Veselovsky would wait until he could arrange their transport back to Leningrad. Many things were found through tip-offs from Russian soldiers. Occasionally, a general in the front line would signal to HQ that he had come across something interesting, in which case Kuchumov might even be afforded a light plane to get him there as quickly as possible. In this way, he accumulated an astonishing number of treasures discarded by Germans and some of them were of prime importance.

Early on, he was told that the Germans had mounted a major exhibition in Riga of 'Treasures saved from the Bolsheviks'. When he got there, the exhibition had been dismantled and its contents scattered but it was clear that a great deal had been taken there. The castle had been used by the Kunstkommission as an entrepot. In it they found most of the collection of negatives of the interiors of Pavlovsk, that had been taken for Alexander Benois in 1900. These would be of incalculable value to the restorers when, later on, they were able to go ahead. Furthermore, Riga yielded up hundreds of pictures stolen from Gatchina and Pavlovsk. Some of them were in such a state that Kuchumov had to have conservation work done before they could be shipped. A large part of Maria Feodorovna's collection of cameos were found in Riga. The city proved such a treasure trove that they stayed there for three months and filled a freight car load of stuff in addition to the negatives.

While Kuchumov and Veselovsky had been quartering the Baltic States, the Red Army had been sweeping on towards Germany with hearts full of anger. The first truly German town it reached was Memel. Memel today is a drab little collection of utility modern houses. Its main claim to interest is that historically it has been regularly flattened every 50 years as great armies have swept through it. It is now part of Lithuania and has been renamed Klaipeda. Perhaps that will bring it better luck. It was duly flattened again in 1944, bearing the first shock of Russian fury, but it was not significant enough to assuage it. Koenigsberg, 70 miles to the south was another matter.

Koenigsberg, as its name suggested, had once been the capital of Prussia and the headquarters of the Teutonic knights who had for so long oppressed the Baltic and Slav peoples. It was in every way an ideal object for a good sacking but it was not the Red Army that started it. During March 1944, the British and American air forces mounted sustained attacks that turned the mediaeval city with its huge fortress and cathedral into a smouldering shambles. The raids were not quite so thorough as those on Dresden and perhaps could claim to be facilitating the Red Army's advance but, whatever their justification, they did half the job of sacking Koenigsberg before the soldiers got there. This did not stop the soldiers from enthusiastically completing it.

It was already known that the Kunstkommission had been using Koenigsberg as a collection point and storage not only for treasures looted from all over Russia but also to safeguard the artistic treasures of noble East Prussian families whose estates might soon fall into Russian hands. Koenigsberg had been the centre of the amber trade and before the war, had contained a famous museum of amber objects. It was known that, at one stage, the Amber Room from the Catherinehof had been reassembled and displayed in the Knight's Hall of the Castle. While Kuchumov was still scouring Riga and the Baltic states, a team of experts, under one Professor Brusov, was sent from Moscow in the wake of the Soviet advance to see what could be retrieved.

Armed only with shovels, he and his team managed to clamber over the collapsed walls of the castle to reach the remains of the Knights Hall, only to find it gutted by fire and knee deep in ashes. They also encountered one or two dazed Germans, including a curator whom they found trying to burn some documents. These revealed the problem the Germans had been facing. Prudently, as their army fell back, they had made arrangements to ship whatever they could to safer hiding places further west but they faced a real dilemma. One thing no-one dared to appear was in any way defeatist and prematurely to start evacuating treasures from Koenigsberg might well give such an impression in the wrong quarters. Hitler's edict was not one step backwards and who could be sure he was wrong? After all, the Russians had passed this way once before on their way to Tannenburg. The war was not going well but it was not yet lost.*

It was not clear to Brusov which of the various evacuation plans had been activated, if any. Then there were alternatives, such as bunkers beneath the town which he tried to examine. Other witnesses came forward to add to his confusion, like a German innkeeper who claimed that the Knights' Hall had not been fired until the Red Army arrived. Brusov was able to find a good deal of material and sent back 12,000 items to Russia, but his key objective, the panels of the Amber Room, eluded him. He concluded that they must have been incinerated in the fire in the Knights' Hall in the ashes of which he had indeed found metal fittings which could have come from the Amber Room. But he could not prove it and it was a conclusion which did not suit the Soviet leadership. The Russians were building up a case for the Nuremburg trials based on their outrage at the Nazi's vandalism in Russia. The last thing they wanted to be told was that the Red Army might have also done its share and destroyed the Amber Room.

So, some time later, Kuchumov was sent to Koenigsberg to check out Brusov's work. Searching had already become less athletic by this time and he duly discovered many things which Brusov had missed. Most notably, in the ashes he found three of the four mosaics from the Amber Room which looked intact but which crumbled at his touch. He might have taken these as confirmation of Brusov's conclusion but he was suspicious. Where was the fourth panel? He also proceeded to re-examine the German witnesses and concluded that they were not telling the whole truth. His report therefore did cast doubt on Brusov's conclusion and he was given permission to follow up such leads as there might be and to travel wherever he needed to in the Soviet zone.

Thus started an intriguing mystery. Perhaps the Amber Room was lying hidden in some disused mine or castle dungeon. Much detective work and a great deal of digging has followed but no-one had solved the riddle until the recent publication of a fascinating book on the subject, which claims to do so. It is called *The Amber Room* and it is by two brilliant investigative journalists called Catherine Scott-Clark and Adrian Levy. The fascination lies in their long quest, trawling

---

* In 1914, the Russians attacked Germany with great élan and initially had the best of it. They swept through East Prussia, capturing Koenigsberg, but fell into a trap set by Field Marshal Hindenberg at Tannenburg, suffering a colossal defeat. It was the end of their offensive pretensions against the Germans.

through the archives, teasing out every loose thread, meeting a wonderful assortment of colourful but unreliable people on the way, and checking out every theory, but concluding, in the end, that Brusov must have been right. But they go further, concluding that Kuchumov was deliberately sent to Koenigsberg to sow seeds of doubt, thus launching a sustained and costly effort to find something they knew did not exist. They accuse Kuchumov, whom they refer to sarcastically as 'the great curator' of being a party to this deception. This particular is not fair and has given huge offence amongst the surviving restorers, who knew him. The authors never met Kuchumov and their opinion seems to have been somewhat influenced by an interview with Alexander Kedrinsky who apparently dismisses him as a peasant, with no artistic talent, and a party hack to boot. Kedrinsky was a man of great charm and stunning talent, but he had a chip on his shoulder. Nor did snobbery die with the revolution and many members of 'the former classes', although they suffered for it as Kedrinsky did, continued to look down on the new men coming up with contempt. Kuchumov never had any artistic pretensions but, despite his humble origins, he instinctively had good taste and an understanding of quality. He was, of course, a member of the party, but so were many of the people involved with the country palaces, like Zelenova or Belekhov. Like them, he found membership helped him to pursue his passion, the saving and restoring of the country palaces. If an angry Politburo wanted the matter of the Amber Room panels left open, it would take a foolhardy man to tell them they were wrong. It is hard to believe that, had he just been a party jobsworth, he would have been so much loved by his colleagues, including those like Valeria Belanina who never joined the party.

It will be interesting to see whether the book's conclusion will be accepted and the missing panels left in peace. Notwithstanding their exhaustive research, it is still just a deduction. The search did not cease when, in 1986, the Soviet government announced that it should. There is no proof and the romance of pirates' gold often transcends the improbability of success. But the book has certainly made success seem much more improbable. But, if you are of a romantic turn of mind, you never know. Perhaps they are lying still in some oubliette, well concealed and long forgotten. After all, those exquisite bronze statues, hidden in 84BC in a cellar by Piraeus harbour as the Roman general Sulla marched on Athens, lay there undetected for 2,000 years.

As if to underline such doubts, a story broke in *Komsomolskaya Pravda* in September 2004, within weeks of the book's publication. It concerned an impoverished couple called Smykov, who claimed, amongst other things, to have some of the amber from the Amber Room and to know who has the rest. Mrs Smykov, though poor, is the granddaughter of a celebrated General Telegin, a key member of Marshal Zhukov's staff in the Second World War and after it in Berlin. He had profited while there by buying whatever valuables he could from their starving German owners. In those days a block of flats could be bought with a few packets of cigarettes or chocolate, these being for a time a more stable currency than the mark. General Telegin had bought voraciously, filling whole railway wagons and keeping the receipts, copies of which the Smykovs retain.

In addition to these purchases, however, Telegin acquired something else. During the course of clearing out the catacombs under the city, so the story goes, a Russian patrol came upon some chests which appeared to be full of bits of amber. Having filled their own pockets, they reported the find which soon reached the ears of Telegin, who promptly had them loaded onto one of his railway wagons. He said nothing about them and paid noone for them. He was looking forward to living, after his retirement, in a dacha fit for an emperor. The NKVD were not so stupid, however, and knew most of what was going on but to do anything immediately would have decimated the Soviet Army of Occupation. When, a few years later, Stalin indicated that he was growing tired of the people's veneration of Zhukov, the great war hero, they conducted a secret search of his dacha and found all or more than they expected. However, Stalin did not think it timely to arraign Zhukov, but no such scruple attached to Telegin, his subordinate. He was arrested and his dacha was emptied. His family were left with a few lumps of amber overlooked and copies of all the general's receipts.

The general was released shortly after Stalin's death but his loot was never restored to him. When he died in 1981, he had nothing of value to leave his granddaughter, Mrs Smykov, who now in her extremity is seeking restitution of his possessions, legitimately if cheaply purchased and wrongly confiscated. Or else she would like a lot of money. The story seems quite improbable and easily dismissed in a country whose history is crowded with false Dmitris.* *Komsomolskaya Pravda* is a serious newspaper and was careful not to express an opinion. It seems unlikely that the FSB, as the former NKVD are now called, will be keen now to disgorge treasures so long concealed by their predecessors, but you never know. The curators have been invited in to have a look. In the meanwhile, the recent book might have done better to conclude that, in so opaque a country, the wisest conclusion is to conclude nothing – advice which we will follow.

In any case, perhaps all the searching was worthwhile, because it brought several items to light, including the fourth mosaic panel which Kuchumov had noted was missing from the ashes. It had been looted by a German soldier and had been hanging in his kitchen ever since, impressing and puzzling his friends, and in particular an art expert of his acquaintance. When he died, his sons revealed its provenance and, after some hesitation allowed it to be sold.** There are thought still to be looted works of art in central Europe many of which have changed hands several times, greatly complicating their authentication and ownership.

Meanwhile, the mystery surrounding the fate of treasures such as the Amber Room and the Samson statue had helped Kuchumov to extend his searches to East Germany and to Berlin where there was a vast warehouse crammed with loot from all over Europe. The victorious allies were working their way through it, trying to discover where it had all come from and the arrival of a real expert like Kuchumov was of immense importance as far as recovering items from the country palaces was concerned. He was able to despatch eleven freight cars of treasures back to Leningrad, and many more to other cities like Kiev and Smolensk.

Just as the Germans had had their Kunstkommission, the Russian armies were accompanied by

* Ivan the Terrible had a son called Dmitri who was secretly murdered by the usurper, Boris Godunov. Boris's reign was plagued by a series of 'false' Dmitris, claiming to be Ivan's son. None succeeded.

** The discovery delighted Kedrinsky who had, in the meanwhile, produced well researched designs for the four panels. His design for this one was extraordinarily accurate.

Trophy Brigades whose job it was to know what to look for and where to look, but they were not just intent to recover what the Germans had stolen. They did their share of looting too but they did not own up. For many years, great treasures, such as Schliemann's Trojan gold simply disappeared and it was feared that some oafish soldier might have looted them and, not recognising their importance, might have melted them down. It was not until the mid-nineties, and then seemingly by an oversight, that the world learned that they had all along remained hidden in the storerooms of the Pushkin Gallery in Moscow. They were then put on display, but the Russians are showing no inclination to return them to Berlin. And, indeed, why should they? Were they not entitled to some sort of reparation for the terrible losses inflicted on them by the German invasion? Most great museums contain items acquired in circumstances even less justifiable. If Schliemann's gold goes anywhere, perhaps it should be to Troy. Other trophies, like the paintings from the Dresden Gallery, were taken to Russia, restored, exhibited in Moscow and then returned to Dresden.

And not all the work of the Trophy Brigades was rapacious. As the armies approached Thorn, the birthplace of Copernicus, they were able to persuade the commanders to pass it by for fear of damaging its many historical monuments. Furthermore, the Germans operated a form of scorched earth policy which, in some instances, the Trophy Brigades were able to frustrate. The Wawel Castle in Cracow, for instance, was set to explode but they got the Russian engineers to defuse the bombs in time. The war was fierce and brutal but they helped to ensure that more was not lost to the world. Perhaps if they had not got there first, some oaf might have melted down Schliemann's gold.

The search for lost treasures has never really ended although Kuchumov died in 1991. There is always the possibility of some looted item turning up in a sale room. Only ten percent of the Russian gold, believed to have been shipped to Germany during the war, has ever been recovered but that does not mean it has not been found. The search for plundered treasure, at one stage, developed into a minor industry and perhaps some of the speculators quietly made a profit, but enough of them ruined themselves to cause a legend to arise that there was a curse on the Amber Room. But in the course of time quite a few items have come to light bearing the tell-tale inventory mark from one or another of the palaces.

Nor has the search been confined to abroad, but has been extended to items misplaced inside Russia like the statue of Hypnos which cost Zubov his freedom in 1922. Then there are all those items that Stalin sold and which, by now, the all-conquering world revolution should have restored to Russia. Their whereabouts are not always known. Joe Davies and his wife eventually divorced and their collection was broken up, but sometimes items can be located and occasionally the Russians try to buy them back. When the publisher Malcolm Forbes died in 1990, the Russians bought back his Faberge Collection. They also tried to buy the Gobelins tapestries from Pavlovsk, whose disappearance once cost that over-curious visitor his liberty, which are now in the Getty Museum. Their proposal was under consideration when Paul Getty died and his successors have not been inclined to give them up.

Not all the items auctioned by Antikvariat went abroad. Russians doing well under the new regime were permitted to bid and many made collections of porcelain and other objets d'art. In an entry in her diary at the beginning of the war, Vera Imber worries what they should do with their collection of tsarist porcelain, should there be air raids. Her husband was an eminent surgeon and she a celebrated poet and journalist and they were probably doing very well. It was to save such collections that Belekhov instigated his system to protect them for citizens at the end of their tether - or beyond it. This produced a macabre harvest of treasures taken into the Hermitage for safe keeping and never reclaimed. From these the country palaces were able to recover items once sold against their will - or at least replacements for items lost.

One of Kuchumov's problems was that Antikvariat had not kept very careful records of what it had sold internally. He kept discovering items in unexpected places. The Leningrad Hotel was well furnished with some of them as was the Sverdlovsk Hospital. Before the war, there had been a set of 300 chairs in Peterhof, all identical and scattered throughout the building. They seemed to have been lost in the fire but one day, he recognised one of them in an administrative office in Leningrad. He set about searching to see if he could find any more and it soon became clear that functionaries had been helping themselves liberally. He managed to find about a quarter of the set, mostly scattered about in government offices. One evening, he and Valeria Belanina took time off to watch the film of *War and Peace*. Greatly struck by the authenticity of a lot of the sets, they made some inquiries and discovered that this was no wonder. The sets were authentically furnished - from Pavlovsk.

Despite the evacuations in 1941 and the recovery of items from so many sources, the loss of beautiful things was appalling. Numerically, about a third of the palaces' possessions were evacuated but inevitably they had taken mostly small easily transportable things. Almost all the bronzes, the porcelain and the small objets d'art and most of the movable pictures were saved but of the 10,655 pieces of furniture on the pre-war inventories, only 712 could be evacuated. Thanks to the intelligent work of the curators, these 712 pieces included the most important and unique items, like the pieces made by the German craftsman, Roentgen. In addition, many exemplars of sets were saved to enable craftsman to copy them later on. Priceless upholstery was often removed and saved even when the chair could not be. There would be no shortage of work for the cabinet makers studying in Belekhov's restorer schools and a lot of the lost furniture has been remade. And where no model existed to be copied, such as the Tsar's bed in Peterhof, presumed burnt in the fire, it could be replaced by a contemporary one taken from a palace in the city. When it became time to make decisions about the future of the ruined palaces, it had become clear that it would not be for lack of contents if it was decided not to restore them.

Chapter 10

PETERHOF'S FOUNTAINS

It sometimes happens that, having fought and won a great battle, a people will decide that they deserve a rest and will even allow their defeated wartime opponents to win the peace. No such relaxation occurred in Leningrad. The citizens did indeed feel that they had achieved a great triumph, and without much help from the rest of Russia. Those who had survived were the tougher ones. If a shell hit a loaded tram, it killed the passengers indiscriminately but the long famine had found its victims amongst the weaker. The stronger who survived felt that their struggle was unfinished. Their Pit'r had been wounded but their love for it had been strengthened. There had even been a rapprochement between them and their austere city leaders who had been at pains throughout the siege to identify themselves with the people. What they had done they had done together. The deputy mayor, Kuznetsov, had even taken his small son with him wherever he went in public to emphasise his humanity. What everyone wanted was to get on with the repair and restoration of their city if only to show those damned Germans that their spirit was unbowed.

The first sign of this mood was the crowd that assembled to witness the dismantling of the sandbagged pyramid which had smothered the famous equestrian statue of Peter the Great. Soon after, when the Anichkov horses were replaced on their pedestals on the bridge, another huge and extremely emotional crowd was there to cheer and to weep. As soon as the country parks were safe enough for the clearing up to start, great numbers of volunteers came forward to help during their spare time. There was no doubt where their hearts lay. They wanted their palace parks back and above all that applied to Peterhof and its fountains. The mere fact that the people might want something had never been, of course, a principle which guided the communist government, but in this instance the idea that the fountains should not be repaired does not seem to have occurred to anyone, not even Stalin.

On the 16th February 1946, the Executive Committee of Leningrad formally promulgated the decision that they must be restored. Water was the first necessity. Before the war it had been brought from the Ropsha Hills, some 14 kilometres away, by a system of dams, canals, sluices and pipes, some of antique lead or even wood, which the Germans had systematically destroyed with dynamite. They had stolen the lead pipes. A large task force was now assembled of 1,000 plumbers, builders and diggers under two lady engineers called Petrova and Soldatova. Delayed by the winter weather, they were nonetheless able to bring water enough to the park to permit the reopening of the main cascade on 25th August of the same year. Of course, there were no statues yet but a huge portrait of Stalin looked down benignly, hiding some of the ruined façade of the palace. All in all, it was a fine display, a token of things to come, and it was greeted by a large and celebratory crowd.

Tikhomirova had been having a difficult time trying to discover what statues had been hidden and where. No-one who had been present when they were buried was still around. There was a map of a *Treasure Island* quality but most of the landmarks and reference points used had disappeared. Looking at the parks with their criss-crossing earth works and slit trenches, it seemed impossible to believe that the Germans had not found some of them - perhaps all. Certainly the ones that had been left exposed had all gone. The others, if they were still there, would have to be sought amongst the dug-outs, the anti-tank ditches and the fields of shell craters. By March 1944, enough of the mines had been cleared to allow the search to begin.

Since the upper gardens were somewhat less disfigured than the lower park, they started there. It was known that Spring and Summer had been buried not far from the square pond which they had graced. Much of the pond had disappeared into the anti-tank ditch but enough was still extant to guide the searchers. Tension rose as, hour after hour, deep trenches were dug across the areas where, theoretically, they should be. After a while, Belekhov, waiting in Leningrad for news, could stand it no longer and came out to see what was happening. So did Joseph Orbeli, the director of the Hermitage. They must have brought luck for soon after their arrival a spade struck something solid. A hectic scrabble revealed it moments later to be the corner of the protective wooden cover over one of the statues. A couple of hours later, and they could lift it up. Summer, underneath, seemed to be alright and there was much rejoicing and hugging. It was the first step on a long, long road but it did a great deal to raise hearts, which was just as well for the difficulties in the Lower Park were of a different order.

Their first objective was the pair of statues, Adam and Eve, which, encircled with jets of water, had matched each other across the canal from intersections a short way up the lime avenue which dissects the park. First of all, the limes and the avenue had been so devastated as to make it quite difficult to find the crossroads where they had stood. Furthermore, it was known that because of their special value - they had been a gift to Peter the Great - the statues had been dragged some way away from their pedestals before they were buried, the better to hide them. By dint of a great deal of digging, and some luck, Adam was found reasonably quickly but not Eve. Many holes and trenches were dug in vain until all the likely open areas had been tested. Thoughts began to centre on a German earthwork in the general area where she had stood. Hearts sank for surely if she had been there, the Germans must have found her. Luckily, it had not yet been filled in by the army of *voskresniks* and they decided to examine it with some care. To their great excitement, they discovered that one of the trenches, instead of ordinary duck-boarding, had quite a solid wooden floor. Under it they found Eve. Unhappily she had been much damaged. Her neck was broken and both legs, one in two places. But she was recoverable and repairable and there was a certain feeling of glee that the Germans had been so close to her without realising it. One wonders what the German soldiers imagined when they found this flooring miraculously awaiting them several feet underground. Perhaps there were shells falling and they put it down to kindly providence.

Twenty-three of the statues and ornaments from around the main cascade had been evacuated to Leningrad where all but one had spent the war in the Moscow Station. The exception was the Perseus which had been such a worry for Belaeva and Zelenova in St. Izaak's. It had been intended to evacuate the rest of them but it was left too late and, at the very last moment, with the Nazis at the gates, somewhere had to be found for them. Someone remembered that there was said to be a tunnel leading from the Grotto, under the parterre, towards the Court of Arms Pavilion. It had been shut up for many years and memories of it were extremely vague but danger concentrates the mind. They found and reopened it. There was by now only a handful of curators and staff remaining in the palace and how these few managed to manhandle such heavy statues and vases into the tunnel is a mystery, but they did so and covered up their work well enough to deceive the Germans. Here they were probably helped by the heavy Russian bombardment which greeted the Germans' arrival in Peterhof, cratering the parterre and churning up the mud so that it hid the entrance without revealing it. But it hid it from the returning Russians too. Nobody present had seen the statues buried or knew whether the Germans had found them. The tunnel was not precisely marked on any of the old plans but if it ran under the parterre it was presumably pretty deep. The thought of prospecting to that depth was daunting. Instead they tried driving down rods, hoping that sooner or later one would yield a clue and indeed one did. With palpitating hearts they dug down to see what their rod had struck and were rewarded. Digging down, they discovered the roof of the tunnel and, inside it, they found eleven vases and 17 statues, hardly damaged at all. When they tried to manhandle them out, they could only marvel at what those few curators had done in 1941.

Repaired and re-gilded, all these statues were installed in time for the spring reopening of the cascade in 1947 but the main statues were still missing. It had not been possible to hide the huge bronze statue of Samson wrestling with the lion which had been the central feature of the Cascade. A newspaper article found on a German prisoner proved that he had been in place at any rate until 1942 and so had survived the early Russian bombardment of the palace. Presumably the Germans had taken him and his attendant river Gods, Neva and Volkhov. They had also taken Neptune from the Upper Gardens and his group of tritons. All these were therefore very high on Kuchumov's list of treasures to be recovered when he set out on his hunt. High, too, were his hopes for surely such huge objects could not easily be hidden. Samson was three metres tall and weighed five tons. There were rumours that he had been taken first to Gatchina but he was certainly no longer there. Another rumour had it that he had been exhibited as a war trophy in Leipzig. Soon after Kuchumov reached Berlin, hopes were raised when Neptune was found and sent back, but the trail of the others seemed quite cold. Gradually suspicions started to rise that they had been destroyed, melted down for their bronze content. Had Neptune survived because he was a German work, bought by Paul I in Nuremburg - while the others were all by Russians and worthless? Furthermore, Samson, by Mikhail Kozlovsky, was a triumphalist work celebrating Peter the Great's victory over Sweden in the Great Northern War - something that *untermensch* had better forget about.

Although no hard evidence of their fate was ever found, hope gradually faded for them, to be replaced by resolution that they must be replaced. Russia's plight might be desperate. The

Germans had destroyed 1,700 towns and countless villages which all needed to be rebuilt, but Samson was too potent a symbol. Whatever he cost, he would be replaced. An old but famous sculptor, Vasily Simonov, who had been a leading artist in St. Petersburg before the revolution was chosen. He had been found more dead than alive in 1942 and evacuated to Tashkent. There he had partially recovered but he was still very weak when he returned to Leningrad after the siege. There was doubt as to whether such a frail old man could undertake so large a work, but the very idea of it seemed to revive him. Indeed, with each challenge that he encountered and overcame, he seemed to grow stronger - and there was no shortage of them. There were no detailed drawings of the original statue and only a few bare statistics about its height and weight. An appeal was sent out through the newspapers for photographs and many were brought in but very few of good quality. All were snapshots taken through a haze of water and almost all from the same angle. Only one showed Samson's backside and then from some distance. None of them showed any detail but they would be a guide to his general shape and attitude. Selecting the best 18, Simonov developed a system somewhere between those little grids used by traditional artists to help them draw their subjects and modern computer graphics. He carefully plotted the exact position from which each snap had been taken and then traced the statue's outline from that angle onto paper. These he then synthesised these tracings into one small scale model which he tested against the photos from all 18 angles. When satisfied, he made a bigger model, one third the eventual size. The final full size copy he left to his assistant, Nikolai Mikhailov, feeling it to be beyond his strength. Just as Grabar had laid down back in the days of Glavnauka, each stage of the work had to be submitted to and approved by Belekhov and his panel of experts on the Inspectorate for the Preservation of Art and History Monuments.

While not sharing the renown of Simonov, Nikolai Mikhailov was a pre-war restorer who had specialised in works of the eighteenth and nineteenth centuries and he it was well able to take over when the strain began to wear down Simonov's health. The final version was approved in early 1947 and taken to the Factory for Monumental Sculpture in Leningrad to be cast in bronze. For this purpose, Samson had to be divided into several pieces and then assembled. By the late summer of 1947, he was ready for his triumphal ride through the city. Surrounded by a guard of honour of foundry workers and draped in bunting, it had been planned to follow a circuitous route so that as many people as possible should see him but they found the lorry and its trailer were too bulky to use the minor roads. Nevertheless, they criss-crossed back and forth as best they could between cheering crowds until finally setting off for Peterhof where another crowd awaited them. Gingerly, they eased him down into the Lower Park where a derrick waited to swing him across onto his pedestal. With much pulling and grunting he was edged along until he hovered above his resting place. Here they struck a new problem which, unbelievably, no-one had thought of.

A length of pipe had been left sticking up from his pedestal to be connected to the spout inside the lion's mouth but how to make the connection? It did not seem possible to manage it from the outside and they were discussing what to do when someone noticed a boy standing in the front of the crowd. He was small but looked quite sturdy and might just fit in. Invited to help by the engineer in charge, he stepped proudly forward to take up his position on the pedestal, pipe in hand. While the huge statue was lowered slowly around him, he kept his nerve and after a few moments, the lion reported in a muffled voice that he was connected up. There was an outburst of applause, halted by a loud shriek. In the silence that followed, they could hear faint sounds of struggle, gradually drowned by a crescendo of wailing. Another problem they had not foreseen - how to get the boy out? Willing hands rushed forward to help but, indeed, there was not much room to get at him, let alone for him to wriggle out. Raising the statue as far as they dared, they tugged at what they could reach of him and bit by bit he started to reappear. Eventually, to a great cheer, he was pulled clear, wild-eyed and bedraggled. While the chief engineer composed himself to say a few suitable words of thanks, the boy thought otherwise. Taking to his heels, he scrabbled his way through the crowd and was soon seen legging it away as fast as he could lest these terrible men should ask him to do anything else. They never even discovered his name.

With Samson steady on his pedestal, it but remained for him to be gilded which was completed in record time for the cascade finally to be restarted before the end of the summer, in September 1947. This was a great ceremony, just as it had been before the war, with the bands playing and a large summery crowd to watch and cheer but it was by no means the end of the road. There were still many details of the Grand Cascade missing. The river statues from around Samson's pool had to be copied from photographs. All the golden masks from its sides had been taken by the Germans except for one, which had been hidden in the tunnel and which served as a model for others to be made. More difficult were the step risers from the cascade. They had been decorated, in golden relief, with scenes from classical myth but all the photographs of them had been made through a curtain of water and were extremely difficult to read. Much time was spent studying works by the various artists involved and, in one or two instances they found models to copy. The interpretation by artists of specific scenes from classical stories tended to run on reasonably predictable lines. Nevertheless, the risers which now grace the cascade are more a matter of reconstruction than restoration. The Germans had left nothing to restore.

Even when the Great Cascade was complete, it was only a start. The Lower Park at Peterhof had been one of the great water gardens of the world, rivalling the Villa d'Este in Tivoli. As Alexander Benois once said, "If Versailles is the marvellous dwelling for a ruler of the earth, so is Peterhof for a ruler of the waters". There are 14 kilometres of pipes leading to about 150 fountains and four cascades in the park, requiring altogether two and a half thousand individual jets, each with its own pipe. The fountains are of all sorts of curious shapes and fantasies. Some create a sort of water sculpture, like the Pyramid where 505 graduated jets sculpt the water into the desired shape. Even more intricate is the Sun Fountain whose central column is topped by a revolving golden ball from which innumerable thin jets spout like the rays of the sun. The so-called Menager or Economical fountains look simpler but derive their name from their cunningly designed jets which send a plume of water high in the air. It looks impressive but is in fact hollow, saving water consumption. Then there are Peterhof's famous trick fountains which look like trees or benches but which soak the unwary visitor who approaches too close. The delicacy needed to control the jets of these fountains was extreme. The volume of water, the pressure and its direction had to be perfect because one rogue jet could ruin the whole effect. All these had been created by master *fontainiers* over the course of several centuries and all had been completely wrecked by the Germans in the course of the 900 days of the siege. Some of the most precious nozzles had been removed before they arrived and hidden in the grotto, but they were found and pointlessly stolen. Luckily, there had survived the siege an old man called Lavrentiev who had been looking after the Peterhof fountains since before the First World War. "A fountain is like a child," he once said. "A little scratch or a bruise can make it cry or waive about. When I saw all the ruined pipes, I could not stay still. I had to go to work to repair them despite my age and health." Taking his son Paul and a collaborator called Smirnov, he set about recreating the 2,500 nozzles. He did not, of course, finish them but he was able to pass on his skills.

Work on the fountains has never ceased. The last major ensemble to be tackled was the Lion Cascade in the western half of the park. Designed by Stakensneider in the nineteenth century, it had been terribly damaged in the war and for many years had lain in fragments behind wooden hoardings. It was decided to restore it in 1986 but this coincided with a marked set-back to Russia's economy and so it took until 2000 before it could be opened to the public. It had been a work of reconstruction rather than restoration. By this time, work had already begun on the refurbishment of the Grand Cascade, 40 years after its reopening. This, however, can be considered as just the normal maintenance needed by a great park, which has been going on at Peterhof now for 300 years. The Germans have proved merely an unfortunate interlude.

Chapter 11

THE LENINGRAD AFFAIR

The survivors of the siege, in later years, often looked back on those days as some of their happiest. Not of course the terrible days during the first year but, even then, it had brought a sort of unity in suffering that overlaid all the years of terror and mistrust that had preceded it. And as the city started to recover and began to believe in its eventual triumph, this glow of pride and happiness could not be suppressed. Even the city leaders shared it. Zhdanov, his affable second-in-command Kuznetsov and the mayor Popkov were full of ambitious plans not just to repair their city but to make it more glorious than ever. It had earned it, all agreed. Well, nearly all.

In 1944, Zhdanov was recalled to Moscow. He had been Stalin's closest friend and presumed successor before the war. He had been very much involved Stalin's pro-German policy and in convincing him that reports indicating a German attack were probably British disinformation. He had even gone on holiday to Sochi on 19th June and was away during those traumatic days when Stalin had to face the fact that he had made a catastrophic error. It was long enough for his competitors, like Malenkov and Beria, to put the blame on him and when he got back, he found that he was to be excluded from the war council and sent to Leningrad. Defeat there would have been the end of him but he was an energetic and capable man, able to take brave, high-risk decisions. His contribution to the survival of the city was considerable and acknowledged by its citizens. And the siege had brought a new closeness between the rulers and the ruled. Zhdanov was not a friendly man, able to talk to ordinary people and reassure them, but his assistant Kuznetsov was all of those things. He had spent a lot of time out and about, in factories, at the front, and talking to the bread queues, usually accompanied by his small son to show that he and his family were sharing their pain. When Zhdanov left, Kuznetsov took over. In one way and another, the people were now looking forward to a better future, to a renaissance of their city. They had earned it. It was this euphoria that brought the *voskresniks* in their thousands to help clear the parks and sort through the rubble, and which brought the crowds into the streets to cheer Samson on his way.

Perhaps it momentarily touched even Stalin when he willingly authorised money to repair the fountains and to conserve the ruins and, indeed, he even allowed them to re-roof Gatchina, perhaps because it seemed the cheapest way to conserve it, but there were already other thoughts in his mind. He knew that, in the desperation of war, he had appealed to the timeless patriotism of the people to save their country, but patriotism was not something he trusted in normal times - unless it was in the form of unquestioning obedience to the Party. He suspected now that it was not and was especially suspicious of prisoners of war and even of returning soldiers whose ideas might have been contaminated by things they had seen in the West. Whole trainloads found themselves forwarded straight on to Siberia to relearn the harsh realities of Soviet life. When, in 1946, Kuznetsov and his colleagues arrived in Moscow to outline their plan for a brighter future for Leningrad, it fell on stony ground.

At about the same time, Stalin gave Zhdanov a new task - to launch an attack on deviationist thinking and on the errors that had crept in during the war. He was to pay particular attention to Leningrad, a city which Stalin had always mistrusted and mistreated. Stalin was determined it would not compete with the glorious defence of Moscow or of Stalingrad or with the great battle of Kursk. It was Zhdanov's chance to regain the ground he had lost to Malenkov and Beria. As a typical first step, the heat was first turned on the intellectuals - the musicians, the writers and the painters. Anna Akhmatova, perhaps the city's best loved poet, was suppressed for writing too much about love and too little about socialist reality. He called her a whore. Perhaps she had been unwise to write, at the height of the terror:

No, I don't live under foreign skies,
Sheltering under foreign wings.
I have stayed with my people,
There where my people unhappily were.

All books and plays recalling the heroic days of the siege were censored. Paintings of the terrible scenes of the great hunger were suppressed. The attack soon broadened onto anything 'cosmopolitan' which could mean either Jewish or belonging to Leningrad, Peter's eye on the west. It also set out to obliterate all memories of the heroics of the siege. The street notices advising citizens to walk on the southern side which offered better protection from German shells were taken down. The Museum of the Defence of Leningrad was closed and its exhibits scattered or destroyed. Its director, Rakov, was arrested. During this time, however, no direct attack was made on the curators, architects and academicians most closely involved with the country palaces. Perhaps Belekhov's links with Malenkov saved them, for while so many others were disappearing, they seemed to lead a charmed life. Nevertheless, the black NKVD cars were back on the streets at night and the shutters came down on the bright future that Leningrad had been dreaming of.

That bright future, as they had presented it in Moscow, had not included the country palaces whose fate was still too undecided. Western advice, in so far as it had been sought, was that restoration was impractical and that certainly they were not offering any help. Most people in Russia agreed. The destruction had gone too far. Two schools of thought predominated, neither of which favoured the restoration of the palaces. One, supported by romantics like the author Ilya Ehrenburg, was to leave at any rate Peterhof in ruins as a reminder of Nazi brutality, rather as the French were doing with the village of Oradour. The other was to reuse them, either repaired or totally rebuilt, for some socially useful object. There were all sorts of ideas of this kind. Gatchina could become a museum of military history, Pavlovsk a rest home for architects. Even many of those most closely involved with the palaces, like Professor Ol who had chaired Belekhov's meeting in 1944, began to assume that their fate would lie between these two. In a way, however, the very fact that they had not featured in Kuznetsov's grand plan for the future now allowed them to escape from unwanted attention. The business of clearing up and conserving was allowed to proceed and small budget projects were still being approved by the city authorities, who saw that the parks were once again full of visitors. Work continued on Monplesir and the Hermitage pavilion at Peterhof. The almost undamaged Chinese Palace in the park of Oranienbaum was opened on 7th July 1946 and at once overwhelmed with visitors. Still, those few curators, architects and academics who still clung to their dreams of restoration, were wary of putting matters to the test lest it should provoke a negative answer. In any case, there were not yet enough skilled artists and craftsmen to undertake really ambitious projects. The Restorer schools were barely starting to release their first students and the better ones were going on to higher courses at places like the Mukhina Institute, the new name for Polovtsov's old Stieglitz Academy.

In 1948, Zhdanov died in suspicious circumstances. This did nothing to alleviate the attack on Leningrad. Indeed, its tempo and savagery changed into a higher gear. Kuznetsov and Popkov disappeared along with virtually all the wartime leaders associated with Leningrad. Even Marshal Zhukov, who had commanded the defence at the most critical moment, was banished to a distant Siberian military district. The city was prostrate before Stalin's fury in a purge which became known as the Leningrad Affair.

By chance, in the middle of all this, a new decree was issued called 'About better measures for the preservation of cultural monuments'. It applied to all the Soviet Union but Leningrad had far more than its fair share of such monuments and so it was of particular significance to the city. As is often the case with decrees, its effect and perhaps its intention was far from what its title implied. It decentralised responsibility for cultural monuments to local authorities and at the same time defined cultural monuments in a very economical way. It suggested that the best way local authorities could look after one was to find a tenant and make him responsible for it. With the decree, the central government made one final handout of which 1,500,000 roubles were allocated to the country palaces. After that, no-one was to expect any more, unless the circumstances were very exceptional. Despite the public protests of Grabar, the restoration work at all the palaces was brought more or less to a full stop, except at Pavlovsk for which Zelenova had managed to obtain a special status. And even there, things began to slow down and had come to a halt by 1951.

However, this did not mean that nothing was going on. By this time, those who still believed that restoration was possible had a clear idea of what it would involve. Although they were experts in their field and knew the palaces well, it was another matter to recreate so much that had disappeared and that remained only in their memories or in the fragments which had been saved. The slow down of the actual work offered them an opportunity for research and scientific study so that they would be ready and confident with good plans and forceful arguments should the situation change. And change it undoubtedly would, one day, for Stalin could not live for ever. In a way, it was a welcome breathing space. There were, in any case, very few really qualified people available but those that were, were destined to play a key role. Zelenova was building her team at Pavlovsk while two leading architects, Vasily Savkov and Alexander Kedrinsky, spent most of their time at Peterhof and Gatchina, mainly working on buildings in the parks, restoring bridges and doing things within the meagre budgets allowed them. In addition, they taught in the Restorer Schools. Kedrinsky was a remarkable man who would play a key role in the restoration of the palaces. His position was based on sheer talent because, before the war, he had not been allowed to attend any of the art schools because he was regarded as one of the 'former classes'. His grandfather had been private confessor to Tsar Nicholas II. He was for this reason debarred from high school and university and the best he could get was entry into an engineering school from where his abilities carried him on to the Institute of Civil Engineering. Combined with his artistic talents, his graduation from this institute qualified him de facto as an architect. Architects in Russia are expected to be more than just designers and engineers. They have to be artists too with a mastery of art history. This was no problem for Kedrinsky. Like many others before the war, he had fed his appetite for art and beauty by studying the country palaces and had found ways of studying with unofficial clubs of artists, one of which was weirdly called 'Russian Disgraced French'. No amount of official disapproval could hold back such talent and he was already well known before the war started.

He had just completed his engineering course and was working in the Urals on his post-graduate thesis when the war broke out. He at once returned to Leningrad and became involved in the building of its defences. He remembers the great hunger but survived because he was young, fit and determined. As the imminence of a German assault on the city receded, he joined up and was sent to the front as a war artist. He barely saw Leningrad again until 1945 when an exhibition was being organised of war paintings and he was given leave to show some of his paintings. They caused a small sensation and some key people made it their business to keep him in Leningrad which needed such talents badly. He was offered a choice - to become head stage designer at the Kirov Theatre or to become involved in restoration. He was attracted to the theatre but his love for the country palaces had been his great consolation during his wilderness years. He decided to dedicate his life to their restoration.

One of his closest colleagues was Irina Benois, also an architect. She had married yet another architect, a nephew of the Alexander Benois of Diaghilev fame, whom she had met at school. They had both practised in the thirties but, in 1938, Irina had given up in order to look after her daughter. In 1940, she started to teach. She and her husband were doing well. On 22 June 1941, she had been in their dacha when a cousin brought her the news. She remembers shaking uncontrollably from fear. Although halfway through his doctoral thesis, her husband resolved at once to join up so they returned to Leningrad. He was quickly allocated to a volunteer battalion and with practically no training and only rudimentary arms, went with them to try to plug the gaps opening up in the front line. With the other wives, Irina marched alongside him to the city boundary where they were stopped and had to remain watching their husbands' figures dwindle until, at last, there was no point in waiving any more. They were gone. She returned to their home where she and her daughter endured the terrible winter that followed. The Construction School where she was teaching was evacuated in 1942 but she refused to go with it because her husband was still at the front and occasionally he could get home for a day or so's rest, but eventually he was wounded badly and brought back to the hospital that had been set up in the Astoria Hotel. She visited him daily, oblivious of the treasures sheltering in St. Izaak's just across the road, until her husband managed to prevail upon her to let herself and the child be evacuated. She did not return to Leningrad until 1945 and at once joined the Restorer Workshops. There was plenty to do, mostly in the city. She was surprised by the amount of money made available for materials but found that this did not apply to wages. They were not only very badly paid but often many weeks late. Nevertheless, she decided to spend her whole life in restoration and her name is linked with some of the most remarkable achievements and in particular with the Cottage Palace which Nicholas I had built for himself in the Peterhof park in the high romantic style of the 1820s.

In the meanwhile, the decree of 1948 had not been good news for the students of the Restorer Schools which Belekhov had set up in 1943. The first trickle of graduates had started to emerge in 1946 but the most talented were sent on to study further at the Mukhina Institute or the Academy of Arts. These offered long courses, up to five years, so many of the best students, like the painter Leonid Lubimov and the architect Evgenia Kazanskaya, found themselves called on to help with restoration once it got going. After all, this also was good training. In the meanwhile, the trickle of those not selected for further education had, by 1948, become a flood and there was almost nothing for them to do. They had had excellent but very specialised training and could find no work commensurate with their abilities. There was a lot of misery and even one suicide, a sculptor who could not bear the humiliation of having to scrub the marble steps of the Metro stations.

The new decree was not altogether bad news for the palaces, however, particularly for the Catherinehof which was handed over to the Navy and used as a cadet training school. For one thing, the Navy had plenty of money. The cold war was getting under way and the arms race was on. The Navy could afford a much better temporary roof than had been achieved by the air raid defence girls, and they had their cadets as a free work force. There were several monuments there which were dear to Naval hearts like the column commemorating the Russians great sea victory over the Turks at Chesma Bay which they were pleased to restore, with the help of advisers like Kedrinsky. The Navy was also allocated the Alexanderhof at Pushkin. Kuchumov had to find new storage for his treasures in a hurry.

The Great Palace at Peterhof was too damaged to be of any use to a tenant and, in any case, in the early fifties, Stalin indicated that he wanted to see it eventually restored. A huge portrait of him had been fixed proprietorially to its facade. In 1953, however, just as his paranoia seemed to be reaching new peaks with the Doctors' Plot, he died. The nation's reaction seemed to be a mixture of lost love, for people can love their torturers, of relief and of anxiety lest the future should produce something even worse. Happily, it did not. Kruschev was able to eliminate Malenkov and Beria and, with his speech in 1956, to launch the idea that paranoia and the cult of the personality were related and should never again be allowed.

One of the first acts of the Politburo, in 1953, was to repeal the decree of 1948. Kruschev wrote however to the Inspectorate, warning that although more funds might now be allocated to restoration, architects would be unwise to indulge extravagant ideas. Nevertheless, to the huge relief of all those trained craftsmen and artists who were scrubbing steps, the Restorer Workshop was now set up as a sort of pool of skills to be allocated as required to the teams tackling restoration projects. The huge question of whether the palaces would ever be restored which had for so long hung in the air now disappeared. It was assumed by all that they would be.

Chapter 12

PAVLOVSK

Although these troubles, like black crows, were once again circling above the heads of the citizens of Leningrad, the growing band of those involved with the country palaces were not directly affected. Partly, no doubt, they had problems of their own enough to distract their thoughts from politics but also they had great faith in Belekhov and his determination and ability to protect them. At any rate, none of them had any political trouble during these difficult years when Leningrad was so much in disfavour. When his predecessor, Pobodenostzev, returned from the war, Belekhov at once offered to stand down in his favour but Pobodenostzev saw how the land lay and declined.

The Inspectorate itself, which Belekhov headed, consisted mainly of academics, art experts and historians and it was on their combined opinions that Belekhov largely relied when making decisions of an artistic nature. No project could get very far without their approval. The doers, however, were organised broadly into two groups. One, known as Lenprojekt, consisted mainly of architects and engineers whose prime responsibility was with the structure of the buildings while Restorer, which included the artists and craftsmen, concentrated on the interiors and their contents. The division was not rigid however. Many architects, like Kedrinsky and Irina Benois were also talented artists and designers in their own right and could operate on either side of the line. Both halves worked under the direction of Belekhov who allocated their resources to projects as they arose. The last word, of course, over the approval of projects and the provision of materials and finance lay with the Leningrad government or even higher.

During these troubled forties, most of the conservation work was of an uncontroversial nature. No-one questioned the need to clear up and save what could be saved. As far as restoration went, priority was given to projects which would have the maximum impact on the citizens, such as the repair of pavilions in the parks which had not been too badly damaged. Work was started on Monplesir which obviously could be and should be saved. The Chinese Palace at Lomonosov had only been hit by one stray shell and that a dud, so it could be repaired reasonably cheaply. Work continued in all the parks to replace the destroyed trees. But during this period it was tacitly agreed not to push for a decision on the restoration of the great palaces themselves, because the money required was clearly not going to be given in the present political climate and, anyway, there were still insufficient skilled restorers to tackle projects on that sort of scale. All agreed to push ahead cautiously without making waves.

Well, nearly all. There was one person who did not agree. This was Anna Zelenova. She was a remarkable woman but compromise had never been her long suit. She did not feel that such patience should apply to her beloved Pavlovsk. She had certain arguments in her favour, some practical, some emotional. There had always been a certain difference in the way people looked at Pavlovsk and the other palaces. They had all been made into museums but Pavlovsk had once been a family home, albeit a very grand one, while the others had been conceived as settings for the extravagant goings on of the Imperial court. Being a home, its contents had been of a more intimate nature - and more of them had been saved. Furthermore, until the war, it had retained its original form, as planned by Maria Feodorovna, and most who knew it would have admitted that it had the best chance of recovering that unalloyed loveliness. Lunacharski had once written 'Pavlovsk Park possesses extraordinary charm. It should have special care'. He was not the first or the last to fall under its spell. Nobody therefore sought to prevent Zelenova if she was going to break ranks and break them she did.

She was a dauntless woman. She was an enthusiastic communist party member and no-one ever doubted where her political loyalties lay, however much she might do battle with one or another apparatchik. This gave her a good insight into how the party worked, and might be made to work. She was always an assiduous maker of contacts - what would today be called a networker. She never forgot someone who might one day be of use. But whether or not she had a contact, she would never hesitate to plunge in and trust to her passion and power of persuasion to get what she wanted. This was how she had been able to commandeer the astonished Captain Sapgir and his company of military engineers - and how she managed to keep them the best part of two years until the ruins of the palace had been firmly supported. It was largely as a result of his work that Pavlovsk now looked the easiest of all the palaces to restore.

Knowing her intentions, Belekhov allocated to her the services of the architect, Feodor Oleinik, whose release from the army he had managed to accelerate. Before the war, Oleinik had done much of his doctoral thesis work in and around Pavlovsk, and he was the ideal choice to join Zelenova. In addition, she had the help of a secretary called Kurovskaya, who was in fact a trained curator, plus a senior researcher called Natalya Gromova who contributed a great deal to her system of cataloguing fragments. Another of the team was the faithful Nikolai Weiss who had struggled back to Leningrad with her under the noses of the advancing Germans. In addition they had the help of students on their days off and lay volunteers from the city. Together, they got down to all the detailed measuring of the building and the analysing what materials they had salved, where they would fit in and what, in addition, they would need.

Before the war, there had been a spur railway leading through the park to the Voksal. This was partly a station and partly a complex which had been built up around it, full of the same sort of attractions that had made Vauxhall in London so fashionable in its day. Indeed, its name was a corruption of Vauxhall. It included a fine concert hall in which most of Europe's leading musicians had performed, earning it fame as the 'musical railway station'. During the war, it was burnt down and the Germans pulled up the rails of the spur line, meaning to make use of them, but they never did. The rails were found, to Oleinik's joy, in a storeroom. Faced with the problem of rebuilding the fallen cupola at a time when materials of any kind were almost impossible to obtain, they seemed like a miracle on which he could base his plan. Crouching over his charts in one of the few surviving houses in the village, he acted as researcher, architect, quantity surveyor and draughtsman all rolled into one until he had planned the rebuilding of the main block down to the smallest detail. They were convincing plans but very ambitious. It was now up to Zelenova.

There was only one source of authority for such an important project as this. She therefore took herself to Moscow, at her own expense and with her own rations. There, she started knocking on the doors of the astonished officials of the Ministry for Culture. At first she met with resistance but Zelenova's reputation was already not confined to Leningrad and she found sympathisers to help her, like Grabar. Even so, it was a slow process and she was half starving when, after a month, she found herself late one night in the great Marshal Voroshilov's office in the Kremlin. He took her very seriously, listened carefully and promised to submit her proposal to Stalin. A few days later she received his approval and she was told she could select a team of experts dedicated to Pavlovsk and not subject to the changing priorities and needs of the Inspectorate. In this particular, Pavlovsk has always been an exception and remains so to this day.

Oleinik knew that it would undoubtedly have been easier to pull down the walls and start all over again but he did not want to do so. He was not of the pedantic school which held that restorers should simply put back whatever original fragments remained and leave a romantic ruin, but he believed that as much as possible of what was left should be incorporated. In order to make this possible and cheaper, he was quite happy to use materials and techniques unavailable to the original architects. With the old railway lines he saw he could steal a march on Cameron, with his armies of serfs, but he never wavered from his aim of faithfully reproducing Cameron's and Brenna's concepts as authentically as possible.

Once the building work started he took firm control. He was allocated a staff, including a colleague from Lenprojekt called Sophia Popova-Gunich, a tiny but indomitable woman who liked best to spend her time up where the work was happening. More concerned about her appearance than her safety she insisted on clicking about the scaffolding in her high heels. In 1953, when the practical work really got under way, a group of building contractors under Belekhov's control and calling themselves 'Facade Repairs 1' was sent to Pavlovsk under the leadership of Oleg Gendelman. Oleinik was a tyrant when it came to detail and anything that erred in the slightest from his carefully measured and researched plan had to be redone. It came to be a shibboleth of restoration to ask: "Would Oleinik accept it?" It was a standard used long after he had departed. Sadly, he did not live to see the completion of his plans. In the early fifties, his 15-year-old son was wandering through the park and trod on a mine. He was killed outright and the father never really recovered. In the words of his friend, Alexander Kedrinsky, 'he half died when his son died'. In fact he continued working until 1954 but was only 52 when he died completely. There is no doubt that he never got over his son's death but his war wounds probably also played a part in so premature a death. He did see the completion of the roof and the new cupola on the main block of the palace, although only through the web of scaffolding which was supporting an army of moulders already at work on the decorative details. Long before he died, this first resplendent triumph of the restoration movement had been having an inspirational effect on all those, sceptical or enthusiastic, who were involved in the restoration of the country palaces. It was not just demonstrating that they could be rebuilt but also how faithfully to the original.

Although Oleinik was officially succeeded by another man called Kaptzug, it was mainly his former assistant, Sophia Popova-Gunich, who now made the running and who soon proved herself to be almost as strong-willed as he had been. Since her arrival, she had been mainly involved in the palace's internal architectural features, such as the colonnaded Grecian Hall and the Egyptian Vestibule. She and Oleinik had worked very closely together and so she could carry his plans forward seamlessly, especially as the emphasis of the work was now turning to the interior in any case. Her relationship with Zelenova was less easy. They were two strong women who did not like to compromise but, of course, one or the other or both always had to. Nevertheless, they worked together successfully for many years, with considerable respect for each other but little affection.

The finance which Zelenova had obtained in 1947 provided several years of momentum towards the rebuilding of the palace but after 1950, no new funds were released and things began to slow down. By the end of 1951, very little work was possible, but, by this time, the main blocks of the palace were intact. Much of Zelenova's time was devoted to dealing with delegations from various organisations interested in using them for their own purposes. The Navy wanted it as an extension of their school at Pushkin; it was wanted as a tuberculosis sanatorium; someone proposed a house of rest for the architects. She managed to fend off these proposals but accepted that some of the treasures being stored in the Alexanderhof could be transferred to Pavlovsk. This brought into her team an able art historian called Valeria Belanina who was particularly highly skilled at mounting exhibitions. To celebrate, they put on a show of the treasures that had been saved. It was the first major exhibition since the war and it caused something of a sensation but did little to raise money for restoration. But the restorers never lost heart. 'Where there's death, there's hope' as the saying goes and, early in 1953, Stalin died.

From then on it was generally accepted that the restoration of Pavlovsk would be brought to fruition. With the building well advanced, plans for the interior could be put in hand. Funds were immediately released that enabled them to resume work on the decorative aspects of the exterior and by 1955 they had rebuilt the southern circular wing of the palace in which they intended to install their administrative offices. It was time to start planning the reopening of the museum.

By the end of 1947, Kuchumov's treasure hunt abroad was becoming less productive and he could turn his attention to what was happening at home. The treasures that had been crammed into the Alexanderhof for convenience needed unpacking, examining, repairing and cataloguing. The collections that had returned from NovoSimbirsk had to be combined with what had been found abroad and what was turning up elsewhere. Curators needed to know what they could expect to put on show, if and when their museums were ever restored. As a bi-product of all this activity, he even managed to put some of his treasures on display which was hugely popular. However, in 1949 the Navy acquired the tenancy of the Alexanderhof, and he was soon asked to get out and all this came to an end. It was not easy for him for none of the palaces were ready to receive them.

Space was found in the stables at Pushkin and in the chapel which, though damaged, still had a roof. Other space was found in disused churches in Pushkin town. Pavlovsk was better placed than the others palaces, having various covered spaces which increased as Oleinik's reconstruction programme progressed. It was not easy however which is no doubt why he detached Valeria Belanina to join Zelenova's team. These storages were, however, at best refuges in an emergency. Where there was no foreseeable likelihood of a palace being able to use its treasures, it seemed only sensible that they should be displayed elsewhere. This worked at least temporarily to the benefit of Pavlovsk whose restoration was well ahead of the other palaces but some of the treasures were sent to museums elsewhere in the country. Nothing was sold however and meticulous records were kept of where everything had gone.

As the fifties progressed and the date for reopening some of the rooms at Pavlovsk approached, Kuchumov felt able to give more and more of his attention to refurnishing them as nearly as possible to how they had once been. For this, he did not just rely on his own memory but spent much time studying the records, the slides he had recovered in Riga and the articles that the Archduke Constantine had allowed Alexander Benois to publish in 1900-1902. In addition, 25 years earlier, Constantine's father had had a comprehensive inventory made and a book written describing in great detail the contents of the palace at that time, which Kuchumov could compare with Polovtsov's inventory of 1917 and his own work of just before the war. He had plenty of evidence of what had been changed and what had gone missing down the years. Furthermore, it had been a discipline laid down by Maria Feodorovna herself to keep meticulous records of such changes and these had been maintained in the archives enabling Kuchumov to reconstruct each room as she had conceived it. They were also invaluable in settling any arguments as to where individual items had come from and who had title to them.

As Head of Central Storage, it was also his task to organise the repair work needed after all the vicissitudes the treasures had been through and, as he began to get on top of this, he was able to commission copies of the sample chairs and tables which had been saved from sets from which the rest had been lost. By this time, highly skilled craftsmen were emerging from Belekhov's schools. He welcomed them but set them extraordinary standards. The names of the original eighteenth century craftsmen were generally known and any attempt to reproduce their work had to be preceded by the most rigorous research. It was not good enough just to make a chair look the same. Every craftsman has his own identifiable way with joints and carving and with the treatment of wood. Kuchumov's aim was that each new chair made should be recognised as authentic, should the ghost of the original craftsman return to see it. He was lucky to have the services of a team of exceptional cabinetmakers, led by Mikhail Kozlov. To aid them, they had had an extraordinary bit of luck. Amongst the baggage evacuated to Siberia had been a trunk which appeared to be full of old rags but these turned out to be a present almost direct from Maria Feodorovna. Always a prudent housewife, if a chair cover wore out, it would not be thrown away but kept as a sample to be sent, if necessary, to the original manufacturer to be copied. Indeed, inside the trunk they found unused materials because living in the extreme East of Europe she had been in the habit of ordering extra material with her original order to avoid long delays should a chair have an accident and need recovering urgently. For the restorers, it was like Aladdin's cave.

In 1956 the need for a Central Storage organisation had decreased and it was closed down. Each museum would henceforth be responsible for its own treasures. This released Kuchumov to join Zelenova as head curator in time to supervise the final months of preparation for the reopening of the first rooms of the museum in 1957. He found the rooms by no means ready to receive furniture. They were still full of rubble, dust and general mess; there was internal plasterwork to be done, wood carving and gilding and, not least, the restoration of the parquet floors. These floors made their own contribution to the controversies which the Inspectorate had to resolve. It was, in fact, an echo of an earlier controversy. In 1803, fire had destroyed some of the parquet floors designed by Cameron and Brenna. Maria Feodorovna had urged Voronikhin to replace them but such floors were going out of fashion and she was persuaded to accept plain carpeted floors instead. It so happened however that amongst the storage in the Alexanderhof had been some badly damaged parquet floors from the Zubov Block at Pushkin. These had originally been made for a mansion Catherine the Great had been building for Count Lanskoye, one of her later lovers but, before they could be laid, he had died. So they finished up in the rooms she built for her very last lover, Zubov. They were in much the same style as those originally designed for Pavlovsk and after much learned argument, it was decided to fulfil Maria Feodorovna's wishes. Even so, it was not easy. They had been badly damaged and many of the panels had rotted. Such exotic timbers were virtually impossible to obtain in post-war Russia but rescue arrived from an unexpected source. At this time, the Soviet Union was spending much effort to support North Vietnam in its struggle against America, which the Vietnamese had no normal means of repaying. However, they did have exotic woods and they sent a large shipload, destined in theory for repairs to the Kremlin. There had been more than enough for the Kremlin however and the ever-nimble Zelenova managed to obtain what was left over for the floors of Pavlovsk. All that remained was to find craftsmen equal to the job but there was now a pool of such skills accumulating from Belekhov's restorer schools. Once again Kozlov with his knowledge of rare woods was brought in, assisted by a skilled and patient carver called V. Fedotov. These two formed the mainstay of the team.

Undoubtedly, however, the greatest challenge facing Zelenova was the restoration of the paintings. Almost all the movable paintings had been evacuated before the siege but, in the days of Paul and Maria Feodorovna, although lavish baroque decoration was already going out of fashion, most ceilings in the palace had been painted and some of the walls. Many were the work of Gonzaga himself but the Cavaliers' Hall had been done by Giovanni Scotti and the State Bedroom by a German artist of totally contrasting style called Mettenleiter. Virtually all this work had been destroyed by the fire leaving but small singed fragments, but even these would prove valuable guides as to the original artist's palette and, indeed the medium he had used. A great variety of media had been used - oil, tempera, faux marbre and grisaille applied variously to canvas, silk, glass, metal, marble, wood and plaster. Where would the master restorer be found who could cope with such a variety of styles and methods? Zelenova knew where.

She had met Anatoly Treskin before the war and was aware of his extraordinary talent. This had been evident very early in Treskin's life, to the dismay of his family. His father was not in the least talented, being a minor clerk in St. Petersburg who hardly regarded painting as a respectable way of life. He wanted his son to follow in his footsteps or, at least, do something safe and respectable. Treskin had other ideas. His grandfather had been Italian and a chef to a great Russian family, on which he built dreams of his own romantic and artistic origins. After all, did not the great French chef Escoffier once describe sculpture as a branch of patisserie. So he wore large floppy black hats and liked to call himself Triskorni. When the Civil War broke out, his father, ever cautious, had decided to take his family out of Petrograd. They sought safety in Siberia only to find themselves in the thick of it, harried from place to place by the fortunes of war and finishing up in Simbirsk, Lenin's birthplace. But whatever might be happening, nothing could stop Treskin from painting. If he could not get proper paint, he would use whatever bits of charcoal and coloured earth he could lay his hands on. This may have dismayed his father but it was noticed by a member of a local trades union in Simbirsk who invited the 16-year-old to become resident artist at a local factory, painting murals and designing scenery for their theatre. His reputation soon spread through union circles and three years later, he was invited to take part in a union sponsored art exhibition which led to him being offered a vocational arts course. This was hardly a commanding height of artistic education but it was a fine testimonial to Lunacharski's new proletarian educational policy. Being somewhat artisanal in its nature, the course did not involve Treskin in the exuberantly futuristic school of painting which was briefly flourishing in the wake of the revolution. His teachers could not have been more conservative, laying great stress on the study of classic composition and on the styles, materials and techniques of the old masters. He was required to copy their works at which he proved so adept that, while still a student, he was invited to help his tutor, Dmitri Kiplik, with the restoration of some paintings in the Leningrad Conservatoire. At about this time, he married, and decided that he must take this as a job. He worked on paintings by most of the great masters and in virtually every kind of medium, always preceding his work with careful research into the artist's methods. In 1938, he was sent temporarily to Pavlovsk to restore the Gonzaga paintings there, which was when he first met Zelenova. Throughout the thirties, he was very happy, working away almost oblivious of the political terror raging around him.

In 1940, it was not a premonition of war that caused him to leave Leningrad but an invitation to become resident artist for the naval garrison on a tiny promontory in the Gulf of Finland which the Finns had been forced to cede at the end of the Finno-Russian War. The attraction for the Treskins was that the use of a charming cottage came with the job. Indeed, had he foreseen the war, he might well have refused the job because almost the first shell fired destroyed the cottage. Luckily they were out. They both played their part in the siege which followed until, in the winter of 1941, the remnants of the starving garrison were withdrawn by night to an almost equally hungry Leningrad. The Treskins went too, clutching two of his pictures. They both survived the great hunger but the rest of his family died. Throughout the siege, he remained in service with the Navy as war artist, often at the front or on Kronstadt, sharing the dangers and deprivations of the sailors. He was decorated for gallantry. When the blockade ended, his talents were immediately in demand and he was soon leading a team of artists repairing the bomb damage done to the Hermitage and many other historic buildings in the city. One of his particular abilities was the speed at which, once started, he worked. There are not many historic buildings in Leningrad which he did not help to restore. Surprisingly, he does not seem to have been asked to teach in the restorer schools, perhaps because of his academic qualifications were not impressive enough.

Zelenova first invited him to join her in the forties but it was not until 1954, when several rooms at Pavlovsk were ready for painting, that she managed to persuade him. He knew what a challenge she was offering him and it must have seemed to him an answer to his dreams. The nature of restoration is anonymous. Restorers never sign their work because it is not their work. They are somewhere in limbo between art and craft. After so many years of being sent hither and thither, the thought of a massive, unified project must have seemed a life-fulfilling prospect. He was now 50. This would be his masterpiece.

The fire had destroyed most traces of the original paintings. There were some sketches and cartoons by the original artists in the archives. There were some black and white photographs of their work from before the war and Alexandre Benois's invaluable articles of 1900-2, with their own archive of negatives. And there were peoples' memories, including his own, of what had been there. Certainly, each room had had its individual integrated theme and design so that its shape, its plasterwork, its floor and its ceiling were all united by the artist's painting to form the harmonious whole which he had envisaged. Each must now be recreated in the style of those artists and follow closely their intentions. Treskin set about studying them, travelling to wherever he could find examples of their work, analysing their pallets and their brushwork and trying to imagine himself into their time and their minds.

Room by room, he prepared his sketches for submission to Belekhov and his colleagues of the Inspectorate. Sadly, however, Belekhov died in 1956. He was only 52 but he had never quite shaken off the effects of the dystrophy he had suffered during the siege. His place was taken by his predecessor, Pobedonostzev who seemed to everyone to be the only person equipped to follow in Belekhov's footsteps and who was greatly respected for the sporting way that he had not tried to reclaim his job. Even so, it was not easy for him. Belekhov had built up such esteem that his decisions were not contested, even by excitable artists like Treskin. Now there were tensions. Great as their expertise might be, these professors of the Inspectorate did not have any Italian blood in their veins and were apt to be alarmed by the exuberance of Treskin's ideas. Nor had they studied the problems with such intensity or in such depth or from so practical a standpoint as had Treskin. There were tricky moments of confrontation for they still wanted their say and he was unwilling to give way. He was backed by Zelenova and was well aware of the fact that, should he resign, they would be hard put to replace him. He was not above throwing a fit of tantrums. The professors faced a formidable opposition but it was not always straightforward. The agreed aim of all was to recreate the original artist's intentions but it was not always clear what these were. In the Cavaliers' Hall, for example, the original Scotti sketches for the painting did not fit the plasterwork, as it appeared to have been at the outbreak of war. Which was right? Treskin stood for the Scottis' sketches and got his way. The plasterwork must be redesigned to accommodate them. The greatest controversy of all, however, arose when they reached the throne room and its ceiling.

The throne room is huge. Because of its size, the ceiling feels much lower than it really is. It is 400 square metres in area and produces a curious echo. In living memory it had always been plain white but it was believed that Gonzaga had started to paint it but had left Russia without finishing it. Indeed, they found in the archives some cartoons by Gonzaga to prove that he had intended to do so. To complicate matters, he had left sketches of three alternative ideas and they did not know which had been chosen. The stage was set for a classic battle between those who merely wanted to restore the status quo ante bellum and those who dreamt of restoring the palace as originally conceived for Paul and Maria Feodorovna. It was generally agreed that Paul would have wanted it painted but maybe something had intervened, perhaps his assassination or the fire of 1803. It had certainly been white before the war. The arguments raged back and forth while Treskin's blood pressure steadily rose. Everything in his nature cried out to paint it. It would be his magnum opus and, eventually, Belekhov's rules came to his aid. How could the Inspectorate forbid him at least to make sketches to show what he could do? He got his way but not until Zelenova had lobbied on his behalf with the Ministry in Moscow, something of great comfort to the academicians obliged to take a perhaps risky decision. Treskin at once redoubled his researches into Gonzaga's work, wherever he could find it. He tried to think himself into the mind of the master, confronted by the problem of this shallow expanse, so wide as to feel repressive. Too heavy a painting could make matters worse which is certainly not what Paul and Maria Feodorovna would have wanted. From the few original sketches, he concluded that Gonzaga must have planned a trompe l'oeuil effect, gently coloured, which would lead the eye up between the tapering facades of houses to a pale expanse of sky, giving an effect of extra height and space. His preliminary coloured sketches took him six months. He made them life-size and affixed them to the ceiling, so that the inspectors could evaluate their effect. The onlooker was given the impression that he stood in the flag bedecked plaza of a renaissance town. The room certainly seemed to gain height and gaiety but it still seemed a step too far into speculation for some. On the other hand, Treskin's sketches were so masterly that it seemed criminal to throw them away. A quick decision was needed if the work was to be done in time for the opening of the throne room to the public, planned for the fortieth anniversary of the October Revolution in 1957. Faced with the combined front of Zelenova and Treskin, as usual, the professors gave way.

There was no time to lose. Tracings had to be made of the sketches and then pierced so that, when positioned on the ceiling, charcoal could be rubbed through the holes to guide the artists with their painting. Only then could the serious work begin. It took two years of intense activity, working to beat the deadline. Four hundred square metres need a lot of painting. All the work was done from on top of scaffolding which had to be regularly dismantled to allow the team to see what they were doing. Treskin's almost uncanny ability to work at high speed was essential but it was not shared by all his team. Nevertheless, the will was there and all were prepared to work whatever hours were needed, whether paid or not. Overtime and work on holidays were not. It was indeed ready for the great opening but at the last minute it was noticed that one of the painters had found time to record in one corner what miserable wages he had received for doing it. Sadly, this has since been painted over.

It is for each visitor to Pavlovsk to make up his or her own mind as to the merits of the work and as to which side he would have taken in the debate that preceded it. Whether or not Gonzaga would approve of it, could he walk in, is unknowable but he would certainly recognise it as a tremendous tour de force by a master restorer. It is indeed Treskin's unsigned monument. But it was not the end of his involvement with Pavlovsk. He and his team restored altogether 28 ceiling paintings and numerous wall paintings throughout the palace. He received many decorations for his art to join those he received for his gallantry during the war. He died in 1986, having worked almost to the end but in his eighties, arthritis began to cause his hand to shake. Unable to paint, life had little point for him. He must have been tough to spend so much time on scaffolding, craning backwards and painting above his head. He attributed his extraordinary strength to ' little glass of spirits and wearing good supportive boots, not too tightly laced'. His last contribution was to prepare designs for the re-creation of the Rose Pavilion, built by Maria Feodorovna and chosen by her son to celebrate his triumph over Napoleon and totally destroyed by the Germans. Treskin loved to paint roses but he did not live long enough to see his designs executed.

This was done by his successor, Leonid Lubimov, a brilliant artist who had already solved many varied and difficult problems in other palaces. He contrasted in almost every possible way with Treskin. Where Treskin was tall and striking, Lubimov was short, almost gnome-like, but with a wonderful twinkle in his eye. He led his team with discipline but immense good humour, so that they all worked for him not just out of respect for his talent but because they loved him. He died in 2001 having just completed the repainting of the palace library. This had been originally restored by Treskin with a trompe-l'oeuil design in grisaille but a hurricane had torn off the roof and the whole thing had to be redone from scratch.

As Zelenova's programme for the planned reopening of the palace got under way, it proved a lifeline for many of the restorers trained in Belekhov's schools. Having gained a start over the other palaces she had her pick of them. Furthermore, unlike the other palaces, she had early on been invited to form her own team which she kept together. The leading wood carvers were Vsevolod Polyakin and A. Vinogradov and amongst the sculptors, Nadezhda Maltseva and Tamara Shabalkina were outstanding. Some were still active into the new millennium, like Tatyana Telukova, a gilder and Valentina Soldatova a very pretty sculptress who was also particularly skilled at restoring porcelain. Soldatova had been one of the earliest to join Zelenova and by the end of the century found herself restoring statues that she had already restored many years before. Russian parks, like parks everywhere, are not immune to vandalism. She and Telukova had both been evacuated from the city during the siege and had been amongst the earliest students in the Restorer Schools. Telukova had originally wanted to be a lorry driver but life does not always go according to plan. She started to train as a moulder and proved very talented but she found that she could more easily get work as a gilder. As one of the early graduates from the schools, her first years had been extraordinarily hard. She had been part of one of the Restorer teams but such jobs as had come their way, rarely required the whole team but she had been luckier than some of the others. Being multi-talented, like so many restorers, she could mould or carve if that was what was wanted but she preferred to gild. It had been interesting in the early days because she had worked all over Russia but she was very glad to be able to join Zelenova. Luckily both she and Soldatova loved their work because, like Treskin's artists, they were paid peanuts for doing it.

In 1957, Zelenova decided that it was time to apply the Belekhov doctrine to the park. It had been cleared of mines and tidied up after the Germans left. All the statues had been dug up again. Some seventy thousand tree stumps had also been dug up and a similar number of saplings planted, but it was now time to start controlling their wild growth and recreating the original park as designed by Gonzaga. Since the Germans had been kind enough to rip up the spur railway which had split his plan into two, they could aim to recreate it as it had been in Maria Feodorovna's day. Zelenova gave the task to her faithful archivist, Natalya Gromova, to restore the alleys and circuses, to tidy up the plantations and avenues, to repair the bridges and the many features some of which had survived but others of which had disappeared. One of the most difficult decisions had been whether to rebuild the Rose Pavilion. At least Treskin lived long enough to throw himself into the argument but the project was not finished until the late nineties. Long before that, in the summertime, the park was once again full of happy groups and families, enjoying the sunshine and Gonzaga's subtly manicured wilderness, just as their forefathers had been doing on that terrible day in June 1941.

In 1979 Zelenova handed over to one Ludmila Kazantseva and, as can happen, died within the year. She was lecturing when she suddenly gave a loud cry and collapsed. She was already dead before anyone could reach her. Belanina had known Kazantseva at university but the appointment was not a success. It was probably an impossible task to follow Zelenova who had not only lived in and for Pavlovsk since before the war but whose fame and stature as a restorer had spread widely across Europe. And then, as Captain Sapgir had once written, there was her radiant soul. Kazantseva elected not to move to Pavlovsk and never managed to convince her team of her commitment. She remained nevertheless for some six unhappy years before being replaced by another woman, Makharova, who handed over after three years to one Ludmila Koval who lasted only three months. After her, they tried a man, Yuri Mudrov who handed over in 1997 to the present director, Tretiakov, who was transferred from Gatchina. Throughout all this period, continuity was provided by Valeria Belanina. Despite never joining the Party, Belanina had been for many years at Zelenova's right hand. She is rightly proud to have reached such a high position while outside the Party but perhaps it explains why she was not chosen to succeed Zelenova. If this was a disappointment to her, it did not affect her zeal and loyalty to the palace she loved. It was she more than anyone who held the team together and who carried on Zelenova's work. In 2002, it was still Belanina who, though retired and working as part time adviser in the palace, was the most powerful personality around. She has devoted 50 years of her life to it. She was exceptionally talented in the mounting of exhibitions. In 2002 she put on an exhibition to celebrate the work of Anatoly Treskin which was both moving and awe-inspiring, for the man's talents were truly extraordinary. She was still guarding the integrity of the palace in a changed era when commercialism was creating new problems for the curators to solve. The best testimonial to her success is the palace itself. It is not just that its extraordinary beauty has been recovered but also its feeling of great intimacy. It is sometimes difficult to believe that Maria Feodorovna is not about to walk into the room. Let us hope that the next century is kinder to it than the last.

Chapter 13

PETERHOF

While Pavlovsk had a special place amongst the palaces because of its artistic integrity and its intimacy, Peterhof was probably closer to the hearts of ordinary Leningraders - and possibly also closer to Stalin's who may have identified more with Peter the Great than with Maria Feodorovna. Peterhof was Peter's creation, containing many personal details and items that evoked his spirit and his vision of the future of his country. Whereas the destruction of the other palaces might be a cultural loss, the destruction of Peterhof had been an insult to the concept of Russian greatness. Furthermore, for the ordinary citizens, it was the most accessible of all the palaces for a day out, by ferry as well as road and rail, and it had its annual gala days like the early summer day when the bands played and the fountains and cascades were brought back to life after the long winter. Its destruction was the heaviest blow of all - and it had been the most thorough. In an access of anger in 1944, the Council of Ministers in Moscow swore that they would restore it and would henceforth call it Petrodvorets instead of the Germanic Peterhof. It meant the same but the new name has never become popular.

The Germans had no sooner arrived on the 21st September 1941 than the palace was set alight. They refused to take any steps to put it out and would not let anyone else do so. The fire could clearly be seen from the naval base at Kronstadt. There has since been disagreement as to who had started the blaze, opinions dividing along a political fault line between those who hated Hitler most and those who hated Stalin most. For those who hated both equally, which must be most people, the balance of likelihood pointed at the Russian artillery although a few locals claimed it was the work of partisans setting fire to the palace while German officers were celebrating inside. Whatever the cause, the German onlookers were probably almost as dismayed as the Russians, seeing vast opportunities for looting going up in smoke. Nevertheless, they stood by and let it burn, having been ordered by their commander, Field-Marshal von Reichenau, 'only to put out fires in buildings needed to quarter German troops. All other buildings should be razed to the ground. No historical objects or works of art in the east are of any importance'. About two thirds of the Great Palace was destroyed, leaving only windowless and roofless outer walls. There are differences of opinion as to whether the Germans did take away much loot. Since Peterhof town was in the front line, within days they evacuated the few Russians who had remained there so, unlike the other palaces, there were no witnesses of laden lorries, carrying loot off to Germany. When, after the war, Kuchumov set off to retrieve what he could, he found much less from Peterhof than from the other palaces.

Throughout the siege, Peterhof was in the front line, even more exposed than Pavlovsk and Pushkin. It was right at the tip of the German salient investing Leningrad from the west. It lay between two Russian forces, but the fiercest fighting took place on the eastern side where the German positions had reached the city's suburbs. It was here that the heaviest shelling took place. Lacking the strength to attack the Germans, the Russians adopted a policy of exchanging shell for shell with the German artillery. As a result, the dachas and palaces in the eastern part of the park suffered the most. The Farm Palace survived but was badly damaged; the Orangerie was burnt to the ground; the Cottage Palace survived slightly better perhaps because the Germans used it as a hospital and therefore did not site any guns too close by. On the other hand, because the main Russian thrust when it finally came was from the east, it was in this sector that the Germans' plans not to leave anything intact were sometimes frustrated by the Russians onslaught. While they had time enough thoroughly to explode Marli, they were only partially successful at Monplesir. They burnt the Catherine block but failed to destroy Monplesir itself.

Having been in the front line, the park seemed like a First World War battlefield to Tikhomirova when she first returned on that February day in 1944. Having taken no part in the evacuation, she felt all the more bewildered. Where to start? What had been saved, what looted? What had been burnt but what might still lie under the rubble? At least she knew that everything in the evacuation plan made by Kwerfeld and Farmakovsky was safe in Siberia. She knew too what was in St. Izaak's and other places in Leningrad. It was too early to worry about such things. On all sides she could see the effects of weather on damaged buildings and she knew her priority was to open a way through the mines so that their conservation could begin. She made an ally of Major Ivanov of the engineers, persuading him to clear the park in accordance with her priorities. Together they investigated the palace cellars where they found one of the masquarones, the grotesque gilded masks that spouted water into the Samson basin. It was heavy but between them they managed to lift it over a huge unexploded shell and carry it out into the daylight. It became the model for restoration of all the masquarones since the others had disappeared, presumably stolen and melted down. The engineers stayed until August 1944 when they were recalled to the front. The war still had many months to run. Although they had cleared some 20,000 mines and countless unexploded shells, they were not prepared to say that they had got them all. In the meanwhile, work to clear up the mess had already started and a little danger was not going to stop it now. As soon as the railway reopened, the crowds of subbotniks and voskresniks began to arrive and the park suddenly seemed less enormous. At about this time too, Tikhomirova was joined by a new Administrative Director called Y. Shurygin, who had been head of the palace's scientific department before the war. He was a great help to her.

From the outset, priority was given to the restoration of Monplesir. It was the least damaged of the buildings but it was no longer weather tight and it needed to be protected until the resources could be obtained to start repairing it. The same applied to the nearby Catherine Block whose walls still stood but whose interior had been gutted. Cleaning up inside, they soon started to make discoveries of great interest and importance for the restorers. In what had been the green drawing room, the decoration had been designed around four wreathlike mouldings which had framed oil paintings. The paintings had been badly burned and when they were removed for conservation, they found behind them demountable alabaster discs. Curiosity overcame them and they discovered that these in turn were hiding four jolly Russian faces, symbolising the seasons of the year. They had evidently been the original decoration, but superseded by something more refined during in the nineteenth century. They had a choice to make, a choice of a kind which would reoccur repeatedly throughout the whole process of restoration. It was essentially the same problem that had confronted Polovtsov and Lukomski some 50 years before when they were preparing the palaces to become museums. Should they leave them as they found them or try to recreate them as they had been originally conceived. They chose the latter.

The other discovery they made in the Catherine Block was more distressing. In the ruined foyer, they were overjoyed to find a particularly beautiful plaster statue of Catherine by Shubin which, although it had fallen off its pedestal, appeared to be undamaged. When touched, however, it crumbled to dust before their eyes. It was a salutary if costly warning that they must handle any remaining decorations with the greatest care and find ways of fixing them. They discovered that an application of thin glue, if allowed to soak in, usually did the trick. It was an important discovery because the number of fragments of plaster decoration saved in this way was enormous. Sifting through the rubble inside the Great Palace, they found that much had survived, protected under a surface of weathered plaster sludge. Eventually they accumulated 54,000 fragments in the Court of Arms wing, filed and classified using the system developed by Zelenova and Gromova. All this, plus the restoration of the fountains, fully occupied the resources of the restorers during the late forties while the portrait of Stalin looked benignly down.

Perhaps it was a symbol of his desire that at the least Peterhof should be restored and, with this to encourage them, steps started to be taken in 1946 to plan how to do it. Professor G.Ol, Belekhov's friend and a much respected academic arrived in that year, with two colleagues, Serebriakov and Kitner, to start taking all the measurements which would be needed before any coherent plan could be made. In September 1948 and notwithstanding their edict about the 'better measures for the preservation of cultural monuments', the Soviet government decided that Peterhof would be restored. This was welcome and perhaps owed something to Belekhov's contact with Malenkov whose primacy amongst Stalin's councillors had become unrivalled since Zhdanov's death. Work which had already started on the restoration of Monplesir, now gained a new momentum and was extended to the Hermitage. However, Professor Ol's work had revealed what a huge task faced the restorers of the Great Palace. For this purpose, a new team was assembled, headed by an experienced architect, Vasily Savkov. Savkov recruited a young assistant, Evgennia Kazanskaya, whose reputation as a brilliant student had been growing. They surrounded themselves with all the most talented restorers available including some like Alexander Kedrinsky who were already experienced. Others represented the cream of the students from the Restorer Schools, moulders like Tsygankov and Nadezhda Ode, the painters Anastasia Vasilieva and Leonid Lubimov and the sculptors Lilia Shvedskaya, Galina Mikhailova and her husband Eduard Maslennikov. During the long period of restoration which followed, many others would contribute the skills they had learned in Belekhov's schools.

The project they faced was of extraordinary difficulty. Braunstein's original Dutch design had been modified by several architects as more flamboyant tastes came into fashion but the most influential hand had been Rastrelli's. A great part of the palace's charm had lain in its roof. This, of course, had gone and there were only memories and a few grainy photos to go by. It had been very subtle with its many curving surfaces blending into each other to create an effect of such airiness and elegance that it seemed more like a tent than a roof. It had seemed almost to relieve the massive building of its weight, but the architects were painfully aware that a wrong curve here or angle there could destroy the whole effect. It was one of Belekhov's more important rules for restorers that their projects must go through several stages of modelling, on different scales and with different materials, each one being approved or not by a team from the Inspectorate. A palace could hardly be modelled full size but it could be done exhaustively and the models could be cleverly photographed from every angle to simulate real life and to compare with pre-war photographs.

But there were other problems. The fire had been so thorough that it was not easy to determine what had been the interior dimensions of the building. With all the redesigning by different architects, interior partitions had moved around, some leaving more traces than others. The restorers' minute studies of the ruined walls led to many discoveries of an archaeological nature and to much argument as to which precedent they should now follow. They worked on the principle that they would reuse every part of the ruin that was reusable although, of course, it would have been much easier to dismantle the lot and rebuild from scratch. It was not until the late summer of 1951 that all the controversies had been settled and the plans approved so that the rebuilding could start. In October of that year, work began dismantling those parts of the walls deemed unsavable and renewing the footings. Once started, and despite the winter weather, progress was rapid and before the end of the following summer, the roof had been completed and the scaffolding on the main block could be brought down. The building was still unadorned with detail but the sight was magnificent. It gave great courage to the assembled restorers. They knew now that they were on the right lines. They could do it although it would not be finished until 1958.

In the same summer, they reopened the Hermitage Pavilion. Despite its use as a gun emplacement, it had not been grievously damaged and all its pictures had been evacuated during the war. They decided not to repair the complicated wooden mechanism whereby servants in the lower floor could hoist meals up to their betters on the floor above. Its refurbishment was therefore relatively easy but its reopening was not without its significance. Along with the Chinese Palace at Lomonosov, it was a token to the public that the restoration of their much loved museums was steadily going ahead. The openings attracted such a great wave of visitors that the curators feared they would do even more damage than the Germans but it provided proof enough of the enthusiasm of the people for the restoration of the palaces.

The following winter, Stalin died. To call it a watershed would be an understatement. The so-called Doctors' Plot was shaping up into a new crescendo of paranoid terror. Several doctors had already been executed. One must wonder that an old man, subject to the infirmities of age, should set out to terrify his doctors but there has never been any evidence that they procured his death. When he died, the executions immediately stopped. Dr Rappaport, a Kremlin pathologist, was in the Lublyanka awaiting death when he suddenly found himself released in the middle of the night. He did not dare go straight home lest his sudden appearance should give his wife a heart attack. Most people treated the news with great caution, however, for who could tell what might follow. Under Stalin they had learned what to expect and despite all the horrors, he had managed to project quite a jolly, avuncular image, which at any rate two of the triumvirate who succeeded him, never were able to produce. Nevertheless, the news was good for Belekhov whose patron, Malenkov, seemed to be the most powerful of the three. He did not last long but when Kruschev emerged the victor, he was quick to reassure the restorers of his support, although he warned them to avoid self-indulgent extravagance.

It was against this background that Alexander Kedrinsky was deputed by Savkov to prepare plans for the restoration of the palace chapel, which had been ruined by that same shell that had started the fire in 1941. He took as his model Rastrelli's five cupola version which was visible in the pre-war photographs. In the meanwhile, however, Savkov and Kazanskaya had been looking through early designs in the archive and found one, also by Rastrelli, which showed only one cupola. After much researching, they came to the conclusion that this had been Rastrelli's original idea, balancing the single cupola above the Court of Arms wing at the other end of the palace. They suspected that Peter's daughter, Elizabeth, a great lover of the high baroque, had prevailed on him, against his better judgement, to provide four more. Perhaps, they thought, it might be artistically correct to go back to Rastrelli's original idea. It would certainly be cheaper. Kedrinsky however had put a lot of effort into his plan and suspected Savkov of artistic default just to save a little money and curry favour with Kruschev and his economical caveat. Disagreement led to argument which developed into a full scale row. Kedrinsky finally lost his temper and threw a bottle of ink at Savkov, missing but hitting a bystander. He stormed out, slamming the door behind him. He never worked with Savkov again but Peterhof's loss was to be Pushkin's gain.

From now on the restoration of the palace, both inside and outside proceeded steadily, step by step, room by room. Internally, they started with the portrait gallery which is the centre point of the building from which one can look in one direction down the Great Cascade and its canal to the waters of the Gulf of Finland and, in the other, along the complementary series of ponds and fountains in the upper gardens. It is one of the few rooms essentially unaltered since Peter's time although Rastrelli had later added much baroque decoration round the doors and mirrors and Vallen de la Moth had covered the walls with 368 portraits by Rotari, each of one of the five girls he used as models, in varying poses and costumes. These had been saved from the Germans but the room had been totally destroyed. This had one advantage. It would test every aspect of the restorers' skills. An impression of its general shape and decoration could be studied from photographs but they were not much help for the details. In particular, the ceiling was indistinct. It was very large, 37.5 square metres, and by the Venetian Bartolomeo Tarsia assisted by two Russian artists, Busuyev and Negrubov, but his work is rare. The project was given to a team under Yakov Kazakov who set out to study early Venetian paintings wherever they could be found. Eventually some sketches by Tarsia were discovered in Italy. Furthermore, some ceiling paintings which had survived in Monplesir were found to be by Tarsia's pupils, Busuyev and Negrubov, and could offer guidance to his style and palette. Sketches of the portrait gallery ceiling showed that, above a plaster frieze there had been another painted frieze curving inwards towards the ceiling painting itself. None of this was very clear from the pre-war photographs. It would once again be a matter of exhaustive trial and error. In all, 37 small sketches were made, then 18 big ones which then had to be transferred onto cartoons before tracing the outlines for marking out on the ceiling itself. At each stage they had to be approved by the experts. Then a special system of hoisting was developed so that the artists could be lowered from the ceiling while the final sketch they were following could be lifted up so that they could check their work. They did not finally complete the project until late in 1962. It was a prototypal triumph of artistic reconstruction and it made Kazakov's name. He later spent most of his time in Pushkin. He came from Vitebsk in Belorussia and had attended art school there in the thirties. The war interrupted his studies but afterwards he gained a place in the Restorer Schools in Leningrad where he was taught by masters such as Pertsev. He was not himself an outstandingly talented artist, but he was a superb organiser and leader with a deep knowledge of monumental art and the techniques of restoration. Very fit, he practised yoga, his team loved him and worked for him in a spirit of collaboration although several of them, such as Ivan Alexeev and Boris Lebedev could outpaint him. He had a sad end to his life when his wife and two sons emigrated to Germany and he was left on his own. He was still active when he died suddenly of a heart attack in 1995, in the courtyard of the Catherine Palace. He and his team carried out many difficult assignments but perhaps the most important, however, was the painting of the ceiling of the Peterhof picture gallery which showed the doubters just what could be done with careful research and dedicated work. Later on, even greater challenges, like the Throne Room at Catherinehof, were undertaken, but in full confidence of success and with the main technical problems solved.

Rastrelli's baroque, gilded flourishes around the Gallery's doors and mirrors could only roughly be seen in the photographs but his techniques and ideas could be studied at Pushkin where much more of his work had survived. However, it was at Peterhof that the first major carving works were undertaken. Rastrelli, in renovating Peter's original palace, had designed some elaborately decorated doorways with interweaving fronds, many cupids and putti all converging around some lovely but sorrowing eighteenth century goddesses above whom spread the wings of mythical birds. The moment had come to test the true skills of the moulders, the carvers and the gilders that the restoration schools had been training. The Restoration Workshop which had been started with such small beginnings in July 1945, had, by the late fifties developed into a string of moderately sized factories, each with their specialisations and bustling with activity. One of the most talented, and most beautiful of the young artists emerging from it to make a name for herself at Peterhof was Lilia Shvedskaya, who would later make a huge contribution to the restoration of the Catherine Palace at Pushkin.

As a small child before the war, she had found herself much in demand from teachers who could not illustrate their lessons on their blackboards which may not have helped her academic progress but convinced her of what she wanted to do. When the Germans invaded, she and her family were caught behind their lines near Pskov and her subsequent experiences and sufferings were such that she spent the rest of her life trying to blot them out of her memory. It was not until 1946 that she reached the Mukhina Institute virtually uneducated but of such shining artistic talent that they arranged for her a general education as well as an artistic one, lasting eight years. Peterhof was her first major task and it was here that she started to wrestle with the problems of immersing herself in the minds of the original artists whose lost work she was trying to replace. Looking around her at the chubby northern faces of her compatriots, she saw little likeness in them to those of Rastrelli's melancholy ladies that had survived. Later, when she reached Pushkin she had similar problems with cherubs and putti but luckily, at that moment, she acquired a small son of her own called Roma. He added somewhat to the practical difficulties of her life but he was a particularly beautiful child and provided her with an ideal model.

Pushkin contains a high population of putti of all ages and virtually everywhere it is Roma that looks down on the crowds passing below. The mannered ladies remained more difficult and Lilia tried placing advertisements for models. Eventually, however, she encountered a slender Osetian girl one day on the Nevski Prospekt who was ideal for her purpose. The girl was astonished so to be accosted but Lilia has a limpid personality which it is difficult to resist or distrust. The Osetian now gazes down on palace visitors almost as universally as Roma. As Lilia studied Rastrelli's baroque decorations, she began to be able to recognise the idiosyncrasies of each of his original sculptors so that the same girl in one design might look subtly different in another. In this matter, Lilia and indeed all the carvers, were much helped by a woman called Elena Gladkova. Gladkova was actually a philologist and had been drawn to Pushkin through her detailed study of the poet's use of language. When she got there, the beauties of the palace seduced her. By a series of small steps, she was drawn into studying these variations of style amongst the old master craftsmen and eventually wrote a thesis on the subject called 'Woodcarvers of the 18th Century'. This made such a huge contribution to the restoration of the palaces that she gave up philology and became a curator. She was able with ease to tell who had carved what.

Although Lilia Schvedskaya had studied painting and was a consummate sculptor, she gradually came to specialise in moulding at which she was quite outstanding. Even so, her mouldings, like everyone else's, had to be twice approved by the inspectors, once in plasticine and then in plaster. The plaster cast would then go to the wood carvers. The leading moulders at Peterhof were the married couple, Galina Mikhailova and Eduard Maslennikov, whose work is to be found in nearly every room in the palace. Finally, it would be the turn of the gilders and for the early restorations they had to rediscover how the original artists had achieve such a smooth and glittering finish. It involved eight or so layers of a gesso made of clay mixed with egg-white and various animal oils and highly polished, onto which to lay the gold leaf. The research and experimentation required was done by Victor Slezin.

Long before the Picture Gallery was complete, work was proceeding in the other gala rooms. Each of these has a different style from the heavy gilded baroque of the Audience Hall [sometimes called the Presence Room], the clean classicism of the White Dining Room to the oriental angularity of the Chinese lobbies. The decoration of the latter centred on a set of ten large lacquered panels which were Chinese from the seventeenth century. Only two of them had been saved, depicting detailed scenes from Chinese country life. One was a seascape and the other depicted the rice harvest. The task was allocated to the youthful Leonid Lubimov.

Lubimov had been at Pioneer camp in the Yaroslavl when war broke out but they were then moved to a camp in the Urals where he had spent an exceedingly cold winter with only his summer clothes. He was allowed to return home in 1943 and as an obviously highly talented youngster, he was able to join the Restorer School straight away. After a short time he was promoted to the Mukhina Institute. Some of the tutors there were old men from Polovtsov's time. Being exceptionally gifted, Lubimov was soon being co-opted to help out with all manner of restoration work but some of his tutors suggested to him that this was a waste of his talent. He should, they said, be a proper artist, using his creativity, rather than a restorer just copying others. He thought a great deal about it but in the end chose restoration. He realised that to exchange the obligation of creativity for the disciplined but endlessly varied work of restoration might seem unromantic, but, in his old age, he never regretted it. This first major challenge to recreate the lost lacquer panels confirmed his choice.

Most of his training had had to do with restoring eighteenth century Italian ceilings. Ancient Chinese panels required him to start again from scratch, the sort of challenge that no self-respecting restorer could refuse. He set about investigating a whole strange new branch of art. He soon found that the first problem to be solved is how to achieve the right surface. This not only requires a perfect and stable panel but then a series of at least six undercoats, each to be dried and then polished, until the surface is level and faultless enough to permit the extremely detailed paintings that Lubimov had now to execute. The panels that had been saved provided him not only with stylistic models but a broad guide as to what the subjects of the other panels might have been. He had some rather poor photographs and spent a great deal studying lacquer work from the same period in the Summer Palace in Leningrad and elsewhere. It was not so much a restoration project as a reconstruction. Everything he planned and did had to be subjected to the approval of the Inspectorate at each stage. One of Lubimov's happiest memories was of the day when the professors from the Inspectorate finally came to judge his work in its entirety. They were no longer sure which panels were original and which were his. He was awarded the golden medal of the Academy of Arts, which was very gratifying for him but turned out to be quite expensive by the time he had stood everyone in the room a drink!

Quite a contrasting challenge was the charming oak-panelled study of Peter the Great with his personal belongings and understated furniture, much of which had been saved. They had saved eight of the 14 panels but the remainder plus all the surrounding decoration had been lost in the fire. Each had its own theme and was carved in bass relief in the renaissance style. The task of recreating these was given to another hugely talented young moulder, Nadezhda Ode. She had been evacuated in 1941. She remembers a long and frightening railway journey. The train was repeatedly bombed but Nadezhda had been given a task which helped her to overcome her personal fear. She was responsible for the safety of a huge pot of butter which she hung onto for dear life. Thereafter she had a rather happy war in various schools near Kirovsk where the good comradeship more than offset the privations. She returned to Leningrad in the winter of 1943, crossing Lake Ladoga in a convoy of lorries and immediately joined the very first course of the Restorer School. In 1947 she could have gone on to the Mukhina Institute but, on the advice of a teacher, declined the offer and joined the Restorer Workshop. She had already spent much time working on the mouldings retrieved from the rubble of Pavlovsk and on a number of projects in and around Leningrad. Peter's study was her first major project and it firmly established her reputation. She had had very little to go on but she studied what she could find in the archives and any other works she could trace by the original sculptor, Nicolas Pineau. As usual, there were photographs but the panels were extremely detailed. The first of her designs was executed by the wood carver, Boris Gershelman. Oak is not the easiest of woods to work and it took him 15 months, using an analogue to ensure that he followed Ode's design exactly. It was installed next to the remaining originals in 1969. Gershelman was joined by Vladimir Ivanov who completed three of the remaining panels, all to Ode's designs.

Ode was also much involved in the reconstruction of the huge Throne Room which had been almost completely destroyed by the fire. Miraculously, they found the remains of one of the four alabaster bass reliefs. This one depicted 'Justice and Safety' and from it the moulders Maslennikov and Mikhailova were able to extrapolate designs for the others which had completely disappeared. The throne room was originally Rastrelli's design but Catherine the Great had had it redone in a more restrained classical style by the Russian architect, Yuri Velten. The result, in subdued greens and whites and with no gilding, is a showpiece of delicate plaster decoration. Many restorers collaborated. Once again, Eduard Maslennikov and Galina Mikhailova recreated the walls, but Ode and Tsygankov worked on the ceiling. The effect of the parquet floor is perhaps especially important in the Throne Room. Luckily, the designs for all the parquet floors in Peterhof were found in the archives in the Hermitage and so there was no controversy about them - just a great deal of careful craftsmanship by a team headed by Igor Antonov. It is a very large floor. During the restoration of the Throne Room, a dilemma arose. No rooms have remained unchanged during the long life of the palace but Velten's design for the Throne Room had provided for a large portrait of Catherine the Great to be given pride of place behind the throne. This had been altered by her grandson Alexander I. He had been presented by Louis XVIII with a large Gobelin tapestry depicting a famous incident in the life of Peter the Great when he saved the lives of some fishermen. Alexander had hung this in the place of his grandmother's portrait where it had remained until it was evacuated during the war. He had also banished the throne itself to Oranienbaum. It was assumed that when the Throne Room was ready again, it would be put back as it had been before the war but in the meanwhile, the portrait of Catherine, missing for over a century, had turned up in the storages of the Tretiakov gallery. In the debate that followed, Catherine won.

With the exception of the ballroom and the gala staircase, the other main rooms on the west wing of the palace had also been redesigned for Catherine in a classical style. The White Dining Room is particularly beautiful with its restrained stucco work but perhaps the most important is the Chesma Room, designed by Velten to display the series of huge paintings by the Dutch artist Hackaert showing each stage in the daylong rout of the Turkish fleet, trapped in Chesma Bay. One of them depicts a Turkish ship blowing up at night and the artist insisted that the Russians must blow up one of theirs so that he could see what it looked like. As a result, these had been amongst the more expensive pictures in the world and the curators took good care that they were evacuated before the Germans arrived. Even so and despite Kuchumov's attempts at first aid, their wartime experiences had not done them any good and Lubimov's team was given the task of restoring them. By a curious chance, the Chesma Room has more or less its complete set of original furniture because its chairs were purloined before the war for use at the Hermitage and in other locations in Leningrad. This is not true of the rest of Peterhof. Apart from Peter's personal possessions, only six pieces of furniture were saved out of all that was in the palace and what is there today is the result of a sustained hunt for replacements through lesser museums and the antique shops. This is not to say that the furniture on show is unworthy of attention. Some items, like the chairs in the Chesma Hall, had strayed from the palace before the war but were recognised by the stamp born by all the Tsar's possessions. Some were found in other museums and some in antique shops. Not everything they collected up had come from Peterhof but nothing that was bought was unworthy of it and some, like the two cabinets by Barbedien in the Blue Sitting Room are priceless. Alongside them is the set of porcelain that was transported so carefully by that Russian unit from Berlin to Siberia while they tried to find out where they should send it. They looked after it with great care. It contained 5,572 pieces.

The last major work of restoration on the western wing of the palace, indeed of the whole palace, was the gala staircase. It was not completed until Gorbachov's day. If the throne room feels restrained this is partly because it is reached by climbing these stairs, which throb with exuberant gold decoration. Only one of the pre-war gilded wooden statues had been saved and the remaining three more had to be recreated together with the banisters and the wall decoration. All blaze with gold. If the throne room is a temple to the art of the moulders, the gala staircase is to the gilders. And yet it was her contribution to the staircase that won for Nadezhda Ode the Lenin Prize, when the visiting Gorbachov stepped aside particularly to admire a pair of putti in animated conversation with each other. The Lenin Prize was the highest award a Soviet citizen could hope for. Nadezhda Ode was gratified - she had been proud of those putti - but she was quite embarrassed to be singled out for something for which she felt dozens of her co-restorers were just as well qualified. Indeed, she felt that the prize could as well have gone to the young lady who, as a preparation for her work on the gala stairway, had given her lessons to show her how our muscles combine to produce what we call body language.

In the meanwhile, the restorers had been working their way eastwards through rooms of a much more domestic character than these great public halls. There was still much work for the sculptors. Ode re-created the moulded swags and garlands of flowers in the Partridge Room, while Mikhailova and Maslennikov executed the new decorations of the Sofa and Crown Rooms. The heroine of these rooms, however, was the painter Anastasia Vasilieva. As great a challenge as any in the whole story of the restoration of the palaces was the recreation of the Chinese silk hangings that had covered the walls in several of the rooms. Some of these had in fact been woven in Russia, in the eighteenth and nineteenth centuries in the Kondrashov and Sapozhnikov factories in St. Petersburg and later in the Krutetsky Monastery outside Moscow which still houses the Silk Institute. Records still existed of the original designs and even orders. Other silks, however, were of antique Chinese origin and had almost totally disappeared in the fire. In one instance, the Divan Room, she had a piece of luck when a roll of the silk was found in store in the Hermitage but for the Crown Room, she had to work from old paintings and pre-war photographs which gave her very little idea of the details of the design. In so far as she found remnants, they were all damaged and often faded. Before she started, she had to discover how to combine the old silks with new and then how to paint on the silk without the paint running. She had to study translations of old Chinese manuals to find out what materials they used and how they mixed their paints. One of the ingredients they used was obtained from a plum-like plant called a feijoa. Anastasia went to the botanical gardens and found they had one in a green house but that it would not fruit so far north. They suggested she tried one of the botanical gardens on the Black Sea. None of them had such a plant but at Batumi, they agreed to obtain some seed and grow some. In due course a parcel was sent to her, care of the Hermitage, but the restorers there appropriated it and she had to ask for a second lot to be sent, this time to her home. Russia is a large country with plenty of room for things to go wrong but, as a result, the Russians have learned the value of patience and persistence. Even more difficult for her, were the problems about the colour and the designs. All the designs were thematic and very detailed, almost impossible to decipher from the pre-war photographs and the colour, where exposed to the light, had faded. She found scraps of the original material trapped under the panelling which glowed with an unfaded lustre quite absent from the photographs. She felt these should guide her but this created a conflict if she wanted to incorporate it with some of the faded original silk. She took her decisions room by room on a pragmatic basis.

The painting was done in a Chinese form of tempera which she made herself but which had the inconvenience of drying out very quickly, before even she had had time to paint with it. She found that the ideal solution was to build a little wooden gallery from which to hang paint-filled condoms but condoms were not easy to obtain. She kept trying in chemist shops but got the feeling that the shops did not approve of a young woman with such a inexhaustible appetite for them so she persuaded an orthodox priest of her acquaintance to help. He had no trouble at all and did not seem to feel embarrassed either.

Anastasia had always shown artistic talent and before the war the family had taken her on many visits to the country palaces which she had been able to appreciate with an artist's eye. In her mid-teens, Anastasia had survived the first winter of the siege in Leningrad, including that distressing incident of attempted cannibalism, but at the end of 1942 the family had been evacuated to Pesochnoye on the Volga where, weakened by his privations, her father died. Soon after, her grandmother attempted to join them and to bring with her as much as she could of their possessions and warm clothing. When her mother went to meet her at the station, she found that she had died on the journey and that all their possessions had been stolen. So she returned sorrowfully to her own children only to find that, in her absence, they too had been burgled. They were now in desperate straits but Anastasia's talent got her a good job painting porcelain in a local factory. The conditions there were primitive and in 1944 her mother had fallen ill just at the moment when the family obtained a permit to return to Leningrad. They could not go and were still there when the war ended. It was only possible to return to the city if invited by someone. On the day of victory, with all the other workers, Anastasia was invited to paint herself a porcelain cup as a souvenir which she kept all her life. Soon afterwards her mother was again able to arrange for the family's return to Leningrad. Better still, one of her mother's friends who worked in the central bookstore knew Belekhov and was able to get Anastasia a place in a Restorer School. She was very happy about this, partly because she did enjoy painting but mostly because it meant regular meals and a warm military uniform. She managed to get one for her brother too. Life was still very hard for the family, however, because at about this time, her mother had an accident and was bed-ridden for several years.

But Anastasia was happy. She enjoyed her studies and found she was one of the star pupils. It was a four year course but long before it ended she had been noticed and was being invited to help with restoration work. When she graduated in 1949, she was offered a further long course at the Mukhina Institute, but she turned it down. She was keen to get on with life and while many of those graduating from the Restorer School were finding it hard to get work, Vasilieva had her contact with Belekhov who fixed her up.

She was a stickler for authenticity and would take great trouble to obtain a suitable model. When in 1956, she joined the team starting on the restoration of Monplesir, one of her first projects was to repair a fresco that had originally featured four monkeys doing antics in some painted fronds, but one of them was missing. She refused to start until she had found, in a zoo, a monkey of the same type and had spent some time watching and sketching him. Despite being a German battery position, Monplesir had been relatively little damaged. However, the German gun crews had treated it with little respect, hacking off wood for their stoves irrespective of the consequences and using its decoration and paintings for target practice. They also left it absolutely filthy. After its liberation in 1944, only the minimum had been done to protect it from further dilapidation and to clear up the worst of the mess. Although there was no money to start a proper restoration, a team including Irina Benois and another architect called Gessen, were given the task of taking all the necessary measurements and making a restoration plan for when the funds would be available. The go-ahead did not come until 1951 when Kazanskaya, with Gessen' was put in charge of reconstructing the building.

The restoration of the interior did not get going until 1955 when a team under a brilliant young artist called Rudolf Sausen started work. Anastasia had worked with him before and was heavily in love with him, so she joined his team with alacrity. Their first task was to clean off the accumulated grime of many decades and to fix the paint underneath it which was starting to flake off. In so doing they found much evidence of clumsy restoration work. They decided to employ X-rays to discover what lay behind it. Some of the most damaged paintings were the work of a French artist called Philipe Pillman in the early eighteenth century. There were documents about him in the archives but they related to his contracts and bills, revealing nothing about him as a man or as an artist. In France and elsewhere he seemed almost unknown but by dint of great persistence and some intuition, they traced him to Lyon where he had been a contemporary and pupil of Claude Gillot, who later became tutor to the young Watteau. The French archives then began to yield quite a lot about him, including his delight in figures from the commedia del'arte which are much in evidence in the paintings in Monplesir. They also solved a particular problem they had with the fourth medallion in the Gala Hall. The three surviving medallions depicted three elements - water, fire and earth. They supposed the fourth must be air but photos revealed only a fuzzy lady seated before a black background which did not seem very encouraging. In

Paris, they found cartoons of the same subjects which had been prepared for Louis XIV. It turned out that the lady was Juno, with a rainbow behind her. Although all the paintings in Monplesir betrayed the influence of Pillman, it was clear that he had not personally executed them all. Further researches brought into the frame those same Russian artists that had assisted Bartolomeo Tarsia a few years earlier in Peterhof's picture gallery. All this preparatory work had taken about three years and it was not until 1959 that they felt ready to start the restoration work. It had been decided to restore the paintings to what they had been originally, as revealed by X-ray, but first, in case things should go wrong, they had to make copies of the existing paintings. Once started, however, and certain of what they were aiming for, these extraordinary artists made rapid progress. The task was completed in 1960 but it was by no means the end of the story of the restoration of this complicated little palace.

Peter the Great had been a lover of Dutch culture and in particular of Dutch tiles. He had sent Russian workers to Delft to learn the trade and set up a factory in St. Petersburg. Tiles from this factory had been used widely in all the suburban palaces. The Germans seemed to have enjoyed destroying them for when the Russian soldiers returned they found themselves crunching on broken tiles. Despite the taking of great trouble to repair tiles wherever possible, Monplesir alone needed 4,500 new ones. A ceramicist called B. Mitskevich was given the task of creating 200 new designs and the factory was recreated. By 1963 the re-tiling of Monplesir was complete.

A few years earlier, another critical problem had been solved. The Lacquer Study in Monplesir had been decorated, so everyone thought, with antique Chinese, or perhaps Japanese, panels. However, some research by N. Arkhipov, the first post-war director, now threw doubt on this. There is, not far from Moscow, a small town called Palekh where they have long had a tradition of lacquer work. Most of the lacquer boxes and souvenirs in today's tourist shops come from Palekh. Analysing the two surviving panels and trawling through the Palekh archives, they were able to satisfy themselves that the panels had been made by Palekh methods and could be again. The venerable Palekh master, Alexander Kotuchkin, came to examine the panels and the Lacquer Room. Seeing that much of the decoration had been in tempera, he confirmed that this could only be Russian work. They still were in doubt about the compositions of some of the panels because the existing pre-war photos were inadequate but knowing their provenance, they were able to make shrewd guesses as to what they had contained. Exhaustive researches were made into other sources of chinoiserie which the Palekh painters of the time might have used as models for the busy landscapes which the panels depicted. Eventually, in 1958 they felt confident enough to make a start on the reconstruction of the room. The restoration of Monplesir was finally completed in October 1964.

Initially, it had been thought that the elegant little Marli Palace at the western end of the Lower Park had been too thoroughly destroyed to make it worth repairing but without it, the whole design of the park seemed unbalanced. The great lime alley leads you to it, and the Golden Hill Cascade and its attendant water gardens seemed pointless in its absence. Kazanskaya was therefore given the task of rebuilding it. She was much aided by good photographs of the pre-war interior. Furthermore, a high proportion of the contents had been saved in those few weeks

Upper Gardens, Peterhof,
ruined by anti-tank ditch in 1944 (top)

Pavlovsk

Marli Palace, Peterhof

The Amber Room (right) in the **Catherine Palace** (below)

The Grand Cascade, **Peterhof** in 1944 (above)
and (below) today.

The Great Hall, **Catherinehof** in 1944 (above)
and (below) today.

The view from the Green Dining Room,
Catherinehof in 1944 (above)
and restored today (below).

The SS cemetery by the entrance to the **Alexander Palace** in 1944 (above) and restored today (below).

before the arrival of the Germans, and what had been lost could be bought in to make good the gaps. One problem remained. A key feature of Marli had always been its Dutch tiles which had been comprehensively ruined. By this time, however, the restorers had become confident in their ability to recreate Dutch tiles.

Once they had got the bit between their teeth, the restorers began to face the problem of deciding where to stop. The Romanovs had been such tireless builders of palaces. It seemed as if a member of the family felt he lacked virility until he had built at least one and between the Lower Park and the suburbs of Leningrad stretched a string of minor and not so minor mansions and palaces associated with various members and generations of the family. With regard to these, the 1948 decree proved its worth. They were found tenants with the resources to keep them in reasonable repair and, in most cases, the wish to do so without destroying all that was valuable and beautiful in them. Thus Strelna had been made a rest home for transport workers while the Cottage Palace, a jewel of Gothic revivalism, became an orphanage. It had been used by the Germans during the war as a hospital and they had done it relatively little harm but the orphans made up for this. Luckily, very little of the gothic furniture remained to be ruined by them. However, in 1969 it was decided that the little palace was something too rare to be allowed to decay and Irina Benois was put in charge of restoring it. It had been designed in the 1820s for Nicholas I by a Scotsman called Adam Menelaws who had clearly read his Walter Scott thoroughly, for its interior represents a high romantic ideal which the author would have loved.

Irina Benois has also more recently undertaken the conversion of the Cours des Frauleins, where all the ladies in waiting had once been quartered. It has become a museum of all the works of her remarkable family. The first Benois to reach Russia had been a French chocolatier and confectioner. He arrived in 1794 and prospered, becoming progenitor of an expanding family of artists and architects. They inter-married with two other talented families. One, called Lanceret, descended from a French officer who had been wounded during Napoleon's retreat from Moscow and rescued by a peasant family who had found him dying in the snow. The other was a Russian family called Serebriakov. Between them, these families had produced an astonishing stream of talent, architects, artists, musicians and men of the theatre, samples of whose work have been gathered by Irina Benois and placed on permanent exhibition in the Cours des Frauleins. which itself was designed by a Benois in 1853. An émigré member of the family, Peter Ustinov, speaking of the uncertainties of an artistic career, once said that to a Benois, it would seem intolerably risky to become a lawyer or an accountant. They preferred to rely on their own creativity.

Some pavilions simply disappeared during the siege and nothing was found but rubble. This was the fate of the English Palace in the Alexander Park, not far from the Cottage Palace, and the nearby Farm Palace had been much damaged. It has been cleaned up and conserved but there has not so far been any attempt to recreate it. This eastern end of the park is now tending to be colonised by 'new' Russians. They build modern houses along its boundaries which threatens the landscape. However, they often like them to be decorated with traditional styles which is good news for restorers looking for employment. While there is still some detailed work to be done, the main public rooms at Peterhof have now been restored and opened to the public. The emphasis is now switching to the problem of maintaining such a huge complex. When Peter the Great chose his site, he had no thought for the battles the curators would one day have to fight against humidity, cold and dilapidation. While on the one hand, the whole point of the palaces is to open their wonders to the gaze of the public, too many visitors breathing can cause havoc. Anastasia Vasilieva worries about the traces of mould she sees already forming on the silk coverings she restored with such loving care. But that is a problem for the twenty-first century. Enough for today to wonder at those whose collective efforts and devotion held at bay all the horrors of the twentieth.

Chapter 14

PUSHKIN

When, on that first visit, Evgenia Turova cried out: "How lucky! They've left us a ruin!" she thought she was being ironical but she was nearer the truth than she knew. Six days earlier, towards sundown, the leading Soviet company under Captain Nikolai Prokhorov had broken into the park of the Catherine Palace, hot on the heels of the retreating Germans. One of his advanced section leaders, Sergeant Alexander Ivanov, on entering the courtyard, noticed some camouflaged wires. He did not know what they portended but, assuming they had been laid for some German purpose, he cut them, thus saving the remains of the Catherine Palace and, most probably, his own and his section's lives as well. They had indeed been laid for a German purpose which was, at the last minute, to blow up what was left of the Catherine Palace and anyone too near it.

The Catherine Palace stands on the site of a small Finnish hamlet called Saar or Saari Mois meaning the 'farm on a hill'. When Peter the Great captured this area during the Great Northern War, the name was Russianised to Saarskoye Selo, meaning much the same. Much later, because of its colonisation by the Tsars, it came to be called Tsarskoye Selo, which sounded the same but meant something quite different - Tsar's Village. This name is now tending to be used again but in between, when Lunacharski was developing his schools and orphanages in the area, it was renamed Detskoye Selo or Children's Village and then, in 1937, renamed once more after the poet Pushkin, on the hundredth anniversary of his death. It was here that he had spent his boyhood and gone to school. It is one of the few names that has not been changed again since the fall of communism. Throughout all this time, however, people have continued to refer to the two palaces and their parks as Tsarskoye Selo.

The Great Northern War was still in progress when Peter donated the area to his second wife, soon to succeed him as Catherine I. She immediately arranged to have a plain stone mansion built by his favourite architect Braunstein which was called Catherinehof. This modest house is still the heart of the central block of the palace although Catherine would certainly not recognise it nor even, perhaps, its location, so much has it been changed. It was Peter's daughter Elizabeth, who decided that her mother's mansion was nothing like grand enough for the ruler of what was now a great and growing nation. In 1743, she commissioned three Russian architects, Zemtsov, Kvasov and Chevakinsky to enlarge it, which they did by adding two wings, similarly proportioned and on the same axis as the mansion and connected to it by single story galleries. This was finished in 1752 but Elizabeth was not satisfied. It was big but too plain and homespun, so she brought in the newly arrived Italian architect Rastrelli to apply his baroque skills which he did most lavishly. Rastrelli was no stranger to St. Petersburg. He had spent much of his boyhood there because his father had been court sculptor to Peter the Great and was, indeed, responsible for his death mask. The son, using an army of craftsmen and serf labourers, brought about a magical transformation. Inside and out, he created a shimmering palace of immense size and grandeur but also of lightness and gaiety. It was blue with white pilasters set off by golden captials, caryatids and atlantes, with at one end a chapel with many golden domes. Not only that, but he transformed the park, digging out lakes and canals, designing and redesigning pavilions and laying out formal gardens which he filled with the statues that her father had bought in Italy for his Summer Palace in St. Petersburg. No visiting diplomat or monarch could possibly now have any doubt but that Catherinehof belonged to an empress of fabulous power and wealth. A great girl for a party, Elizabeth believed in show rather than aggression. Her reign was peaceful but she left an empty treasury, and wardrobes containing 15,000 dresses. Apparently, she never wore a dress twice.

However, the next empress, Catherine the Great, was still not satisfied. In the first place, by this time fashion had moved on. Catherine was genuinely much interested in the Enlightenment, provided it did not subvert her subjects. She had invited to her court European philosophers like Voltaire and Diderot, and she gradually became aware that such modern thinkers were not impressed by all this barbaric splendour. Taste in western Europe had moved on to neo-classicism and that was what she must have. Furthermore, she did not think Rastrelli's Catherinehof was yet big enough. She started to develop it with two Russian architects who shared her views, Velten who had done so much work at Peterhof and Neyelov who had been developing the park at Tsarskoye Selo. Soon afterwards, two foreign architects arrived, Quarenghi, an Italian, and Cameron, a Scot who had studied for many years in Italy. Both were arch-exponents of the style she was seeking. Happily, she was persuaded that Rastrelli's work was not barbaric but a superb example of a very beautiful style and that different styles, in the hands of really capable architects, could be made to combine harmoniously. If there is anywhere in the world where this theory has been proved, it must be the Catherinehof. Not only does the new Zubov block added at each end by Velten and Neyelov seem to grow naturally out from Rastrelli's palace but Cameron's agate rooms and his Gallery add a hugely satisfying extension. Finally, deciding that the Catherinehof was still inadequate, the Empress commissioned Quarenghi to create a wholly new palace for her grandson Alexander. This was purely classical until Nicholas II, the last of the Romanovs, had its inside rather heavily redecorated in the art nouveau style of his day.

The inside the Catherinehof, a combination of the baroque and the classical was achieved with the equal felicity. Rastrelli's vista of golden doorways, his picture gallery and above all his Great Hall, shimmering with light and golden fantasy, seem to lead naturally into the Cameron's calmer but no less exquisite neo-classical designs for the rooms Catherine prepared for her son Paul and herself, at opposite ends of the palace. Presumably one advantage that such a huge palace had for both of them was that they hardly ever had to meet.

During the siege, Pushkin had not been quite so much in the front line as Peterhof but it had not been far behind. The Russians positions on the hill at Pulkovo were only seven kilometres away. The park, like Pavlovsk, was turned into a defensive area with many of the pavilions converted into blockhouses and many trenches and barbed wire entanglements spread around but there were not quite so many mines as in the other palaces. The Alexanderhof had initially been used to quarter Spanish troops but later it had become the HQ of the Gestapo. German soldiers had been quartered in the Catherinehof. They had used the chapel as a motorcycle workshop and the Cameron Gallery as a smithy and stable. The officers' mess had been in the Agate Rooms and seemed to have been witness to some riotous parties. At some stage, a bomb or large shell had hit the palace above the Great Hall, bringing down its roof and that of the main entrance, and all the way along to the Picture Gallery. Floors had fallen in, leaving the big stoves hanging on the wall like huge martins' nests. Miraculously, quite a lot of the carved decoration still clung to the walls of the Great Hall but elsewhere, the subsequent fire seemed to have been catastrophic. It had destroyed two thirds of the palace. Of Rastrelli's golden suite of doorways, nothing remained but charred brickwork. Underfoot lay piles of rubble, containing thousands of shards of tiles from the stoves. It is illustrative of the thoroughness of the German character that they should feel this destruction to be insufficient and to require them to place in the cellars those eleven 1,000lb bombs, rendered inoperative by Sergeant Ivanov. When Turova arrived in that bus on the first of February, a covering of snow added to the desolation of the scene. It says much for her resilience that she felt like making a joke, even if a sarcastic one.

If Turova had her moment of despair, it did not last for long. Whatever might or not be the long term possibilities of restoration, there was clearly so much practical preservation work to be done at once that already by the time of Belekhov's meeting on the 18th February, she was talking positively. She was given the support of a unit of air raid defence girls who had learned a lot about coping with bomb damage during the siege. Under the supervision of Turova and her curators, they set about collecting and recording some of the more fragile bits of decoration. More important, they tried to stabilise the walls and to rig up shelters to keep out the worst of the elements. They bricked up the gaping windows. Soon they were being reinforced by students from the Restorer Schools for whom this was as good a training as any they could receive in the classroom. Within a year, the Leningrad government had agreed to erect a temporary roof.

Apart from one portico which had collapsed, the Alexanderhof was much less severely damaged. It had been initially used as a barracks, housing both German and Spanish units but later the Gestapo had taken it over as their headquarters. Both had done a great deal of mindless damage but perhaps their most striking legacy was the number of empty wine bottles left around which had filled eight huge lorries. Evidence of their occupation was to be found in virtually all the pavilions in the park. Some had been adapted for defensive purposes but often the damage seemed quite wanton though there was also evidence of their determination to loot whatever could possibly be of value. In the middle of the large lake in the Catherine Park stands the Chesma Column, designed by Rinaldi to celebrate Russia's great naval victory over the Turks. They were able to prize off and steal most of the bronze panels with their base reliefs although they had dropped one in the lake and left it there. They had also coveted the great bronze eagle at its summit and decided that the only way to reach it would be to pull down the whole column. A long cable was attached to a tank on the lake's shore but at the critical moment it broke. Disheartened, they gave it up, having inflicted much damage. Although the park was less heavily mined, much damage had been done to its trees.

As with the other palaces, Turova's first priority was to start with the sifting of the debris to find salvable remains but she was also very keen to try to find the statues they had hidden. She had a particular reason for this in that, in the scramble of the evacuation, no-one had kept a note of what statues had been buried where. She was pretty sure that certain statues had not been buried. The Rape of Proserpine from the roof of the Hermitage and the Flora and Hercules that had stood each side of the stairs leading down from the Cameron gallery were no longer there but she thought they had been considered too heavy and awkward for the men to dismount and bury. Presumably the Germans had them. But as to the rest, she was not sure. Perhaps the Germans had had them too. A certain architect called Ermoshin had refused to be evacuated from Pushkin with the rest of them. Perhaps he had given them away. He was interrogated, shaking with fear, but could not or would not help. Turova had a sketch map she had tried to make while in St. Izaak's but she knew her memory had been unreliable. The park was a big place. She could not even remember how many statues there had been. Where should they start? Some of the pedestals were still in place and old photos revealed where many of the statues had once been. The gardens had been rich in them and many were the old Italian statues purchased by Peter the Great himself, originally for Peterhof. The anxiety was almost unbearable and she longed to get digging. It would be a bit like playing the game of Jutland whereby each player tries to guess on which squares his opponent has placed his ships. She assumed that they would not have buried them right next door to their plinths but, on the other hand, they would not have wanted to drag them too far away either. She decided she could only offer very general advice. It is hard work digging down two metres and she did not want to be the one to blame when nothing was found. The diggers knew what they were looking for. Let them play battleships, not her. Happily, it was not long before the first reports of success started to come, encouraging everyone, not least those whose digging had so far born no fruit. Little by little over months, more and more statues were found but, gradually the ratio of digging to finding began to grow longer, and the diggers morale less bouyant. Eventually the search was called off. No-one knew for sure whether they had found everything. If not, was this because the Germans had got there first? Kuchumov had found Flora and Hercules but no others. Or had they merely not dug in the right place? A doubt remains. Perhaps someone some day will happen upon a treasure trove like those road builders did in the Piraeus. There is currently a retired admiral still searching the park with a sophisticated mine detector. He claimed he knew where the Tsars had buried treasure there and he persuaded the authorities to equip him for the search. Excitement rose to great heights when, in the expected place, he obtained a strong signal. The press and TV were invited to the exhumation which made the disappointment all the greater when they discovered an iron pipe and a bed-head. Disappointed but undismayed, he continues his search during the winter months when he believes the frost aids the signal. No-one now has much hope that he will find any treasure, but he just might find a statue.

Another of Turova's early concerns was to take stock of what had happened to the treasures of the two palaces. She found that 17,600 items had been saved or recovered which were soon placed in storage in the Alexanderhof. However, that implied that over 42,000 items had been lost that had been listed in the pre-war inventory. Because of the combined size of the two palaces and the fact that they had contained so many rooms of a domestic nature, the amount of the loss seemed the greater but proportionately it was no worse than for the other palaces. Although expectations of major new recoveries began to fade, they have never disappeared altogether and never will. However, it has long since been the policy not to wait for some miraculous reappearance like that mosaic from the Amber Room. The emphasis has been on replication, where possible, or replacement.

The general conservation of the ruins of Pushkin was nearing its end in 1948 when the new decree 'About better measures for the preservation of cultural monuments' was issued. This was followed up fairly quickly by a decision of the Leningrad government that Pushkin, both Catherinehof and Alexanderhof were going to be leased to the Navy, one as a cadet training school and the other as a research institute which it still is. At first this fell like a thunderbolt on the heads of the restorers. For what had they spent the last four years collecting, preserving, listing and filing every little fragment that could one day serve as a guide for restorers? The fact that much restoration work had been approved and was going ahead at Pavlovsk and Peterhof, made the decision all the more bitter. Why had they been singled out for this? Unable to see into the future, they were in despair but, with the benefit of hindsight, most would now admit that they were wrong.

The Cold War was by this time well under way and the Soviet Union hell bent on overawing the West with its armed might. It might not have as much money as the West but what it had would go to the armed forces. The Navy had ample funds to patch up the palace even if only for its own purposes. It was soon improving the temporary roof and repairing walls which been no more than propped up. Furthermore, they proved sensitive to the anxieties of the restorers and, indeed, helpful. What better training for the cadets than to don diving equipment and to dredge up the plaque from the Chesma Column that had fallen into the lake. They took a great interest in the Chesma Column which, after all, had special significance for them since it celebrated the Navy's greatest victory. They agreed, in conjunction with the restorers, to restore the column. This required them to reopen a disused quarry at Olonetz in Karelia to obtain marble to repair the base. Comparing the one saved relief panel with the many pictures of the famous battle, Kedrinsky felt confident he knew how the original artists would have designed the others. Under his guidance, they were executed by a craftsman called Poliakov and replaced on the column. It all took rather a long time because the island on which the column stood was small and sheer. Trying to repair the column from a boat proved very difficult until General Winter came to the rescue. Only when the lake was frozen over, could they get on with the job.

On the other hand, working with the Navy had its inconveniences too. They wanted Kuchumov and his stores out of the Alexanderhof as soon as possible. Some of the palaces like Pavlovsk already had space and already could foresee the day when they could reopen as a museum but this did not apply to Catherinehof or indeed to Alexanderhof itself. In this way their exhibits came to be spread about to other museums around the country. None were lost track of but it made life very complicated for Kuchumov.

In the meanwhile, the restorers had no need to be idle. They never lost sight of the possibility that one day restoration would be given the funds to go ahead, a day for which a vast amount of planning needed to be done. Each item and aspect had to be carefully researched. To take, for an example, the missing statue of Proserpine. It had originally been acquired by Rastrelli in the mid-eighteenth century. There were some photographs of it, of course, but as it had stood on the Hermitage roof, these did not show the detail. A drawing of it, found in the archives, was much more useful but still not adequate. A search was launched for other renaissance versions of the same subject and it was this that led to a real discovery - a statue in Florence by Chiaffino on which Rastrelli's appeared to have been based. Further research in the archives revealed that a bronze copy of Chiaffino's statue had indeed been sent to St. Petersburg where Rastrelli saw it. The problem was solved. Now they knew what to copy. Once the funds were available, a team of restorers could be put together to go through all the now well established phases of plasticine, plaster and marble to recreate the original.

As elsewhere, Stalin's death in March 1953 was to prove the turning point although this was not obvious straight away. Russians had learned to be cautious for who could tell what might come next. But soon a sense of relaxation became perceptible, like the scent of early spring flowers. Then, in July, the hated Beria was seized when he arrived to attend a meeting of the inner circle, an operation reminiscent of the mafia. Kruschev and Malenkov, who had planned it in nervous detail, had come secretly armed, while Marshal Zhukov with ten trustworthy soldiers hid in the room next door. With Beria's death, the Russian people definitely started to breath more freely. For the restorers, however, release came in 1954, when the decree of 1948 was revoked, opening the way to the real restoration. This was a moment of quiet rejoicing not only for the leading restorers like Belekhov, but also for the rank and file, the skilled craftsmen and artists that had been graduating from the Restorer Schools, only to find that there was no restoration work for them. Now it was going to change.

All through this difficult period, funds had nevertheless been made available for relatively modest restoration projects, mainly on the various buildings in the park. These may have fallen short of the ambitions of the restorers but it had one huge blessing. It led to the study on a small scale the sorts of problem they would have to cope with on a much greater scale if and when the restoration of the main palaces became possible. For instance, it was agreed that the exterior of Rastrelli's Hermitage pavilion should be restored. Two experienced moulders, called Kalugin and Stryzhov, were put in charge. Quite a lot of the intricate stucco work had survived but it was all damaged and large chunks were missing. Studying the remains, they made an important discovery. While modern craftsmen normally made a mould with which they could consistently repeat intricate designs and apply them ready-made to whatever wall they were decorating, this was not how the craftsmen in the eighteenth century had worked. For them, each decoration, however simple or complicated, had been created individually. Each feature had been built up, bit by bit so far as the gypsum could be persuaded to hold fast while it dried, and then fashioned as a sculptor might have fashioned it out of stone. This discovery also threw light on how the eighteenth century artists had been able to make repeated patterns that still remain so lively and interesting. Each plaster motif or Corinthian capital was individual and its tiny differences from its neighbour subliminally created a little drama which, multiplied many times, brought a wall or a room alive. This was the moulders' equivalent of the discoveries Elena Gladkova had made with respect to woodcarvings. As a method, it was of course much more demanding but perhaps it was the secret of why these huge buildings and halls managed to look so light and airy. At any rate, it became a principle which the restorers henceforth always tried to follow. They would steep themselves in the individualities and idiosyncrasies of the original craftsmen who had created these palaces. They were helped by the scientists, who developed a more durable formula for gypsum which dried more quickly and was easier to fashion. It was such an improvement that even where undamaged eighteenth century mouldings remained, they started to relegate them to the storerooms and replaced them by new ones in the new material.

In a parallel exercise, a team of artists led by Lubimov was working in the Hall on the Island, in the artificial lake south of Cameron's Gallery. They had fragments of the pre-war murals to guide them but found that they were but the last of several paintings which they were able to peel back until they found what Cameron had intended. In the last days of the Tsars, the Hall had been used by guards officers for military exercises in close combat and the walls were adorned with rather incompetent illustrations of these exercises. It was not difficult to decide to go back to Cameron's concept.

All these projects, however, were just paddling in the shallows compared to the challenge of the Catherinehof itself. It was small wonder that many people had doubted the feasibility of its restoration. It was not just the variations in its styles and the skills the restorers would require; it was also it sheer size. If a cardboard model of Catherinehof could be unfolded into a straight line, its facades would stretch about a kilometre, all of the most varied and intricate design. A first step, however, was authorised in 1954. This was the replacement of the temporary roof of the Great Hall. The problem was not easy. The original roof had been supported by massive wood beams. Such beams were not easily found and needed to be well seasoned. The original Hall had had problems when one of the walls had started to shift which noone wanted to repeat. The problem of re-imposing this heavy wooden structure on walls already shaken by wartime damage was daunting indeed. However, an architect-engineer called Alexander Titov thought he had a solution and wanted to try it. The Soviet steel industry had developed a steel alloy that combined strength and lightness. The aircraft industry had produced a helicopter capable of putting heavy loads accurately into position. Titov was sure that he had the solution to the roof of the Great Hall. Not many agreed. Helicopters were newfangled and had never been used for such a task anywhere in the world but he was persistent. They told him that if he was allowed to go ahead, he would be held personally accountable for any failure. He was a brave man and still wanted to try and, in the end, he was given permission to do so. First the temporary roof had to be dismantled and the old wooden beams removed. The positioning of the new metal beams depended on placid weather which usually accompanies the white nights in June. It was therefore in June 1954 that the attempt was made. It was a triumphant success and, of course, the technique has since been used by architects all over the world. Titov having proved his theory and done such singular service to the cause of restoration, decided on a change of career. He left Belekhov's team and went to the Design Institute where his delight in innovation could have greater scope. However, the walls of the Great Hall were now bearing a roof both lighter and stronger than the original. Rastrelli would have been envious.

By this time, the responsibility for the conservation of the remains of Catherinehof had been taken over by N. Kreshemskaya, a senior architect on the staff of the Inspectorate. The successful replacement of the roof now added credibility to the idea of restoring the Catherinehof but still there were no funds. It would be a tremendous undertaking. Only to restore the facades of the great building, with all the battered atlantes, caryatids, balustrades, copings, acanthus leaves, ogee curves and every other baroque device was not made to seem easier by the decision that each plaster detail should be built up individually by the eighteenth century method. It would take an army of skilled men and women. But before any of that could start, several decisions would be needed. For instance, in the nineteenth century Alexander II, who loved a parade, had converted the garden in the courtyard into a parade ground. Tarmac had been poured onto it half submerging the circle of offices and servants quarters that surrounds it. Furthermore, he had built a rather pompous new portico with a reviewing stand. The restorers would certainly want to dismantle all this, dig out the tarmac and revert the whole area to what it had been in Catherine's day. There would be arguments about other details. The Tsars had replaced the coat of arms which had surmounted the centre block with a rather ugly clock - which luckily the Germans had stolen! Broken cornices above the first floor windows revealed that underneath there were eighteenth century bass reliefs which could be re-exposed. The damaged paintwork showed them the blue colour Rastrelli had intended as the background to all this decoration. In these matters, restorer sentiment was for a reversion to the palace of the eighteenth century, using the techniques used by eighteenth century craftsmen, even though this would take longer and cost more.

In 1957 a decision was reached. The Council of Ministers of the USSR voted to allocate the necessary funds for the Catherine Palace to be restored and the Navy was invited to move out of it, though not of the Alexanderhof. Soon after, Alexander Kedrinsky was appointed as head architect to supervise the whole enterprise, both external and internal, and in the park. It became his life's work. He was strongly of the opinion that the nineteenth century changes to the outside should be changed back again. To prove his point, he got Stryzhov to make a huge model, on a scale of one in ten, on which to demonstrate the changes and improvements he was recommending. With the help of this, he got his way in just about everything. With the help of the Inspectorate, he was able to collect together an extraordinarily talented team led by four outstanding sculptors - Kalugin and Stryzhov who had worked on the Hermitage Pavilion plus Tamara Shabalkina and Nadezhda Maltseva who had been repairing the buried Italian statues. In addition, he had the services of an exceptionally talented gilder called Maurichev. And of course, he was provided with a small army of craftsmen and builders. The start to the work was not long delayed and it progressed at a rate that might have surprised even Rastrelli. Perhaps most important of all was the presence of Elena Gladkova. She had now become Head Curator and her remarkable eye for detail helped Kedrinsky insist on a standard of quality that would have satisfied Oleinik. By 1963, the exterior was once more immaculate, save in one detail. There had not been enough money to replicate all the gilding that Rastrelli had specified. Instead, a newly developed gold paint had been used which looks, well, different. The Russia of Kruschev had different priorities to that of the Empress Elizabeth. It intended to impress the world with the number of its tanks and submarines rather than the lavishness of it palaces. Nevertheless gilding was allowed for the cupola of the Chapel Royal which had been badly damaged in the war.*

The overall effect is grandiose and it had been achieved remarkably quickly but it was only a beginning. There had been 55 staterooms in the palace of which all but 16 were completely wrecked, to say nothing of the innumerable smaller domestic and service rooms. If the restoration of the external walls had seemed daunting, it was nothing to the problems offered by the interior. These would not be completed in a few years and, long before they were finished, it would be time to renovate the exterior again. It had been Kedrinsky's ambition to complete it all in his lifetime but, by the end of the century and in his eighties, although still at work designing, negotiating and supervising progress, he knew he would leave much behind for others to complete. It was not just the scale but also the complexity of the problems.

The worst of the damage had destroyed all Rastrelli's golden suite from the Great Hall to the Picture Gallery, and beyond. Probably the most famous of these rooms was the Amber Room. While many treasure hunters were searching Europe for the original panels, a small local mystery arose soon after the end of the Navy's tenancy, when a family called Blynov from Lithuania came to Pushkin offering to restore the Amber Room. There is, of course, amber along the coast of Lithuania but there was a whiff of Rumpelstiltskin about this offer. They seemed to be offering magic and might, like Rumpelstitskin, demand a terrible reward. At that time, no-one felt like asking for the sort of money that might be needed. The Blynovs' offer was refused and for a long time, the restorers had to content themselves with reconstructing in amber the skirting of one panel, just to give visitors an impression of what the whole room must once have been like. Even this required a great deal of research to discover how the original craftsmen had achieved the limpidity of the amber and the variations in its colour. It involved clarifying it by boiling in honey and oil and judiciously applying heat to fix the colour. The room's restoration remained a dream however until the fall of communism. One of the economic consequences of this was the huge contract made by the German company Ruhrgas to pipe Russian gas to Germany. In recognition of the value of this contract, Ruhrgas proposed to sponsor the restoration of the Amber Room. Instead of jumping at this proposal, the Russian Treasury tried to tax it and so for some time nothing happened. It took the approaching tri-centenary of the foundation of St. Petersburg to clear peoples' minds and find a solution. By the turn of the century, work on the Amber Room had at last started and it was duly completed by 2003.

If work on the Amber Room was delayed by the problems it involved, the same logic in reverse dictated that priority should be given to the rooms of Paul and Maria-Feodorovna at the north end of the palace. They had been damaged but they had escaped the fire and some of them posed no tremendous problems. In each room, enough remained to guide the moulders to repair the decoration. In the Green Dining Room, one of the doors had survived with enough of its graffiti decoration for the painters to repair it and repeat it on the others.

---

* Four different gold paints were developed and applied to four atlantes. Only one resisted the weather.

The Germans had stripped the walls of the Blue Drawing Room but some of its chairs had been evacuated and could provide a sample of the same fabric for the Krasnaya Roza Factory near Moscow to replicate. All this could go ahead while work was going on the outside walls. These two rooms plus the Butlers' Room and the Choir's Anteroom were opened to the public as early as 1959. They were followed in the early sixties by four more rooms including Maria's bedroom. This offered a real difficulty in that its most prominent design features were the slender and highly decorated faience columns that Cameron had specified many of which had been wantonly damaged. Where fragments could be recovered, they were used but some columns had to be completely remade. Here modern technology came to the rescue, using polymers developed by the moulder Eduard Rodonov to replicate the originals. Visitors are challenged to say which are the original columns and which the replacements. This was so successful that it was used also to repair and replicate the tiles for the stove in Crimson Drawing Room but traditional methods were used to replace tiles elsewhere.

The first of Rastrelli's rooms to be opened, in 1967, was the Picture Gallery. The walls of the gallery had been completely covered by a mosaic of paintings of various subjects and by different artists, relieved by two immense tiled stoves and highly decorated doorways, which provided Lilia Shvedskaya with her first major restoration project in Pushkin, where she was to spend the rest of her working life. 115 of the pictures had been evacuated and the 16 that were lost were replaced from the huge resources of the Hermitage. The ceiling painting had entirely disappeared but a study of the archives had proved that the original painting of 'The Banquet of the Gods' by Dizziani had long since been transferred to the Hermitage in St. Petersburg where it had come to rest on the ceiling of the Jordan staircase. Kazakov and his team were selected to make a copy and place it in the Picture Gallery. From there, the restorers started to work their way towards the Great Hall which, everyone agreed, would be one of the greatest tests of the restorers in any of the country palaces.

The first rooms they tackled offered, in many ways, good training for that test. Rastrelli had been liberal with his gilded surrounds to the mirrors and his elaborate dessus-de-porte which were at the heart of that beautiful vista of gilded doorways disappearing into the distance. It kept Lilia busy recreating Romas and Ossetians, which she had to learn to distort so that, seen from below, they appeared lively and graceful. In the meanwhile, Gladkova had learned to distinguish the work of four eighteenth century masters - Dunker, Stalmeyer, Karnivsky and Valekhin, each with his own distinctive style. Their modern restorers had to try to immerse themselves into the style of whichever of these masters they were re-creating, copying the way he used his tools and created his effects. It was, perhaps, easier for them if the piece they were working on had completely disappeared so that they could start from scratch to copy Shvedskaya's design. Much more work was needed when enough of the original carving had survived to be worth keeping. Then it was their job to repair the damage and replace the missing bits. This required them to chip off centuries of gesso and gilding until they regained the original wood which they had to match. They did not then add more than the basic eight layers of gesso before gilding. The new parts were always visible at the wood stage but when gilded, no-one could tell. A curiosity arising from this is that the gilded woodwork at Pushkin is more slender than the same at Peterhof although the originals were by the same designer, Rastrelli. The reason is that the restorers of Peterhof had only fragments of the decoration to copy which they did not try to scrape down to the underlying wood but simply copied as they found them, bulked up by generations of re-gilding. Although it meant extra work and expense, Kedrinsky insisted on observing the basic rules that had governed all the restorers, to save and incorporate anything salvable. He was lucky to have an outstanding team of wood carvers, led by Yevgeniy Kozlov and Vladimir Bogdanov and including such masters as Vinogradov and Constantine Kochuev, all of whom were later to head their own teams of carvers.

Rastrelli was fond of using mirrors and foil. In the Green and Crimson Drawing Rooms he had used coloured foil backings but in the Great Hall used clear mirrors to create a lightness and exuberance to offset its sheer size. While windows make up a large proportion of the long side walls, mirrors lighten the spaces in between them and the end walls and themselves are enlivened by gilded carvings of great intricacy. To re-create such a hall would have daunted most people but the experience that Kedrinsky's team had obtained already gave them the momentum to tackle it. More of a problem was the ceiling painting which had completely disappeared. It had originally been the work of the highly talented Italian, Gaspari Valeriani, but early in the nineteenth century, something had caused it to start sagging down and it was removed, but no-one recorded where to. It was thought to be lost. The ceiling remained white for about half a century until it was painted again, this time by two second-rate artists. They were given for their subject a celebration of the way in which science and the arts were flourishing under autocracy. It involved goddesses sitting on clouds operating milk churns and gods carrying locomotives. They were required to indulge these fantasies within Valeriani's general schema and the result was faintly hilarious. Everyone agreed that if the ceiling was to be restored, it would not be to this nineteenth century curiosity. However, memories of it were about all they had to go on in trying to re-create Valeriani's original design until Kazakov made an exciting discovery. He was engaged on the cleaning and restoration of two paintings from the ceiling of the Court of Arms Hall in the Mikhailovski Castle in Leningrad when it struck him how inappropriate was their subject for the position they were in. They depicted architectural elements which were simply not at home in this location and then, in one corner, he found that the monogram of Paul I had been super-imposed on an earlier one, Elizabeth's. This proved that they had not been painted for the Mikhailovski Castle, which was built long after Elizabeth's time. An intensive search through the archives soon revealed that a part of Valeriani's ceiling had indeed been used in the Mikhailovski Castle when Paul I was preparing it for himself. Then, better still, a verbal description of the whole ceiling was found, which dated from 1795. It confirmed the authenticity of the two parts Kazakov had found and gave invaluable guidance about the centre part which was still missing. It remained a mystery where it had got to. It seems to have been still extant in the middle of the nineteenth century because Stakensneider, an architect much favoured by the tsars in the nineteenth century, made a sketch of it when he commissioned its replacement. This sketch was found but not the painting itself. The suspicion is that the painters of the later version disposed of it. Nevertheless, all these discoveries gave Kazakoff and his team great courage. They needed it. The ceiling area was 860 square metres, most of which was the missing centre panel, but they knew what they wanted to do. The restoration of the Great Hall took 20 years and was arguably the most ambitious and demanding of all the restoration projects undertaken in any of the country palaces. It involved a galaxy of artists in all fields of restoration.

Much progress was being made elsewhere while it was going on. Some of it offered problems which were no less acute, though they were on a smaller scale. The Blue Chinese Dining Room had been hung with old Chinese silk with a complicated hand-painted design. It had been torn off the walls and stolen by the Germans, leaving only a tiny fragment which had been trapped under the wood surrounding the fire-place. A study of this proved that, though it might be antique Chinese silk, it had been painted by Russian artists. This did not make it any easier for Raisa Slepushkina, the young artist chosen to recreate it as her diploma work for the Mukhina Institute. She only had that fragment and the usual fuzzy photographs. These indicated a typically Chinese landscape full of animated little figures engaged in every imaginable activity. Happily there were other silks of similar provenance in other palaces to be studied and there was the earlier work of Anastasia Vasilieva to guide her with problems of painting tempera on silk. With most reconstructions, it is not possible to say how close the result is to the original but subsequently the original stolen silk was discovered decorating a house in Switzerland. It testified to the accuracy of her work.

By the end of the century, there was still a great deal to do. Most of the exteriors of the palaces and the many pavilions had been repaired and they looked alright from the outside but internally there remained much to do. The anti-chambers behind the Great Hall were ready for restoration in the sense that the elements of their decoration had all been fabricated but, during the nineties, shortage of money delayed their installation. Of the south wing of the palace and the Cameron Gallery, only the Agate Rooms had been opened to the public. With the approach of the 300th anniversary of the foundation of St. Petersburg, a big effort was planned to complete all these in time for it but it was only partially successful and afterwards the momentum has slackened. The same applies to the pavilions in the park. All look pristine from the outside and some, like the Hall on the Lake have been finished internally as well. Most, however, have work to be done inside. A high priority was being given to the Hermitage Pavilion although it was not intended to fix the main hoisting machinery though the method will be demonstrated with one of the sidetables which could be hoisted individually. Kochuev is the only survivor of the original team of wood carvers and, although not well, he continues to carve in his workshops but has given up leading the team. The leading wood carver is now, Adolf Zabrovski, who produced most of the intricate baroque work in the Hermitage. His grandfather had been a carver too with his own workshop before the revolution. Adolf was born in 1933 and acquired his rather Germanic name because, at that time of his birth, his parents had the smaller part of a very cramped flat shared with an Estonian woman. Seeing their discomfort, she had offered to swap her bigger room with theirs, and, in gratitude, they named the baby after her father. Adolf went to the Architecture and Art School No 9, where Kedrinsky used to teach, and qualified initially as a moulder, first class. He had emerged from it just at the time when things were at their worst and he had to get himself a job outside restoration. In any case he was due to start his national service. When he returned, he was persuaded to switch from moulding to carving and he found himself working in the team led by Kochuev. He was working at Pushkin when Titov pulled off his feat with his helicopter and the roof beams. When Titov quit the Inspectorate for the Design Centre, Adolf decided to go too.

His hobby was the fabrication of very detailed model cars, capable of speeds up to 150kph, and he felt that he would find great pleasure tackling the design problems that the Institute was required to solve. He did indeed enjoy the life but he never forgot his delight in working with wood and after ten years he returned to Pushkin. Kochuev, at the end of the century, was still active but he had given up leading his team. Adolf is now the most experienced and arguably the most skilled wood carver but, he is a very modest man. He prefers to lead by example rather than hold any formal position. He has young colleagues, none more than 30 years old. During the nineties, they decided to leave Restorer to work freelance which had not been without its problems. They had difficulty finding an honest book-keeper. None of them wished to give up carving for something so boring as counting the money and, perhaps as a consequence, none of them has become very rich. Adolf is not sorry. He has a brother who is a banker and has made more money, but he still envies Adolf. He wishes he could carve wood too. There is enough to do at Pushkin to keep Adolf and his team busy for many years.

Although the outside of the Chapel Royal, including the damaged cupola, was repaired early on, it is only recently that serious work has started to rehabilitate the interior. It was dreadfully vandalised by the German motor-cycle engineers. The decoration of the walls was not destroyed but much damaged and the iconostasis disappeared with all but two of the icons. The work is being led by Natalia Formichiova who is a gilder but with experience as a carver too but gilding is the skill that will be most be needed. During the nineteenth century, the chapel suffered a fire and the restorers have discovered that the repairers of those days were not above taking a few shortcuts. In order to tidy up and re-gild the decorative motifs, they found that the original carved wood, where damaged by the fire, had been replaced by papier mâché. Oleinik would not have approved.

The Navy has never completely relinquished the Alexanderhof although the public are now permitted to visit one wing. The collapsed porch and other superficial damage to the outside has long since been patched up but the palace is a little bit shabby compared to the Catherinehof. The damage done inside during the war has been repaired and the Corner Sitting Room had been restored to Quaranghi's original neo-classical designs. Others, including the billard room, had kept their heavy art nouveau encrustation. The palace is very sparsely furnished, but contains a display of the innumerable uniforms once required by Nicholas II. They make one realise how important a part uniforms played in the life of those days.

In his eyrie in the Chapel Wing of Catherinehof, Kedrinsky, in his mid-eighties, still supervised what was going on and still hoped to see it completed. It was a large and chaotic office, strewn with many years of plans, sliding off the tables and scattered on the floor. Amongst the mess of papers could be seen drawings and designs of great beauty. Kedrinsky had at some stage a hand in the design of practically everything in Pushkin and the walls of his office were covered by his exquisite drawings. He remembered his boyhood visits to his grandfather's dacha at Gatchina when he was still the Tsar's confessor. He had lived through whole cycles of destruction and danger to see his beloved palaces rising again like phoenixes from the ashes. He was one of the great heroes of their resurrection. He died in 2003.

Chapter 15

GATCHINA

In the days of the Princes of Novgorod, there was a village called Khotchino in land dominated by the Teutonic knights until taken by the Swedes in the seventeenth century. It was finally captured by Peter the Great in 1700 at the start of the Great Northern War. It emerged from these adventures with its name slightly changed to Gatchina and so it remained until communist days when there was an attempt to rename it, first Trotsk and then Krasnoyeguardesk or Red Guard Town. It is now Gatchina again.

Its prominence dates from 1765 when Catherine the Great commissioned Rinaldi to build a country seat for her lover Gregory Orlov. By this time, Rastrelli's baroque style was already out of date and Rinaldi designed an austere facade in local limestone, flanked by curving galleries leading to two low blocks, all enclosing a peaceful meadow where sheep grazed. Internally, his decoration was neo-classical with understated plasterwork on Pompeiian themes but he also designed some exuberant parquet floors. The effect is of restrained elegance resulting in some quite beautiful rooms such as the White Hall and the Marble Dining Room. These are lovely but perhaps his greatest legacy was the park. He chose the site and developed and dammed its natural lakes to wind in and out of a maze of spits, promontories and islands, offering romantic sites for temples and pavilions all connected by graceful marble bridges. There were pleasure boats of all manner of historical designs for the courtiers' amusement. Rinaldi did not live to complete the park himself but he launched the ideas which others were able to fulfil.

Gregory Orlov died in 1783, and Catherine bought it back, lock, stock and barrel from his family and gave it to her son, Paul. While Paul's wife Maria Feodorovna delighted mainly in their other palace at Pavlovsk, Paul loved Gatchina but he was anxious to banish the memories of the hated Orlov, his mother's lover who had killed his father. Employing his favourite architect, Brenna, they heightened the galleries and the two blocks and converted the meadow in between into a parade ground where Paul could endlessly drill his private army. Without departing from Rinaldi's basic designs, and, thank God, not changing his glorious floors, they made Orlov's plainspun decoration more luxurious with gilding and new furnishings, more fit for an emperor. And they modified the Orlov's secret stairway to provide private access for the emperor to the empress's boudoir.

When Paul was assassinated in 1803, his son Alexander I neglected Gatchina and it stood unused until Alexander's brother Nicholas I came to the throne. It was Nicholas who instituted the annual Russian army's manoeuvres in the country around Gatchina during which he made it his HQ. He decided not to disturb his father's apartments in the main block which were to remain as a museum in his memory. Instead, he had a more modest suite prepared in the Arsenal Block. It was his grandson Alexander III who, unnerved by the assassination of his father and alarmed by the unrest of his people, came to live in Gatchina, hiding himself away in an obscure suite of rooms and provoking Karl Marx to refer to him contemptuously as 'the revolution's military prisoner in Gatchina'.

It was therefore in Gatchina that the last Tsar, Nicholas II, spent his childhood. During all this period, treasures steadily accrued to fill Gatchina's five hundred rooms. By the time Nicholas fell, there were 4,000 paintings, mostly portraits, vast amounts of Chinese porcelain and walls decorated with antique weapons. Small wonder that Zubov and his friends were so excited at the chance to discover it all and make it into a museum. When it opened, it was Gatchina that drew the most visitors. Unfortunately, for the same reason, it was also Gatchina that most excited Gokhran and Antikvariat when they started to sell treasures to the west, to Seraphima Belaeva's great grief. Nevertheless, there were still nearly seventy thousand museum items for her to evacuate before the Germans came. She managed to save about a third. The Germans did their best to leave nothing behind. In his farewell message, Herr Wurf had not been joking.

Unlike the other country palaces, Gatchina had not been right in the front line during the siege. It had not suffered like Peterhof and Pushkin. Nor had the Germans cleared all the inhabitants out of the town and there were plenty of eyewitnesses to describe the convoys of laden lorries departing towards Prussia. It had been thoroughly ransacked and seems to have been used by the Germans as an entrepot to which they brought loot from other palaces for onward shipment. When they left, they did not place bombs in the cellars but they started the fires in three places with true German thoroughness. These had brought down the roofs and the floors but the outer walls remained fairly intact. There had been no dome to come crashing down as at Pavlovsk. So Belaeva had been full of hope as she walked from the bus across the parade ground to open the doors. Her first sight of all the tangled, smouldering wreckage within had therefore been all the more bitter but with a few hours reflection, she began to feel that her troubles might be less severe than those of her colleagues. The decoration of Gatchina had relied less on carved, gilded wood and much of the internal stucco work appeared to still be in place. The fire had been so recent that the weather had not had time to get at it. The outer walls still seemed sound. If they could get a new roof over it quickly, a lot might still be saved. The palace had never had a particularly complicated roof.

In the very early days there was general agreement that the repair of Gatchina should be given priority. No doubt the character and seniority of Belaeva contributed to this decision. Also, she was backed by her former mentor, Vladimir Makarov, now occupying an influential position in the Museum Collegium. Of course, all the first steps had to be taken at Gatchina as elsewhere - the mine clearances, the filling of trenches, the digging out of tree stumps. They were quickly able to retrieve all the buried statues which had been scrupulously charted by Belaeva but two others appeared to have been stolen by the Germans. These, depicting Poetry and Culture, had been left on their lakeside pedestals below the private garden. They were gone.

They had by no means finished clearing up, however, when Gatchina received a real mark of preference. Before the end of 1944, Lenproject was given the go-ahead to reroof all three main blocks. Sophia Popova-Gunich, who later played such a key role at Pavlovsk, was put in charge. It was, in truth, a much less complicated and artistically fraught operation than the re-roofing of any of the other palaces; nevertheless, it took until 1948 to complete. The interior was still a damaged shell but Belaeva, with Sophia Popova-Gunich, did her best to make it look respectable enough for the modest exhibitions she now started to organise of the treasures she had managed to save. She had hardly got going, however, when the decree 'About Better Measures for the Preservation of Monuments of Culture' was issued. As a consequence, work at Gatchina virtually stopped and it would be some years before much more was done. In 1953 tenants were found, another naval cadet school. Belaeva had to move out and set up her office in the Aviary. Her exhibitions had to stop and, indeed, there would no longer be storage for all the treasures she was guarding. She had to find new homes for them and trust that, if and when things improved, she would be able to get them back again.

In the meanwhile, reconstruction had been going ahead in the park. The Germans had blown up most of the bridges although the Hump-backed Bridge survived because the charges placed under it had failed to go off. All the temples and pavilions were to some extent damaged, some lightly but others, like the Birch Pavilion, had disappeared. They had done their best to destroy the Priory Palace but its manner of construction with beaten earth had largely frustrated them. To his delight, Alexander Kedrinsky was given the project of restoring the park. It was a job after his own heart. His grandfather, the Tsar's confessor, had lived in Gatchina which was full of boyhood memories for him. There was not much money but he contrived to make it go further by first replacing the destroyed bridges with wooden ones. This was how they had originally been designed by Rinaldi and there were plenty of eighteenth century drawings of park to guide him. He was able to continue with this work despite the 1948 decree and several of the pavilions were carefully restored. The Venus Pavilion on the Island of Love had been the site of many a romantic concert, reached on a summer night by pleasure boat. The Germans seemed to have used it for drunken parties, using Mettenleiter's ceiling painting of the Triumph of Venus for target practice. Leonid Lubimov was charged with its repair, one of his earliest projects.

The naval cadet school was not good news at all for the interior of the palaces where they did almost as much harm as the Germans had done but they took a useful interest in the park. The Germans had left the dams and sluices much damaged so that the lakes had been partially drained and areas turned into swamp. The Navy brought in contractors to repair these and to restore the level of the lakes. They had the Holland boathouse restored too, according to its original design, but the boats they installed were alas no longer the historical models of former days. These were nevertheless frustrating days for Belaeva, locked out from her palace and striving to do what she could to contain the harm that she knew was being done. In 1959 she died. It was a sad end to her life. She was not immediately replaced. Gatchina was removed from the list of monuments for which the Inspectorate was responsible. Shortly afterwards, however, the Navy decided that Gatchina was no longer suitable for them and left in 1960. Gatchina was left orphaned for a while but eventually another tenant was found called Electronstandart, a highly secret organisation, even by Soviet standards. This was a disaster for the palace. The new tenants could do whatever they wanted without hindrance or conscience.

Although no new curator was appointed, an architect called Plotnikov was given the project to study what would be involved if the main gala rooms were to be restored to their former condition. Plotnikov had qualified as an architect in the early thirties but, shortly afterwards, one of his relatives had been branded an 'enemy of the people'. Just to be on the safe side, the authorities banished him and his family too. While in exile in Siberia, he made an extensive study of oriental architecture which was to stand him in good stead later on. He was allowed back to Leningrad in 1941, arriving shortly before the Germans attacked. He joined up at once and went to the front, but not for long. He was recalled to resume his studies and evacuated, with his family, to Uzbekistan. In 1943, he returned to Leningrad and became one of the first teachers in the Restorer Schools, but soon moved on to practical work. He was put in charge of the restoration of the Elagin Palace at which task he spent many years. He also gained a reputation as a doughty fighter for the principles of restoration. Perhaps it was hoped that, by employing him to survey Gatchina, some relaxation of the tenants' iron grip might be achieved but, after three years and a completed survey, nothing came of it.

In 1968 a new curator was appointed, a lively girl called Adelaida Yolkina. She had worked at Pavlovsk and was a great friend of Zelenova. Zelenova was aghast at what was happening to Gatchina. Her grandfather had worked there as a cabinetmaker before the revolution. Furthermore, she had been a great friend of Belaeva and of Belaeva's prewar assistant, Irina Yanchenko. Yanchenko with her two daughters had shared their miserable lodgings in St Izaak's during the first winter of the siege and one of the girls had died of starvation. In 1942, to her great joy Yanchenko was allocated a flat that had become vacant. Everyone helped her move and had waived her goodby but as she awaited her tram in the Nevski Prospekt, the shelter was hit by a shell. Yanchenko died instantly and her other daughter a short time later. Zelenova had been very fond of the family and had never got over her grief. She did not just want to do something for Gatchina but also for the memory of her two friends who had given so much of their lives to the palace. She was forming some idea in her mind of merging the curatorship of Gatchina with Pavlovsk. So, in the early sixties, she, Kuchumov and Yolkina had gone to the palace to see what could be done. They were met at the entrance by two enormous women with security armbands and had to leave without even getting near it. Zelenova was not one to be easily deterred however.

In 1968, her efforts bore fruit. Adelaida Yolkina moved to Gatchina with her new appointment in her hand but that was all. She had no idea where to start. The palace was still guarded. She could see it in the distance but no more. She could not even find out who the tenant was. She started writing letters but no-one would help. Eventually, she wrote a letter to every minister in the government in Moscow asking each one if he was responsible for the tenant in Gatchina.

Of course, she got no replies. All the letters were intercepted in Leningrad. The situation was becoming more and more like a Kafka novel when she had a bit of luck. She discovered that one of the managers of this mysterious tenant was wont to attend meetings the town's Executive Committee. There she managed to get into conversation with him without telling him who she was. He was called Gaagin and she found him perfectly charming. They were soon getting on like a house on fire so she decided to hoist her true colours. He was highly amused. "Well," he said, "We know how we stand. You must do whatever you can to get us out of the palace and I will do everything I can to stay there. But let's be friends nonetheless."

She realised that a frontal attack would be hopeless so she applied to the Inspectorate to get it reinstated onto their list. This succeeded and an architect called Kapilian was appointed to represent the palace but he was not much help. He was quite unable to stand up the military, under whom Electronstandart evidently came. However, after a few months Adelaida managed, without any help from him, to wangle her way into the palace. She was horrified by what she saw. The White Hall and Marble Dining Room had been turned into electronic laboratories. The Anti-room where Paul I had daily inspected the guard had been made into a lavatory. The Arsenal Block seemed to be some sort of factory. Perhaps worst of all, all the thousands of decorative fragments that Belaeva had so lovingly collected, preserved and logged had been thrown out. She was shown the dumps in the park and allowed to hunt through them for what she could find. But she was still far away from getting permission to do anything inside the palace. It was not until 1976, and thousands of letters later, that she got the matter onto the agenda of the 25th Party Congress. As a result, Electronstandart was advised to look for another home. There was no date set but they started to evacuate one or two of the gala rooms. At this point, Zelenova had a brainwave. She pointed out that under the terms of such tenancies, outgoing tenants were required to restore the property to the state they had received it. Suggesting there might be room for compromise, she got them to agree to a definite programme by which one room after another would be restored to her. She even managed to get them to pay towards the restoration.

Of course, initially she still had no cash for any serious restoration but she felt it would be wise to move in as soon as a room was vacated. A few bottles of Vodka procured a load of scaffolding from Pushkin which she had quickly erected in the Marble Dining Room. Adelaida was summoned a few days later to the Ministry of Culture in Leningrad and accused of theft but they did not take the scaffolding away. The next problem was that the regulations governing the contractors the Inspectorate used restricted them to a range of 25 kilometers from Leningrad. Gatchina is 45 kilometers away. The local contractors were not only unused to restoration work but were also heavily involved in working for the military on local collective farms. Of course, having got this far, a woman like Adelaida was not going to give up but it was not until 1985 that the first rooms were ready to be opened to the public.

Because of all these exceptional difficulties, Adelaida has been criticised on the grounds that some of the restoration work is not up to the rigorous standards of the other palaces. Oleinik might not have approved of all of it. It is not easy to tell. The magnificent floors have been beautifully restored. During the nineteenth century, many artists had been encouraged to make watercolours of the palace interiors and these were an excellent guide, preventing the restorers from straying. Also, Kedrinsky from Pushkin was a great support both in obtaining for her the right craftsmen and solving her problems over contractors. Perhaps also the decor of the rooms offered less of a challenge than had the baroque decoration and the silk wall coverings of Peterhof and the Catherinehof. If there is an artist whose name should be particularly linked with the restoration of the gala rooms at Gatchina it is Lydia Stryzhova. She was the daughter of Alexei Stryzhov who made the model of the Catherinehof for Kedrinsky. He had had a sculpturing workshop before the revolution. As a young man, he had made the death mask of Alexander III. He became one of the leading sculptors in Russia between the wars. During the siege, the family were evacuated to Yaroslavl but in 1943, her father was recalled to help set up Belekhov's restorer schools. Lydia became one of his first pupils - and one of his best. She had not wanted to be a sculptor. She wanted to sing but her father pressed her to it. She never quite reconciled herself to it but it did not affect the quality of her work. Adelaida had gone to great trouble to persuade her to come to Gatchina. The two of them worked very happily together until in 1997 when Adelaida was transferred back to Pavlovsk.

There were eight rooms open in Gatchina by the end of the century. That is perhaps sufficient for the amount of the contents which survived both Stalin and the Germans. Belaeva had only been able to evacuate some 11,000 items. Kuchumov found many of the paintings from Gatchina in Riga but there was never likely to be enough to furnish more than a handful of the 500 rooms. The items now on display were recovered from the other palaces, that had borrowed them, plus no fewer than 49 other museums all over Russia. Luckily, Belaeva had scrupulously recorded where everything had gone. Finding them was one thing. Getting them back was another but Adelaida is persistent. She struggled for years to recover two Gobelins tapestries from Pavlovsk, only giving up when she herself was transferred there. Nevertheless there are some exceptionally beautiful things on display, including the rest of the tapestries presented to Paul and Maria-Feodorovna by Louis XVI. They even found the statues of Poetry and Culture one day when dredging the edges of the lake. The Germans had not taken them after all. They just pushed them into the lake for fun. Electronstandart finally moved out in 1993 but since then, new smaller tenants have moved in, occupying the two blocks and some of the pavilions. There is still work to be done over the presentation of the central block but not much likelihood of extending the museum beyond it although there has been talk of reconstituting Alexander III's secretive suite of rooms. Kedrinsky's wooden bridges have long since been replaced by marble copies of those the Germans destroyed. The Birch Pavilion has been rebuilt and is once again in need of restoration. Since Adelaida left, there have been a series of curators but none of them has settled. Lydia Stryzhova died in November 2002. There is talk of reverting to Zelenova's old idea of merging the organisations of Pavlovsk and Gatchina. If Gatchina is a little off the tourist track, it is a great pity. It is worth going to see it just for the floors and the park. It is all very beautiful but Zubov might feel a little sad. I asked our guide if she knew into which room he and Schakhovskaya had locked themselves with their treasures as the red guards advanced. She had no idea what I was talking about.

Chapter 16

OTHER PALACES

In 1917, the first intrepid curators concentrated on those palaces which were especially vulnerable because their owner, the Tsar, had abandoned his title to them, but these were only the greatest palaces amongst many that dotted the landscape and filled the little towns. Many of these were historically important and very beautiful. They were often owned by relatives of the Tsar or important courtiers who initially saw no reason to follow Nicholas into perdition, but as the Provisional Government became increasingly beleaguered, they felt an increasing need to find a way to protect them. This was why the Grand Duke Ivan had invited Polovtsov to Pavlovsk and why, shortly afterwards, Bernstam had been asked to take the Menshikov Palace at Oranienbaum and its satellite pavilions under his wing. Polovtsov, without taking responsibility for their palaces, tried to help some of these owners because he could not bare the thought of beautiful things in danger. The Princess Palei, the morganatic wife of the Nicholas's uncle, the Grand Duke Paul, had implored his help to save her famous collections of French porcelain and her lithographs and he had given it, but the three curators soon had to make it quite clear that they could not accept responsibilities outside the briefs they had been given.

One cannot blame them. They could not defend the wealth of the whole of the upper class. Many of these properties had been built by tsars or empresses, either to reward a favourite, like Menshikov, or for a utilitarian purpose. For instance, in the days before the railway or steamboats, Peter the Great had found a staging post at Strelna to be convenient. Of course, a staging post for a tsar could not be any ordinary sort of staging post. Other palaces, like the Chinese Palace or the Switchback Pavilion at Oranienbaum, had been built by Catherine the Great purely for fun, there being no provision for anyone to stay after the party was over. Others, like the Cottage Palace were built for tsars who preferred something more bourgeois for a family home than their grandest palaces could offer. Yet others, like the Palace of Peter III or the Catherine Block beside Monplesir, had been used to house members of the family temporarily unwelcome at court. Most of all, however, wherever the tsars chose to live in state, the courtiers and great families would build themselves properties nearby of a grandeur suitable to their wealth and place in the order of things. Many of these were very beautiful and contained things of great beauty. When George Lukomski in exile was writing about how much better the Russian Revolutionaries had cared for their country's treasures than had the French sans-culottes a hundred years before, he was not thinking of all these lesser but valuable properties. They had really suffered. Lunacharski had tried to take into safe keeping their choicest treasures if the owners asked him to, but a great deal was lost. Often beautiful things were vandalised in an orgy of hatred against the 'reptiles' who had for so long battened onto the wealth created by the poor. The houses themselves were soon given to less artistically sensitive tenants, like orphanages and agricultural colleges. Inevitably, a great shabbiness began to characterise what had once been so brilliant.

When the war came, while the Germans did not bother to do them any deliberate damage, many of these palaces were terribly exposed. The towns of Pushkin and Pavlovsk had been bitterly defended, first by the Russians and then by the Germans and the result was havoc. The great houses, like Mikhailovka and Constantinovka at the eastern edge of the Peterhof Park had been right in the front line, and used tactically by soldiers, who reckoned that victory and their own lives were much more valuable than the preservation of architecture. Only the Cottage Palace survived relatively undamaged.

On the other hand, the palaces and pavilions of Oranienbaum survived the war fairly unscathed because the Germans did not bother to attack the Russians in this western enclave. The Chinese Palace received only one direct hit, from a shell which did not explode. Peter III's palace too was struck once by a stray shell but it had done little damage. But both it and, especially, the Switchback Pavilion had suffered a great deal from the damp and the cold. Immediately after the siege, while arguments still were raging about the future, if any, of the great but ruined palaces, resources were authorised to refurbish these undamaged buildings in order, as quickly as possible, to reopen to the public some part of the parks they had so much loved to visit before the war. One of Lubimov's first tasks had been to join the team restoring the paintings in the Switchback Pavilion with its beautiful scagliola floors. Unfortunately, in the hurry, insufficient thought was given to what they were doing. Inappropriate materials like concrete were used and the work needs now to be done all over again but with the added complication of the consequences of the mistakes. Luckily, this did not happen in the Palace of Peter III. Lubimov also worked here on the lacquer panels, while the main work, on the restoration of its wall paintings, was by Anastasia Vasilieva with her close friend Rudolph Sausen.

The exquisite Chinese Palace required less work and was partly opened on 7th July 1946. It contains Rinaldi's delightful fantasy on the Orient as imagined by an eighteenth century Italian. Its reopening proved hugely popular and visitors were soon arriving at a rate of 2,500 a day. Unheated and anyway prone to damp, the palace soon began to suffer the consequences of so much breath being exhaled into its rooms. Eventually visits had to be curtailed and they still are, which makes it almost impossible to finance its maintenance. Luckily it is one of the few palaces that has the benefit of its own charitable foundation, called the Friends of the Chinese Palace. It was set up by an English businessman called Thomas who had spent many years in St. Petersburg, and who had learnt to love this little palace, with its swirling parquet floors. Thanks to his efforts, it has been listed by the World Monument Fund as one of its 100 most valuable sites and is under restoration.

The problems offered by the great Menshikov Palace were of a different order. They were of long standing. After the Menshikovs were banished by Peter I's grandson, the estate had become just another of the Tsar's possessions. Peter III however had loved it and had started to build Peterstadt nearby, a sort of private fortress with a little palace in its midst. However, he was interrupted when Orlov, Catherine's lover, came to take him off to prison. The palace remained but the fortress was made of wood and disappeared. Despite this, Catherine liked Oranienbaum and built her two pleasure palaces there, the Chinese Palace and the Switchback Pavilion. Eventually the Menshikov Palace was given to Paul I's youngest son Michael and inherited by his only surviving child, another Catherine. She married the German Duke of Mecklenburg-Strelitz, whose descendants lived in the palace until the revolution. Unfortunately, they had already used concrete to repair the building which has since caused great problems.

Having plenty of property abroad, the family did not hang around to see how the revolution would work out. Since the estate had been abandoned, the communists quickly confiscated it, giving the main building to an agricultural college and only the smaller palaces in the park to Lunacharski. It was with this difficult situation that Bernstam was expected to cope in 1918. As far as the main palace was concerned, he did not succeed. After the Agricultural College had left, it became a School of Forestry while much of the palace was made into apartments for the poor. This situation remained until the war, after which the Navy was given the palace in which to set up a highly secret torpedo research establishment. Some effort was made by the Inspectorate to look after the palace. The architect, Kazanskaya, was allowed to carry out preservation work on some of the internal decoration but it was not until the nineties that there was any real talk of opening the palace to the public. The Navy relinquished the main block but retained the wings facing the restorers with serious problems. The palace had been built on a hillock in the middle of a swamp and had begun to subside. There was fierce controversy over what to do. The geo-engineers wanted to, and did drive some 500 piles into the ground to hold it up. The restorers, on the other hand, wanted to drain the marsh which was the cause of the problem. In the meanwhile, no-one felt it would be wise expensively to restore the interior. It has been opened to the public as is. Its most popular feature is its famous summer-house in the Japanese style, as it was imagined in the eighteenth century.

Two other small palaces that lie to the west of Peterhof had had the misfortune to come within the German perimeter and both were very severely damaged. One, the 'private dacha' had been built by Peter's daughter Elizabeth and later developed by Nicholas I and his son Alexander II. The communists nationalised it but by the end of the war, it was a wreck. However, in 1963 it was decided to make it into a sports centre for the Leningrad Institute of Engineering and Architecture. Two architect-restorers, Kuznetsov and Yakovlev, were given the task of recreating the original exterior. The other, called Sergeievka, was built in the mid-nineteenth century by Stakensneider, based on antique Roman lines. In the sixties, it too was rebuilt retaining its external appearance and leased to a biological research organisation.

The situation to the east of Peterhof was quite different because this is where the battles had been fought. Three important palaces dominate the landscape - Znamenka, Mikhailovka, and Strelna. The Znamenka had been built by Peter I as a country dacha for his favourite, Menshikov. It had subsequently passed through several hands and been much developed by 1850 when it was given to the Grand-duke Nicholas, a younger son of Nicholas I. It had become a complex of 15 separate buildings by the time of the revolution, all of which were more or less destroyed during the war. For some time it remained derelict until it was allocated to the Organisation of Leningrad Transport Workers who determined to convert it into a rest home. They selected the excellent Michael Plotnikov as architect. Plotnikov's main achievements had been the restoration of several important buildings in Leningrad, including the Elagin Palace. It was he, also, who prepared the first plans for the restoration of Gatchina. He found the challenge of Znamenka one of the most difficult of his life. He was expected to meet the requirements of his employers, the transport workers, to provide about a thousand of them with comfortable quarters and recreational facilities, while preserving the historical and cultural aspects of the building. He was conscious at every moment that the Inspectorate was watching everything he did. Reflecting on the job afterwards, he complained that "it was really very difficult to combine the original architecture with the modern functions expected". The interior had been grandiose, with much ornate marble and plaster work from the workshops of one Triscorni. Perhaps it was he who had inspired the artist Treskin centuries later to fantasise about his origins. The palace had been intended for the luxury of a few rather than the comfort of many. All this, said Plotnikov, "made our work much harder." In the end, it got too much for him. Asked by the transport workers to add on some further conservatories, he rebelled. Stating that it would ruin the balance of the building that he had been at such pains to preserve, he resigned with all the drama he could muster; but they built them just the same.

Mikhailovka, next door to Znamenka, offered much the same problems. Perhaps it was not so hawkishly watched over by the Inspectorate because the palace had only been built by the Grand Duke Michael in the 1860s. It too was a complex of buildings with Kitchen, Cavaliers' and Stable Blocks plus extensive conservatories of which there was precious little left by the end of the war. It was allocated to the workers of the Kirov Factory and the construction of a rest home for up to 1200 of them started in 1968. There had been a particularly beautiful park, full of oak trees, fountains and granite bridges, the restoration of which was undertaken by the architect, Gromova.

The last of this string of great palaces, now on the very edge of St. Petersburg, is Strelna, the post house used by Peter I on his way to and from Peterhof. Once its original function was no longer needed, it had passed into the hands of the Grand duke Constantine, Paul I's second son who had declined to become Tsar after his brother Alexander I died without an heir. By the time of the revolution, the buildings had been poorly maintained but they were converted into a house of rest for the workers and were popular. Their ruin was completed by the war. For some time nothing was done about them until in the early fifties, they were leased to the Arctic Institute, a military establishment. They carried out the repairs they needed to perform their training functions but, as is normal with military places, the details of what went on were lost from view. In the 1970s, Lenproject developed a plan to restore the overgrown park and to replant some of the lime trees which had been its former glory. Thus matters stood until, towards the end of the century, a project was started to make it into an official state residence where important guests could be housed and functions held. For this purpose, the restorers are charged to recreate it as nearly as it had been in the days of its greatness, a long time before. This was clearly going to cost a great deal and it arose at a time when the Russian economy had not been at its strongest, so a charitable fund was instituted to enable 'new' Russians, who had so greatly benefited from the changed economic circumstances, to repay some of their gains. The work was pressed ahead under the spur of the oncoming tri-centenary of the city's foundation so the government probably supplemented these private contributions. It is now functioning as a rather grand state guesthouse and is the centre of a little community of dachas built by these same new Russians. All this has proved a valuable source of work for our restorers.

As St. Petersburg prepared for its great centenary, many of the aristocratic palaces in the city were hastily restored but this is less true in the suburbs. Here and there a dacha which escaped serious damage has been done up, like the Yusupov dacha outside Pushkin. Inside the towns however, concrete Kruschev blocks of tiny apartments now line the once elegant boulevards. In some instances, commercial sponsors have come to the rescue. A Danish group has been given a long lease to use the Chinese Village in the Alexander Park at Pushkin as a hotel. The search for such sponsors is nowadays one of the key activities of the museums' directors, and they are not without success. Their commercial skills are becoming more valued than their architectural knowledge or their political standing, a pointer to the palaces' fate in the twenty first century. It is difficult to maintain buildings that serve no economic purpose but commercial exploitation cannot be worse than what befell them in the twentieth.

Chapter 17

RESTORATION UNDER CAPITALISM

Before the Second World War, the maintenance of the country palaces depended to a large extent on an ageing pool of craftsmen who had learned their trade in pre revolutionary times. The most talented might obtain a place in a school, like the Stieglitz that Polovstov had run. More often, they were just following a family tradition. In this way the art of fountains had passed from Lavrentiev to Lavrentiev down the generations. Until the revolution, tradition lay heavy on the land and it was not easy to break away. Lydia Stryzhova, the talented daughter of Alexei Stryzhov who made the model for Kedrinsky, wanted to be a singer but she finished up a sculptor like her father. The new impetus which Lunacharski had brought to education and indeed the whole surge of hope and ambition which then filled bright young hearts, caused many to question such family traditions. Surely they could do better than dad, especially with the country girding itself to give chase to the west in terms of industrialisation and modernisation. And, indeed, there were new opportunities. Clever pupils were given higher education courses. If they did not get to a university or an academy of art, they could expect excellent training in a technical institute. Good people got quick promotion, not least where the care of historical monuments was concerned. Belekhov, Kuchumov and Zelenova were all extremely young when they were given important responsibilities. No doubt Stalin's purges had been good for promotion and so probably was the war. Wars always are. There were of course cases, like Kedrinsky or Plotnikov, where some blot on their CV was held against them and could deny them the opportunities their talents merited. Even so, between the wars, no-one had felt it necessary to make special arrangements for the development of new craftsmen to look after the palaces.

As the shells rained down on Leningrad, battering chunks off the city's best loved buildings, Belekhov could see that what had done before the war would not be enough after it, if there was going to be any realistic attempt to repair the damage. It was not just his foresight that brought about the establishment of the first Restorer School in 1943. Even though he now enjoyed considerable authority, it would have been unthinkable for him to take such a step without some high level sanction but, with contacts in the Politburo, he was well placed to get it. It was Stalin himself who signed the order but it was Belekhov's baby. Given that, in 1943, the siege was still far from over, let alone the war, he demonstrated considerable confidence in the future.

Initially, he set up three schools. The first, a school for restorers, was in the Peterschulle,

Zelenova's old school. It was followed in 1944 by two Architecture and Art Schools, one in the former Catholic Church on the Nevski Prospekt and the other, the smallest, near the Mariinski Theatre. For some reason they were numbered respectively 9 and 11. They were at once popular if only because, as Vasilieva discovered, they supplied a warm uniform and reasonable rations. They were divided into departments covering almost every skill from painting to jewellery, from sculpture to gilding to cabinet making. No one school catered for all the skills covered but all had the services of outstanding teachers. At first, these tended to be old men like Ernest Kwerfeld and Vasily Simonov who had, before the war, been responsible for the first evacuation plan. However as architects and artists like Kedrinsky started to return from the front, they enrolled as teachers with alacrity, since it classified them as workers, qualifying for a more generous food ration. Lubimov's first tutor, whom he admired enormously, was a painter called Vladimir Bellaev who had graduated from the Stieglitz in 1910. So had both Olga Borodina who taught graphics and Dietrich who taught sculpture.

Having just returned with her family across the ice road, Nadezhda Ode was on of the first intake in November 1943, and she studied for three years. Afterwards, she could have gone on to spend years more at the Mukhina, but her teacher advised her not to, which in after life she often regretted. She was a searcher after perfection and, while others thought she achieved it, she always felt she fell short. Perhaps those extra years would have made the difference. Leonid Lubimov joined a year later by which time there were already 200 students in his school. Unlike Ode, he did complete the full eight years although much of it was spent working on restoration projects around the city, often with established masters like Treskin. He enormously enjoyed his time in the schools because of the wonderful standard of the tuition.

By the time Anastasia Vasilieva joined the school a year later, her intake was already numbered 23. A veritable army of restorers with all manner of skills was being trained and assembled, the historical equal of which is hard to recall. There have been tremendous flowerings of artistic talent in various places at various times in history but restoration is something different. Lubimov chose it rather than creative art because it offered a greater variety of challenges and also, perhaps, because artists creativity was circumscribed by conditions in the Soviet Union. Although Stalin by this time was dead, artists were still expected to be socially useful whereas restorers faced endless but fascinating new technical problems. Furthermore, although not at all well paid considering the skills required, it promised a more secure life. And not least, he really enjoyed the challenge and variety. Most of the restorers looked back on their days in the schools as a halcyon time, with warm clothes and enough food, although not enough to prevent the art students yearning to eat the white bread they were given with which to clean paintings.

Not all the students succeeded. Some, probably well connected, had joined more for the warm uniform than because of any exceptional talent. These received at best the basic three year course and many, particularly in the early fifties, found it impossible to get work. Indeed, during this period several tutors lost their positions in a climate of retrenchment and economy. Happily, it turned out to be a fairly short phase and after Stalin's death, things began to get easier again. The normal move from the schools was to join the Restorer Workshops which not only provided working places but became their regular employer, paying them a wage and hiring them out to the architects and directors in charge of the various projects. Only Pavlovsk, for reasons to do with the way Zelenova had first obtained the go-ahead to restore it, kept its own in-house team and still does. But Pavlovsk too from time to time had to call for help from the outside. Restorer Workshop was thus not only a location where artists and craftsmen could do their work. It was also a sort of labour exchange of a highly specialised nature.

With the exception of a few brilliant individuals, most artists and craftsmen were organised into teams, under an experienced leader. They might be sent anywhere. The scale of the projects required teamwork. After all, the original artists of the eighteenth century, faced with 400 square metres of ceiling, had not worked alone or without help. By the end of the fifties, these teams were recognised and well established although they remained flexible, adaptable to the job in hand. Artists worked with leaders they found not only stimulating but also congenial and if things went wrong, they were free to change to another team, if they could find one. By the sixties, when restoration was going ahead full bore in all the four palaces and there was plenty of work, the stronger teams began to break away from Restorer Workshop. They found they could negotiate marginally better terms for themselves and could also arrange their work the better to suit them. The painter, Yakov Kazakov and the carver Constantine Kochuev were the first to go private, having their finances looked after by the Artists' Union. The funds, of course, still came from the same sources. It might be a local government fund or an allocation from the central government but it was all public money. The amount the palaces could earn for themselves was negligible and was swallowed up by the cost of routine maintenance. The teams also began to accept and train talented newcomers so that the influence of the Restorer Schools became less dominant. In any case, by the mid-sixties, these schools had been absorbed into the long established higher education system of Leningrad. The Restorer School, for instance, had been merged into the Mukhina. The method became more formalised with a rigid grading system, which would determine what sort of wage a restorer could expect during his working life. Thenceforth, students were divided into those studying art and those studying to restore. The former were encouraged to be creative but the latter were not. Instead, they had to go into all the science that lies behind the development of different forms of painting and other arts, and undergo the discipline of discerning and obeying some other artist's ideas, while suppressing their own. They had to become experts in archive material and in assembling and marshalling all relevant information they could find before they attempted even a preliminary sketch. At the summit of these seats of learning, a new Institute of Restoration was established in Moscow bearing the honourable name of Grabar.

A change began in the mid-eighties. It was not just the arrival of Gorbachov and perestroika. The Soviet economy was already on its last legs, operated by a system of corruption that everyone knew was dragging the country to ruin but which no-one, least of all Gorbachov knew how to stop. He tried but all he achieved was mounting chaos. It was a sort of chaos that might have felt familiar to Zubov, Polovtsov and Lukomski except that, unlike the events of 1917, it all happened in slow motion. For Russians who had been through the civil war and collectivisation, it may have seemed a fairly small earthquake but, its consequences for the restorers were dire. Financial support was rapidly cut back. Palace directors were told that they could not expect much in future and should look to ways to raise money themselves. Projects in hand, like a second refurbishment of the fountains at Peterhof were stopped in their tracks or had to be spread out over many years. The Restorer Workshops collapsed and the few restorers still dependant upon it were told they would have to seek their own livelihoods themselves. In desperation, many of the teams formed themselves into private companies. Nadezhda Ode's son, with some friends, formed a company called 'Style', aimed at helping the so-called new Russians, those who had been quick-witted enough to profit from the chaos around them. In a seething world where today's success could collapse tomorrow, the newly rich wanted to enjoy it while they could and wanted houses and apartments to match their new status. It became fashionable to build smart country dachas again, called kotedzhi in a charming misconception of English. Style was one of the many little companies formed to help them achieve their dreams. Style did not last long, but long enough to see Ode through the worst years. During these years she had started once again to go to church and had formed a friendship with one of the orthodox priests called Father Vasily. When Style failed her, she thought to retire but Father Vasily would have none of it. He chided her that she, with such abundant gifts, could contemplate retiring without passing them on to a younger generation. So she formed a new company, to be run on co-operative lines and concentrating on what she knew best, plaster moulding. She called it Vasily and the timing was right. But not every restorer was as talented as Nadezhda Ode. Most went on working for as long as they could because they could only expect a pittance for a pension. Many, like Anastasia Vasilieva, had to give up for health reasons, often brought on by having had to work with noxious materials without proper protection. Some, like Lydia Stryzhova, felt very bitter because she felt that her whole life had been misdirected. But she was an exception. Most felt their lives well spent. Certainly Adolf Zabrovsky would not have changed it for more money.

By the time Vasily opened, Russia was beginning to pull out of its economic nosedive. The landscape was utterly changed but for all the crudity of the Yeltsin's so-called privatisation, the new businesses were beginning to get their bearings and some people were becoming amazingly rich. Furthermore, and providentially, the price of oil rose to enable Russia to earn foreign currency and stabilise its own. Although the new government's revenues were cruelly reduced, it was spending less on arms and, in addition, it received massive support from the west which was aware of its faults but suspected that almost any alternative would be worse. In one way or another, as things got better, more funds might be spared to continue the preservation of historical monuments, and in particular, the country palaces, one of communism's success stories. Furthermore, Yeltsin favoured decentralising more power to major cities like Leningrad where a sprightly new mayor called Anatoly Sobchak started off well by changing its name back to St. Petersburg. He had a clever deputy called Vladimir Putin, who was in charge of foreign affairs and well aware of the city's potential for tourism.

Circumstances began to favour the palaces again but there had been a change of scenery. Whereas the project leaders like Kedrinsky had once held most of the power, now it was transferred to the palace administrative directors. Their responsibilities were increased to include not only the restoration of the palaces but also all aspects of their finances. It was up to them not only to decide on how to spend the subsidies which began to come available again but also to find ways by which the palaces could raise more funds by better use of their assets. This latter task made them look at what they had got from a different point of view. The Rose Pavilion might be a cultural and historical monument but it is also be a grand place for a party, which was, after all, its original purpose. If such a potential was to be realised, a lot of preliminary work needed to be done to the infrastructure in the form of toilets, canteens, restaurants, kitchens and so on. The palaces had to be made user friendly. Curators saw money they felt had been allocated for them for restoration, diverted to commercial uses. It was not always just a conflict of priorities. Commercial requirements could encroach in ways which the curators felt could damage the integrity of their palaces. There was a furious battle at Pushkin over an idea to convert the ground floor into a tourist centre with shops, restaurants and all sorts of other facilities. Some of the plans even envisaged removing pillars which were, in fact, holding up the palace above. Because the directors were in overall charge and held the purse strings, even of the curators' wages, the battles could be a bit one sided but their outcome was in fact reasonably well balanced. Nothing outrageous appears to have been done to the museums or their contents, but quite a lot for the comfort of visitors. Indeed, by western standards the palaces are still rather under-exploited but in the meanwhile, restoration projects were being held back due to this diversion of funds. The anti-chambers beyond the Great Hall in the Catherinehof have remained for a long time like warehouses, full of beautiful woodcarvings and pillars while the funds were lacking to assemble them. Nevertheless, in key ways the concerns of the curators are still paramount. Visits to Monplesir and the Chinese Palace, for instance, are strictly controlled lest too much humidity should damage them. The atmosphere is still one of conservation, protecting the palaces for posterity rather than exploiting their tourist potential in the way that a Disney or a Madame Tussaud would.

The privatisation of the teams of restorers has brought new anxieties. Although they are mostly the very same artists who have always worked in such a disciplined way for the Inspectorate, there is worry that the profit motive might tempt them to take short cuts. The Inspectorate still exists and exercises its control over important public buildings but where private patrons have acquired works of art that needed attention, restorers may be tempted to take risks. Anyone who has restored anything will know that the cost of the care and patience involved in the work cannot be translated into a price that seems reasonable to a layman. Nor is it only private patrons that cause anxiety. Smaller museums, strapped for cash, have begun to employ private contractors to restore their exhibits, presumably because they are cheaper - but how are they able to be cheaper? By the end of the century, there was much talk of the need for a licensing system and a code of practice for restorers. People were looking to the Grabar Institute to give a lead.

In the late nineties, however, a new factor began to exert an influence. St. Petersburg's foundation dated from 1703 when Peter decreed that it should arise fully formed like Venus from out of these northern marshes. Its three hundredth anniversary was due in 2003 and the new government which had succeeded the chaotic Yeltsin years, was resolved to use it to good effect. Project after project was revived and the drive was on to complete as many of them as possible by the anniversary year. Many of these projects are to restore the great palaces of the aristocrats in St. Petersburg and there is a growing realisation of what touristic treasures the city is heir. Perhaps one day Polovtsov's palace on Stone Island will be done up. It stands sadly alone behind its trees after many vicissitudes. It is at present empty although for some time one room was rented by a firm making hand made quality furniture. That at least might have pleased him. Many of the projects relate to the country palaces, especially Pushkin, which is far from complete. Work has been going ahead in the Chapel, the Anti-chambers, the Zubov Wing and the interior of the Hermitage but not much was completed in time for the anniversary. The Amber Room however was ready. Kedrinsky's dream of seeing the restoration of Catherinehof completed in his time did not come true. He never gave up working but died, well into his eighties, in 2003. In the meanwhile, it has been a good time for restorers. Many of the old hands are still active. The carvers Lilia Schvedskaya, Constantine Kochuev and Adolf Zabrovsky and three of the painters Kazakov's old team - Boris Lebedev, Ivan Alexeev and Yuri Zhuravliov - are all busy once again but the wages paid for public work are still shamefully low. There is still plenty of woodcarving to be done in the Catharinehof, but Adolf Zabrovsky could not manage financially without his private commissions.

It is too early to say what will happen now that the anniversary is over and the bands have marched away. It is difficult for these great palaces to generate enough income through gate receipts even for their maintenance needs, let alone further development. Great houses everywhere in the world have tended to become financial burdens and the tourist season in St. Petersburg is extremely short. Furthermore, the great army of restorers which was launched by Belekhov in 1943 has begun to fade away as the older soldiers are not replaced. The new commercially savvy museum directors may show much talent in finding sponsors and uses for their palaces, but they will not achieve much without the skills and dedication of the artists and craftsmen to whom they owe the assets they are managing. Problems however always mean opportunities for someone and it is difficult to imagine that the new century will offer such formidable problems as the last one did. Let us be optimistic. As Churchill once said at a low point in the war, there is not much point in being anything else. And indeed, the gathering signs that Russia may be reverting to something resembling a tsarist autarchy may presage a new golden age for palaces. Already Strelna has been refurbished in record time and there are rumours that the authorities may be eyeing the Chinese Palace for their parties.

Chapter 18

WAS IT WORTHWHILE?

Apart from the terrible human misery it caused, the Second World War was one of the most destructive events in history. Nearly all European nations suffered but those in the eastern half suffered the most. Furthermore, they emerged with totalitarian governments, so that the two halves of Europe went different ways in most things but not least as far as their policies on reconstruction were concerned. While western nations tended to regard the razed areas in their cities as opportunities to build something modern - or at least economical - those in the east showed a great resolution to re-create what had been lost. In most cases, this did not go further than rebuilding the mediaeval exteriors of houses while designing new interiors to suit the needs of the twentieth century. Heavily damaged cities like Warsaw, Danzig and Dresden have scrupulously and beautifully restored their historical centres but only as far as their superficial appearance goes. The great exception to this was Russia. The arguments and politics surrounding the question of what to do about their devastated monuments continued for a decade and even when, after Stalin's death, the new leadership showed itself at once to be more open to the proposals of the restorers, there was never a formal comprehensive decision taken as to what should be done. One reason was that the restorers were proposing something fundamentally different to what was being done anywhere else - or had ever been done. They wanted to re-create something in its entirety something which had existed in the past but was gone. In so far as ruins remained, they would conserve them. Broken fragments would be rescued and incorporated rather than replaced, although it would have been much easier to replace them. Tottering walls were not demolished but stabilised and made part of the reconstruction.

In the city of Leningrad itself, this was a relatively easy policy to follow. Although nearly all the city's historical buildings had been hit, mostly it had been by artillery shells which caused less damage than bombs. Indeed, the city probably suffered less from aerial bombardment than had most German cities or even English ones. There was no reason in the world to hesitate before restoring the city but the country palaces were another matter. They really had been wrecked and could not just be restored. It would have to be a mixture of restoration and reconstruction. Was this feasible? What would the results be like? Disneyland did not yet exist but there was always the danger of producing a pastiche. Many people both in Russia and, especially, in the west, thought that the attempt would be misguided. It would be breaking new ground - and very expensive. That it was allowed to go ahead, in a country so impoverished by war, surely owes much to the passion of the small number of architects and artists from Leningrad. Men and women like Belekhov, Zelenova, Oleinik, Kedrinsky, Kuchumov and Tikhomirova have figured repeatedly in the history of the great restoration effort, but many more were influential and supportive albeit from the sidelines. Men like Makarov, Shusov, Orbeli and Grabar must all have helped and, of course, their efforts were hugely supported by the new restorers who were reaching the fore-front of their profession - artists like Treskin, Kazakov and Lubimov, craftsmen like Ode and Vasilieva - who were showing just what they could do. It is impossible to list all the skilled and dedicated people who contributed.

The key movers were not only passionate but very shrewd. They did not try to obtain a general policy decision to restore all the palaces and their parks. Instead, they went about it step by step, only putting forward projects of an imaginable scope, which would not frighten away the authorities, but which would enable them to demonstrate that their dreams were feasible. So they were given the chance, initially at Pavlovsk, to show that, with care, sensitivity and a willingness to relearn the old ways, they could reconstruct and restore a wreck so that it did literally become what it had been before- or at least seemed to do so. Each visitor to the country palaces today must make his or her own mind up as to whether they have succeeded.

Their first important objective was achieved which was to convince those in authority at the time. This was quite a feat when it is recalled that at the outset of war, the Soviet Government had only just ceased selling off the tsars' treasures and threatening to close the museums. An extraordinary change of attitude had taken place. No doubt the war itself had thrown into doubt everyone's pre-war certainties, not just the Russians'. The very fact that the Germans had tried so hard to take something from them no doubt filled them with a resolution not supinely to allow it to happen. Perhaps also the truth that, for all its Marxist dialectic, the Soviet Union was by no means yet a materialistic country, made the loss of these palaces seem the more grievous. Anyway, from the mid fifties when Stalin's successors were in the saddle, there was never any real doubt that the reconstruction and restoration would go ahead. The speed of progress would clearly depend on the economic situation.

Possibly the most satisfying testament to the restorers' success is the way that their example has been followed abroad. The Royal Castle of Warsaw, for instance, is a major work of reconstruction, very much based on the techniques developed by Grabar and Belekhov in the Inspectorate and by Zelenova, Oleinik and Gromova at Pavlovsk. More recently, other countries have started to follow along the same lines. In France, very ambitious reconstructions have been made of the castles at Chinon and Saumur. They are no longer picturesque ruins but appear to have jumped straight off the pages of the Duc de Berry's Book of Hours. There must, however, be a limit somewhere to how long a gap in time and culture can be bridged, and how big an exercise of the imagination can be justified. When that limit is reached and perhaps overstepped, it will no doubt be recognised but it will not invalidate the pioneering work done in the country palaces of Leningrad.

One of the sadnesses is that the art of the restorer is anonymous. During our researches, we were presented with a pair of impressionist landscapes, very beautiful but unsigned. They were by Ivan Alexeev, one of Kazakov's team but when asked to sign them, he refused. Restorers never sign their work on the grounds that they do not regard it as theirs. In compensation, they are able to range far and wide in what they do, one day making Chinese panels, the next an Italian ceiling. Once, during our researches, having watched one of Lubimov's team called Viktor Khmelevsky painting the trompe l'oeuil ceiling of the library at Pavlovsk, and discussed with him how he had made the delicate rose garlands that festoon the ball room in the Rose Pavilion, he showed us round the private apartments of Maria Feodorovna. Stopping in front of a charming 18century sepia drawing of figures in an Arcadian park, we asked who it was by. "Me," he said. There is no end to their versatility. In 1795, an excited Maria Feodorovna wrote a long letter to her mother describing in great detail each room of the palace, a letter which has been of great value to the restorers. If she could come back, one wonders if she would detect any change.

Well, of course, she would. These rooms today - indeed the whole palace - cannot be exact copies of what she knew if only because the restorers had nothing to copy. In any case, no copy can be exact. No two artists think and act exactly the same. Occasionally artists copy their own works themselves. There are apparently identical landscapes hanging in both the Prado and the Kunsthistorisches Museum in Vienna, both by van Ruysdael, but who knows which was a copy of which - and what does it matter? What did matter in the restoration of the country palaces was that the restorers took no short cuts. They were not just seeking to replicate the appearance of things but, after exhaustive study, to repeat step by step what the original artists had done. For, had they done otherwise, who could tell what detail would fatally be missing from the overall effect? The result seems so successful that, even if Maria Feodorovna should detect some changes, it is difficult to believe she would not still feel at home.

It is hard to say what sacrifices the Russian people had to make to fund this extraordinary achievement. Attempts have been made to estimate the cost. One came to five billion roubles but with changing values and exchange rates, who is to say what that really means. It is certainly less, however, than the original cost of the building of St. Petersburg under the driving hand of Peter the Great. At least no serfs lost their lives. There is no doubt that the restorers themselves do not regard their lives as wasted. They have been poorly paid, their health has often suffered from the materials they were required to use and the awkward places where they had to use them and many of them died rather young. But, with very few exceptions like Stryzhova, we met none who regretted it or felt that their stupendous work had not been worthwhile. They felt they had done something not just for St. Petersburg or even for Russia, but for the whole world. A common tag they quote comes from Dostoyevsky – 'Beauty will save the world'. If before the war the Russians had taken so much pride in these palaces, which were a legacy to them from an earlier and different time, how much more should they do so now that they are all their own work. Perhaps, however, our final judgement on their worth should be a democratic one. Vadim Znamenov, the Director of Peterhof, reported that, by the end of the century, over five million people were visiting his palace and its park every year.

Appendix 1

The Romanov Succession

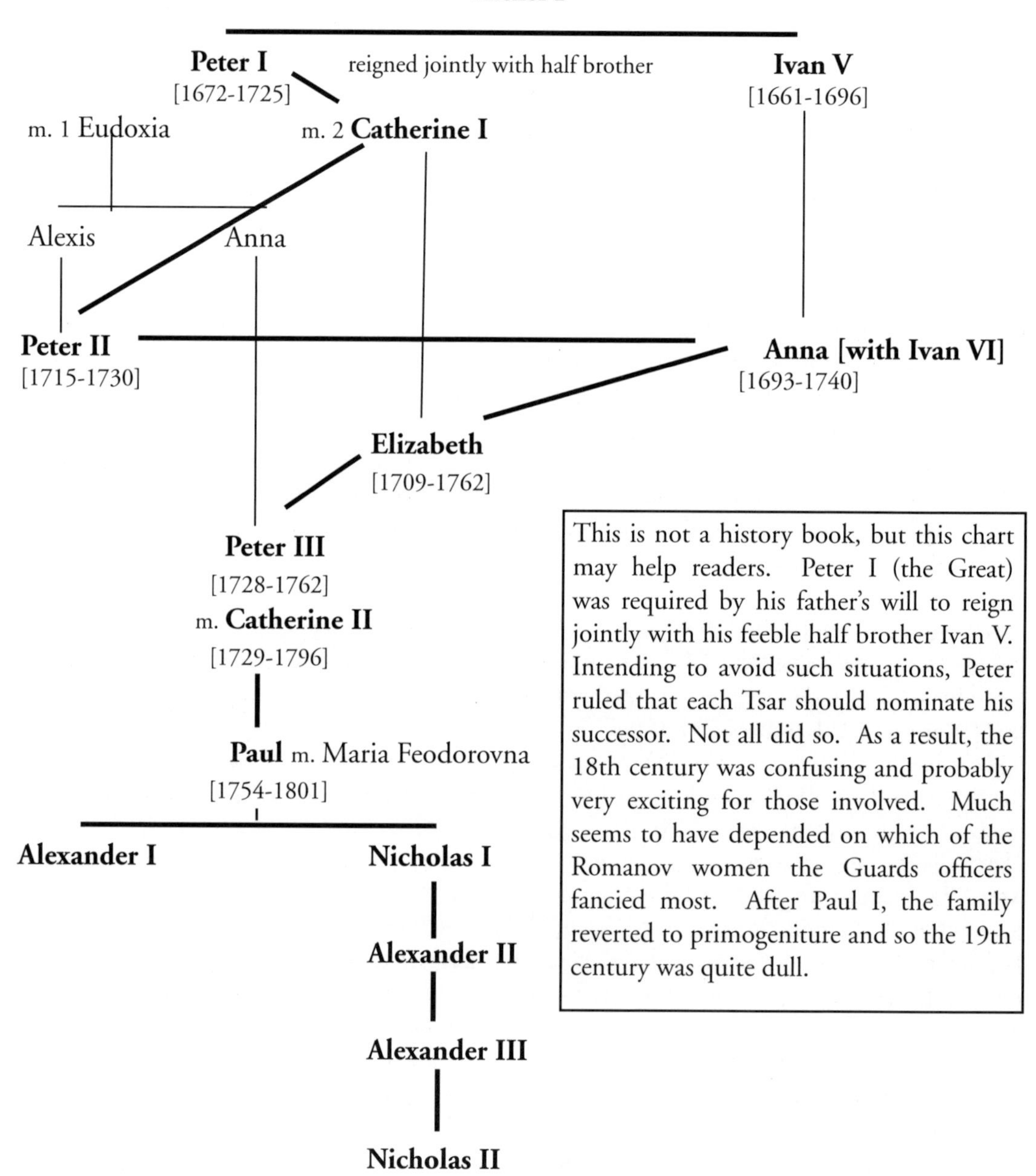

This is not a history book, but this chart may help readers. Peter I (the Great) was required by his father's will to reign jointly with his feeble half brother Ivan V. Intending to avoid such situations, Peter ruled that each Tsar should nominate his successor. Not all did so. As a result, the 18th century was confusing and probably very exciting for those involved. Much seems to have depended on which of the Romanov women the Guards officers fancied most. After Paul I, the family reverted to primogeniture and so the 19th century was quite dull.

BIBLIOGRAPHY

All sources are in Russian unless indicated by an asterisk

Books

Baranov, N. *Silhouettes Of the Siege*/Notes of the senior architect. Leningrad 1982.

Bardovskaya, L; Khodasevich, G; *Catherine Palace in Tsarskoye Selo.* St.Petersburg 1999

Benkendorf, P. *Last Days at Tsarkoye Selo*/Heinemann 1927.*

Bobrov, M. *Angel's Curators*/Notes of a siege mountain climber. St. Petersburg 1998.

Bunatian, G.; Lavrov, V; *Suburbs of St. Petersburg.* A guidebook. to St. Petersburg 2004.

Glinka, V. *Peterhof*/Leningrad, 1944.

Grabar, I. *My Life.* Studies about artists. Moscow 2001.

Granin, G; Gurevich, I; Kohodasevich, G; Belanina, V. *Risen from the Ashes: Petrodvorets, Pushkin, Pavlovsk. Leningrad*/Aurora 1992.*

Iljin N.; Semionova N., *Sold Treasures Of Russia.* Moscow. 2000.

Imber, V. *Leningrad Diary.* Hutchison 1971.*

Kedrinsky, A. *Restoration of the palace and park ensembles of the suburbs of Leningrad*/Best in architecture. Collected articles. Moscow, 1987.

Kedrinsky, A. *Chronicle Of The Revival: Restoration of the architectural monuments of Leningrad and its suburbs destroyed in the time of the World War II by the Nazis,* Leningrad, 1971.

Kedrinsky, A; Kolotov, M; Ometov, B; Raskin, A. *Restoration of the architectural monuments of Leningrad.* Leningrad, 1987.

Khodasevich, G; Voronov, M. *Architectural Ensemble of Cameron in Pushkin.* Leningrad.1990.

Khordikainen, L. *Life in the Occupation.* Pushkin, Gatchina, Estonia. Publication and commentaries by S. Nuriganova. St. Petersburg 1999.

Klementiev, V. *Chinese Palace in Oranienbaum.* St. Petersburg 1998.

Levit, E. *Left Only On The Photographs; Monuments - damaged and destroyed, pieces of art - stolen and lost.* Moscow 1978.

Maksakova, L. *Rescue of the Cultural Treasures in the time of the World War II,* Moscow, 1990.

Massie, S. *Pavlovsk, The Life of a Russian Palace*/St. Petersburg 1990.*

Moynihan, B. *The Russian Century*/Chatto & Windus 1994.*

Petrov, A. *Restoration of the suburban palace-museums of Leningrad* (1944-1967)/Works of the research Institute of Culture. Problems of preservation, restoration and propaganda of the art and history monuments,1971.

Polovtsov, A. *Les Tresors d'Art en Russie sous La Regime Bolsheviste*/Paris 1919.*

Priyutko, Y. *Gatchina*/ Artistic monuments of town and outskirts. Leningrad 1979.

Ravikovich, D. *Preservation of the art and history monuments in the Russian Federation* (1917-1957)/Works of the research Institute of the museum management studies and protection of the art and history monuments, 1970.

Razgonov, S. *Left by the Centuries.* Moscow, 1986.
Razgonov, S. *Keepers of the Eternal,* Moscow,1975.
Scott-Clark, C. & Levy, A. *The Amber Room*/ Atlantic Books 2004.*
Telemakov, V. *Beauty Should Live Forever.* Leningrad, 1981.
Tikhomirova, M. *Monuments. People. Events;* notes of a curator. Leningrad, 1984.
Tretiakov, N. *Rescue of the art and history monuments in the suburban palaces of Leningrad, 1941-1948.* Author's dissertation/St. Petersburg University, 1991.
Stein, A. *Blood and Ruins*/Heroic deed of Leningrad, 1941-1944. Moscow, 1960.
Velichko, M. *Lomonosov*/Palaces and parks. Leningrad 1968.
Zelenova, A. *Palace in Pavlovsk..* Leningrad 1986.
Zubov, V. *Stradnyie Gody Russie*/ Wilhelm Fink 1968.
Great Deed of the Century; painters, sculptors, architects, art critics in the time of the World War II. Leningrad, 1969.
Leningrad in the Siege. Documents relating to the defence (1941-1944). St. Petersburg 1995.*
Monuments of art destroyed by the German occupants in USSR. Collected articles. Moscow 1948.
Restoration of the Monuments of Culture/Problems of Restoration. Collected articles, Moscow 1981.
Report of the special Commission on the Nazi war crimes. Moscow 1944.
Pavlovsk. Historic anthology II. Pavlovsk. 1996.
Photoalbum. Introduction by Dimitry Shostakovich and Nicholas Tomsky, Moscow ,1978.
900 Days. Collected literary and documented articles dedicated to the heroic defence of Leningrad in WW2. Leningrad 1962.

Newspaper Articles

Alexandrova, M. *The Kingdom Of Beauty*/Leningradskaya Pravda, 1979.
Alexandrova, T. *Singed By The War*/Pravda, 1984. No. 246.
Basmanov A. *Recovered from the Ashes*/Leningradskaya Pravda, 1986.
Faltz-Fein, E. von. *Curse of the Amber Room*/Argumenty I Facty 2004.
Foniakov, I. *Contemporary Chronicle of Catherine Palace*/Literaturnaya gazeta (Literary newspaper), 1976 28 April.
Fridman, M. *Let's Enter The Palace*/Leningradskaya Pravda, 1985 No.103.
Grabar, I. *Palaces-museums of the suburbs of Leningrad:* Report/Vechernaya Moskva (Evening Moscow), 1944 17 February.
Koroleva, I. *Master Plotnikov*/Vecherny Petersburg (Evening Petersburg), 1991 29 October.
Gerasicheva, G. *Workshop In The Palace*/Leningradskaya Pravda, 1968 18 April.
Gessen, A. *Revival From The Ashes*/Soviet culture. 1959 5 May.
Koval, L. *Architect & Restorer F. Oleinik*/Pavlovsk reports. 1994 No.18.
Kuchumov, A. *Beauty Revives The Human Being*/Literaturnaya Rossiya (Literary Russia), 1989 11 November.
Metlitsky, B. *Fairy-tale Wooden Pattern*/Vecherny Leningrad (Evening Leningrad), 1974 23 July.
Metlitsky, B. *True Story or Legend*/ Leningradskaya Pravda, 1990 13 May.
Munshtukova, N. *Behind The White And Gold Door*/ Leningradskaya Pravda, 1986 No.40.
Mudrov, Y. *A Word About A. Kuchumov*/Pavlovsk reports. 1992 No.11.
Nesterenko, A. *By The Hands Of Restorers*/Vecherny Leningrad (Evening Leningrad), 1985 25 November.

Nikolaev, A. *Dream And Reality*/Smena, 1978 No.16.
Nikolaev, L. *Third birthday of 'Samson'*/Evening Leningrad. 1987 12 September.
Noskov, Y. *By The Hands Of Restorers*/Vecherny Leningrad (Evening Leningrad), 1985 No.34.
Ol, A. *Revival of Petrodvorts*/Vecherny Leningrad (Evening Leningrad), 1946 15 July.
Patrunov, F. *Deed Equal To The Heroic One*/Sovetskaya kultura (Soviet culture), 1977 10 May.
Poroshina, Y. *Working-days and Holidays of Old Park*/Vecherny Leningrad (Evening Leningrad), 1981 26 March.
Smirnov, A. *Pavlovsk Owners.* Empress Maria Fiodorovna/Pavlovsk reports. 1993 No.17.
Taube, N. *Pavlovsk Palace Is Being Restored*/Leningradskaya Pravda, 1946 19 June.
Tolstoy, V. *Deed Of The Revival; Monuments of Fatherland*/Pravda,1986 15 June.
Trofimova, M. *Pavlovsk Museum is 75.* Pavlovsk reports. 1994 No.18.
Vishnevsky, A. *Second Birth of Rose Pavilion*/Pavlovsk reports. 1992 No.11.
Zelenova, A. *Chronicle of Revival*/Pavlovsk reports. 1991 No.5.
Zhukova, N. *Masters*/Leningradskaya pravda, 1984.
Lenin prize of 1986/Literaturnaya gazeta (Literary newspaper), 1986 23 April.
Lion Cascade in Scaffoldings/Leningradskaya Pravda, 1986 No.10.
Lenin Prize Awards, *Pravda* 1986.

Magazine Articles

Aliansky, Y. *30 km. Away – XVIII century*/Neva, 1969 No.6.
Alexy, Patriarch. *German crimes in Peterhof and Pushkin*/ Magazine of Moscow patriarchate, 1944 No.2.
Azarov, V. *Germans in Peterhof*/Leningrad, 1944 No.3.
Basmanov A. *'And once again I see in front of me…'*, Pamiatniki Otechestva (Monuments of Fatherland), 1981. No.1.
Basmanov A. *Reviving the beauty*/Leningrad panorama, 1986. No.5.
Basmanov A. *Restoration of the Leningrad Palaces*/Literature and art, 1944 27 May.
Betaki, V. *Opening of the Opened*/Aurora. 1970 No.8.
Chamot, M. *The Palace of Pavlovsk, near Leningrad*/Antiques. May 1971.
Davydov, S. *Revival from the Ruins*/Construction and architecture of Leningrad, 1965 No.5.
Palaces Rise from the Ashes/Soviet art, 1945 23 June.
Evseviev, M. *Artistic life of Leningrad in the year of great victory*/Vestnik LGU (Leningrad University Bulletin), 1985.
Gaziants, S. *Pass On The Baton Of Creativity And Craftsmanship*/Construction and architecture of Leningrad, 1978 No.5.
Gessen, A. *Revival of Petrodvotets*/Construction and architecture of Leningrad, 1954 No.1.
Glinka, I. *Gatchina*/Leningrad. 1944 No.5.
Ivanova, O., Ilynskaya, N. *Revival of the historical park ensembles*/Construction and architecture of Leningrad, 1973 No.6.
Kadina, I., Kharlamova, A. *Pavlovsk – Monument of the history of culture*/Pamiatniki Otechestva (Monuments of Fatherland), Moscow, 1972.
Kalinin, V. *Revived Beauty*/Artist. 1961 No.2.
Kalinin, V. *Revived Beauty*; Restoration of Pavlovsk palace-museum/Artist. 1961 No 3.

Klokova, G. *Restorer's Education in Russia*/Museum. 1995 No.2.
Krashennikov, A. *Pavlovsk Park*/Artist, 1991 No.9.
Krestovsky, Y. *Given Back Beauty*/Avrora, 1984 No.8.
Lazarev, V. *Revived Pavlovsk*/Tvorchestvo (Creativity), 1974 No.5.
Lazuko, A. *Second Birth Of Masterpieces*; restoration of decorative and monumental paintings in Catherine palace in Pushkin/Leningrad panorama, 1986 No.9.
Leliakov A. *Under The Protection Of Old Parks*/Construction & architecture of Leningrad. 1979 No.11.
Leskov, A. *'Samson' of the Perestroyka Epoch*/St. Petersburg panorama, 1993 No.6.
Likhachev, D. *Restoration Or Falsification?*/Sovetskaya kultura (Soviet culture), 1968 No.2.
Lubimov, L. *Pearl Necklace*/Zvezda (Star), 1963 23 April.
Martynenko, O. *Revived Masterpieces*/Sovetsky Soyuz (Soviet Union), 1986 No.8.
Metlitsky, B. *Secrets Of Old Plafond*/Vecherny Leningrad (Evening Leningrad), 1974 3 June.
Mudrov, Y; Koval, L. *Restoration of Rose Pavilion*/Museum world. No.1997 No.2.
Ol, A. *Our Work On The Revival of Petrodvorets*/Construction and architecture of Leningrad, 1946 No.19-20.
Piliavsky, V. *Vandalism of Nazi in the suburbs of Leningrad*/Architecture of the USSR, 1944 No.7.
Piliavsky, V. *Destruction of the suburbs of Leningrad*/Architecture of Leningrad, 1944 No.1-2.
Piliavsky V. *Visibly Immortalized Biography*/Construction and architecture of Leningrad. 1973 No.6.
Piotrovsky, B., Tikhonov L. *Revived from the Ashes*/Pamiatniki Otechestva (Monuments of Fatherland), 1985 No.1.
Piotrovsky, B. *Restoration of the Palaces-Museums of Leningrad*/Museum, 1985 No.147.
Raskin, A., Sautov, I. *Like A Miracle*/Artist, 1985 No.9.
Raskin, A. *Craftsmanship and Inspiration*/Construction and architecture of Leningrad, 1973 No.5.
Razgonov, S. *Raised Echo*/Pamiatniki Otechestva (Monuments of Fatherland), 1987 No.1.
Rozadeev, B. *Revival*/Construction and architecture of Leningrad. 1970 No.5.
Severov, I. *Revived From Ashes*/Leningrad panorama, 1984 No.1.
Snytko, G. *Descendants of the masters of the past*/Construction and architecture of Leningrad. 1979 No.11.
Staleva, T. *On Behalf Of Mankind*/Selskasya molodiozh (Country youth), 1977 No.11.
Telemakov, V. *How To Create The Masterpieces*/Constructure and architecture of Leningrad, 1977 No.7.
Tikhomirova, M. *Like A Heroic Deed...*; restoration works of the Pavlovsk park and palace/Zvezda (Star), 1972 No.2.
Tolstoy, V. *Incarnation of the Soul Forces*/Tvorchestvo (Creativity). 1986 No.8.
Tolstoy, V. *Restoration Of The Palace*/Sovetskoye iskusstvo (Soviet art), 1945 24 August.
Ulanov, N. *Medal On The Banner Of Petrodvorets*/ Construction and architecture of Leningrad, 1974 No.1.
Yaglova, N. *Notes of the Siege*/Art of Leningrad. 1990 No.5.
Znamenov, V. *Revival of Peterhof*/Museum, 1994.
Znamenov, V. *Revival of Peterhof Palaces*/Construction and architecture of Leningrad, 1979.

Znamenov, V. *Revival Of Peterhof*; Conversation with the director of Peterhof Museum, 1994.
Official report of the special Commission on the Nazi crimes and their allies in the time of the war; destruction of the art and history monuments in the towns Petrodvorets (Peterhoff), Pushkin, Pavlovsk. Architecture of Leningrad, 1944.
On The Podium Is A Restorer/Interview with the participants of the 2nd exhibition
Restoration of the museum works of art in Russia, December 1966/Museum World, 1997 No.1.
Palace-Museum Is A Medal Holder/Construction and architecture of Leningrad. 1978 No.5.
/Leningrad panorama, 1984 No.8.

Archives

Zelenova, A. Private archive of the director of Pavlovsk museum in the time of the World War II (kept in Pavlovsk).
Proceedings of the Council of Curators of the Country Palaces 1918-1925.
Oranienbaum after the Revolution 1917-22.
Activities of the Tsarskoye Seloe Art & History Commission 1917-18.
Minutes of the Tsarskoye Seloe Art & History Commission 1919.
Oranienbaum Salary Lists 1918-22.
Copies of orders of Gatchina administration. (1917-1918).
Copies of orders of Gatchina administration (9 December 1919 – 9 February 1920).
Copies of the orders of Peterhof administration (January 1919-April 1919).
State Museum Salary Lists 1919-1925.
Orders of the Gatchina Administration 1917-20.
Orders of the Peterhof Admninistration 1919.
Reports of the meetings of the union of workers of Administration of Gatchina palace-museum and employees of Detskoye Selo Art Commission (10 December 1917 – 18 January 1919)
Staff lists of Gatchina (1921-1922)
Reports of proceedings of the meetings of council of the curators of country palaces of Petrograd, Gatchina, Pavlovsk and Peterhof (August 1918 – January 1925).
Evacuation of the museum treasures from Gatchina palace.
Revived from the ruins (an article by Kuchumov dedicated to the opening of all halls of Pavlovsk palace after the restoration – 1970).
Scientific conference dedicated to the restoration of suburban palaces (Peterhof, Pushkin, Pavlovsk and Gatchina) 21 March 1944.
Lists of workers of the Department of Preservation and Registration of the Art Monuments.
Report of the activity of Tsarskoye Selo Art and History Commission (October 1917-October 1918).
Notes on meetings of the Peterhof Workers Union 1918.
Tikhomirova's deathbed statement to E. Chalikova 1991.
Tikhomirova's Diaries.
Tikhomirova's Situation Report on September 1941.
Lemus, V. Unpublished article from the archive of Tsarskoye Selo museum. 1980.
Manuscript of Kuchumov.Report given in the Architect's Club in Leningrad, 25 April 1972 on the results of scientific methods of restoration of Pavlovsk palace.

INDEX